THE WAY
SCIENCE
WORKS

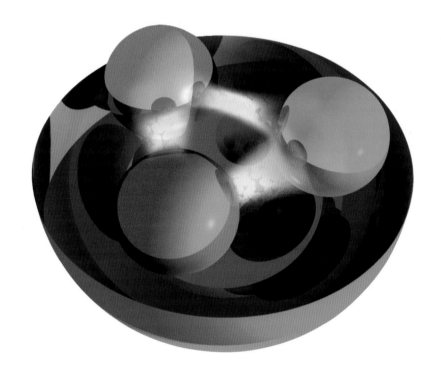

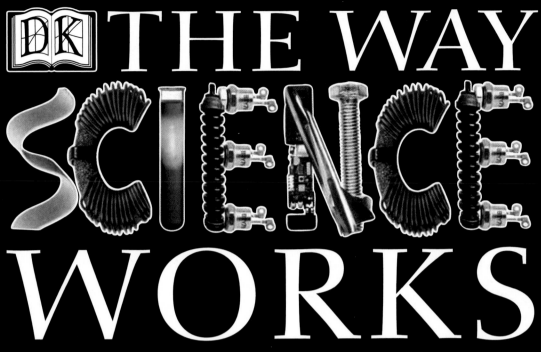

THE WAY SCIENCE WORKS

Discover the secrets of science with exciting, accessible experiments

By Robin Kerrod and Dr. Sharon Ann Holgate

A DK PUBLISHING BOOK

Dorling Kindersley

LONDON, NEW YORK, MUNICH,
MELBOURNE, and DELHI

Project editors Kate Bradshaw, Maggie Crowley,
Caryn Jenner, Amanda Rayner, Sadie Smith
Art editors Sheila Collins, Guy Harvey,
Joanna Pocock, Wilfred Wood
Senior editor Kitty Blount
Senior art editor Martin Wilson
US editors Gary Werner, Margaret Parrish
Category publisher Jayne Parsons
Managing art editor Jacquie Gulliver
Art director Cathy Tincknell
Picture research Marie Osborn, Sarah Pownall
Picture librarians Sally Hamilton,
Rose Horridge, Sarah Mills
Jacket design Dean Price
DTP designer Siu Yin Ho
Production controller Erica Rosen
Special photography Trish Gant
Digital artwork Robin Hunter, John Kelly
Science experiments adviser David Phillips

First American Edition, 2002

10 9 8 7 6

Published in the United States by
DK Publishing, Inc.
375 Hudson Street,
New York, NY 10014

Copyright © 2002 Dorling Kindersley Limited.

All experiments in this book have instructions that include
safety warnings where appropriate. In addition, the "safety box"
on page six details the precautions that you should take when
performing any science experiment. The publisher cannot take
responsibility for any accident or injury that occurs because
the reader has not followed the instructions properly.

A CIP catalog record for this book is
available from the Library of Congress.

ISBN 978-0-7894-8562-5

Color reproduction by Colourscan, Singapore
Printed and bound in China by Toppan

See our complete product line at
www.dk.com

CONTENTS

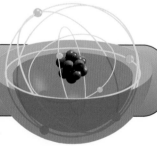

FORCES AND ENERGY 60–81

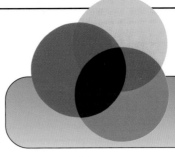

LIGHT AND COLOR 100–121

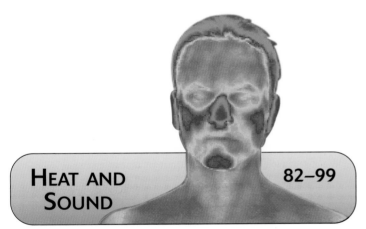

HEAT AND SOUND 82–99

ELECTRICITY AND MAGNETISM 122–149

THE WAY SCIENCE WORKS

SCIENTISTS CAN MAKE MOLECULES THE SIZE OF pollen grains that spin around like propellers. They can do this by using devices that can pick up and move individual atoms. Using chemical "scissors," they can cut and splice genes and transfer them from one living organism to another. They can make electricity from sunlight, peer into the brain, and probe deep into space to unravel the secrets of the universe. However, science is not just about the amazing and the fantastic. There is science behind everything that happens in our world – when a ball falls, or a rocket takes off; when lightning flashes and thunder booms; when birds fly and fish swim; when water freezes and lava flows; and when a match burns.

THE BIG THREE

Let's examine the science behind a match. When you strike the match, the muscles in your fingers produce a force that pulls the match over a rough surface. The friction between the match head and the rough surface produces heat energy, triggering a chemical reaction in the head that gives out more energy as heat and light. If you let the match burn down, it will burn you. Nerve endings in your fingers will send messages to your brain to say "pain" and force your fingers to release the burned match. All three main sciences are involved in striking the match – physics, chemistry, and human biology. Physics is the study of energy, forces, and matter. It has many branches. For example, in nuclear physics, scientists investigate the forces and energy within the nuclei (centers) of atoms. Chemistry is the study of the properties of the

EXPERIMENTS – SAFETY FIRST

Before conducting any experiment, be sure to read it carefully. Think of the things that could go wrong first, and be prepared. You should consider whether the experiment could injure yourself or somebody else. This is called risk assessment. Here are a list of things that must be considered before conducting any kind of scientific experiment:

General points to remember
• Tell an adult immediately if you have an accident of any kind. Do not attempt to clean up any breakages yourself.
• Always follow instructions carefully. Ask if you are unsure.
• Do not use chemicals or equipment unless you have permission.
• Wear eye protection when necessary.

Heating
• When heating anything, always wear safety goggles and tie back long hair and loose clothing.
• If heating liquids in a test tube, always hold it correctly – use tongs and point away from yourself and anyone else. Never look directly down a heated test tube.
• If you need to pick up hot equipment use tongs and/or heatproof gloves. Allow equipment to cool before putting it away.
• Always have a fire extinguisher or fire blanket on hand in case of an accident. If burned, hold the burn under cool running water and tell an adult.

Breaking surface tension with detergent

Using chemicals
• Never put chemicals in or near your mouth.
• Always wash your hands after experimenting with chemicals. If chemicals get on your skin or in your eyes, wash immediately with water only and tell an adult.

Electrical equipment
• **NEVER EXPERIMENT WITH HOUSEHOLD ELECTRICITY.**
• If using electrical equipment, other than battery powered, ensure that the equipment is not near water. Never touch electrical equipment with wet hands.
• Never dismantle electrical equipment.

Testing for acidity

SAFE SCIENCE

In this book symbols are used to indicate whether an experiment is safe to do at home with adult supervision, or should be demonstrated in a school laboratory. If an experiment has no symbol at all, it is safe to do on your own. However, always tell an adult first.

LET'S EXPERIMENT
THE LAWS OF REFLECTION

Adult supervision
Experiments shown with this symbol must only be done with the help of an adult.

DEMONSTRATING
MELTING POINTS

Laboratory experiments
You must not attempt to do these experiments at home. Ask an adult, such as your science teacher, to demonstrate them in a laboratory for you.

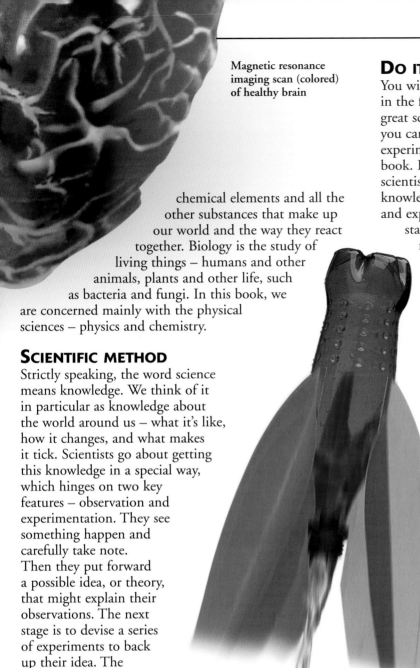

Magnetic resonance imaging scan (colored) of healthy brain

chemical elements and all the other substances that make up our world and the way they react together. Biology is the study of living things – humans and other animals, plants and other life, such as bacteria and fungi. In this book, we are concerned mainly with the physical sciences – physics and chemistry.

SCIENTIFIC METHOD

Strictly speaking, the word science means knowledge. We think of it in particular as knowledge about the world around us – what it's like, how it changes, and what makes it tick. Scientists go about getting this knowledge in a special way, which hinges on two key features – observation and experimentation. They see something happen and carefully take note. Then they put forward a possible idea, or theory, that might explain their observations. The next stage is to devise a series of experiments to back up their idea. The results from the experiments may be favorable, in which case the scientists may be able to convert their idea into a law. If the results are unfavorable, they will be forced to try other ideas and other experiments. Along the way, the scientists may come across all kinds of interesting things they didn't know before. William Henry Perkin discovered one of the first synthetic dyes, mauveine, while he was trying to make artificial quinine. When they were researching uranium radiation, Marie and Pierre Curie found a new radioactive element, which they called polonium.

Homemade rocket blasts off, propelled by a water jet.

DO IT YOURSELF

You will be following in the footsteps of great scientists when you carry out the experiments in this book. Like those scientists, you can gain knowledge by observation and experimentation. Before starting an experiment, read the instructions carefully. Ask an adult for explanation if you don't understand what to do. Take your time to think about what you are doing. If the experiment doesn't work the first time, double check that you have done everything correctly. In electrical experiments, for example, check that all the connecting wires are making contact. Keep an experiment notebook and record the date of your experiment, what you did, what you observed, and note any results. In some experiments, for example, with a swinging pendulum, you will need to compare your results to work out the basic laws of the pendulum.

Light-bulb filament glows white-hot.

AT THE CUTTING EDGE

As you read through the book and carry out the experiments, you will realize that science is one of the most fascinating subjects there is. Scarcely a day goes by without the announcement of new scientific advances. In the years ahead, you could be at the forefront of the continuing revolution that is science. You could be creating new drugs to combat cancer; building intelligent robots that could think for themselves; or designing nuclear fusion reactors that could give the world energy forever. You could even be among the first scientist-astronauts to set foot on Mars and hunt for fossils of ancient Martian life.

Cross-reference boxes
Boxes like this occur on some of the pages. They cover an aspect of the particular science discussed but also relate to the science on another page. For example, this box (right) on radio telescopes appears on page 147 and cross-refers you to page 112, which discusses telescopes.

‹ TUNING IN ›
In 1932, a US electrical engineer named Karl Jansky detected radio waves coming from space and launched radio astronomy. Astronomers pick up radio waves from space with huge, dish-shaped radio telescopes. Their study of the radio universe led to the discovery of new astronomical bodies, such as quasars, pulsars, and radio galaxies. 113▶

Parkes radio telescope in New South Wales, Australia, has a dish 210 ft (64 m) across.

LOOKING AT MATTER

Picture: *Liquid crystal photographed in polarized light through an optical microscope.*

STATES OF MATTER

EVERYTHING AROUND US IS MADE FROM MATTER,
including our own bodies. Matter is made from atoms,
and the amount of matter in an object is known
as its mass. The most common types or "states" of
matter are solids, liquids, and gases. However there
are other states of matter, including plasmas, that
can form at either extremely high or extremely low
temperatures. Under certain conditions, matter
can change from one state to another. When
solids melt, for example, they turn into liquids,
and when liquids boil, they become gases.

to fill whatever space is available
to them. However, the atoms
do come into contact with each
other, since they constantly
move around bumping into
things. Most gases are
invisible. Even steam from
a kettle can't be seen
until it condenses into a
mist of liquid droplets.
But some gases can
be detected by
their smell.

SOLIDS

Atoms and molecules in solids
can't move around like those
in liquids and gases. This
means you can pick up solids,
whereas liquids just slip through
your hands. The arrangement of
atoms in a solid can either be crystalline
or amorphous. If crystalline, a particular
pattern of atoms is regularly repeated. If
amorphous, the atoms are arranged
much more randomly.

*This rock and the yellow
diamond embedded in
it are both solids.*

LIQUIDS

The structure of a liquid is halfway
between the structure of a solid and
that of a gas. Unlike solids, which
remain the same shape if they are
put into a container, liquids flow to
take the shape of whatever is holding
them. Their atoms and molecules can
move around more than in a solid, but not
as much as in a gas. They can slide past
each other, so a liquid can flow. Some
molecules find it harder to slide along and
the liquids made from these don't flow as
easily; they are said to have a high viscosity.

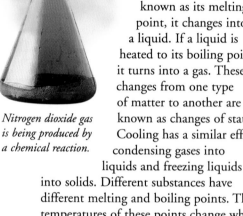

*Nitrogen dioxide gas
is being produced by
a chemical reaction.*

CHANGING STATE

If a solid is heated to a
particular temperature,
known as its melting
point, it changes into
a liquid. If a liquid is
heated to its boiling point
it turns into a gas. These
changes from one type
of matter to another are
known as changes of state.
Cooling has a similar effect,
condensing gases into
liquids and freezing liquids
into solids. Different substances have
different melting and boiling points. The
temperatures of these points change when
the surrounding pressure changes, or when
another substance is added. Increased
pressure lowers the melting point of ice,
so pressing down on an ice cube melts it
without using heat. Adding salt raises the
boiling point of water, so salted water
takes longer to boil, but boils at a
hotter temperature than pure water.

*If liquids, such as this cranberry
juice, are poured quickly, they
can produce enough force to
knock over a glass.*

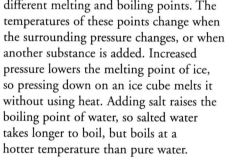

GASES

The molecules in a gas are farther
apart and move even more freely
than those in a liquid. They
behave as though they are
completely separate, which
means gases have no
structure, and expand

PLASMA

As well as the familiar states of matter
of solid, liquid, and gas, there are also
some more unfamiliar states like plasma.
Plasma is a special type of gas made from
parts of atoms. Plasmas form either when a

c. 265 BC Greek mathematician Archimedes discovers relative density.

1644 Italian physicist Evangelista Torricelli constructs the first barometer.

1662 Irish scientist Robert Boyle makes the link between a gas's pressure and volume.

1738 Swiss mathematician Daniel Bernoulli describes liquid and gas movement.

1774 English chemist Joseph Priestley produces oxygen.

1781 French mineralogist René Just Haüy discovers the internal shape of crystals.

Timeline

Electricity has created streams of plasma from the gas inside this plasma ball.

gas is heated to an extremely high temperature, or when an electric current is passed through it. In both cases, this causes electrons to be separated from their atoms. The Sun makes plasma naturally, but scientists are currently experimenting with artificially created plasmas to see if they can be used to help generate electricity in the power stations of the future.

ANTIMATTER

The Universe is made from matter, but modern experiments suggest that when the Universe was created in the Big Bang,

equal amounts of matter and antimatter were formed. Antimatter is like a mirror image of matter. Every particle of matter has a corresponding particle of antimatter, and when they meet they annihilate (destroy) each other. Nobody knows how we are living in a Universe made entirely of matter, since the equal amounts of matter and antimatter originally created should have destroyed each other. By investigating antimatter, created in special experiments, scientists hope to work out the answer and discover how the Universe exists.

DARK MATTER

Around 90 percent of the Universe could be made from a mysterious type of matter known as dark matter. Scientists do not yet know what dark matter is made from, but it could contain new types of particles that have not yet been discovered. Dark matter cannot be seen or detected directly, but scientists believe it is there because of the effect it seems to be having on matter that we can see.

Antimatter can be created in particle physics experiments. This picture shows the tracks made by electrons (green) and positrons (red). Positrons are the antiparticles of electrons.

Erupting volcanoes throw out molten rock in the form of liquid lava. The lava in this picture is flowing into the sea, which is cooling it. When lava becomes cool enough, it changes state and becomes solid rock.

1783 French chemist Antoine Lavoisier explains that water is composed of hydrogen and oxygen.

1787 French physicist and chemist Jacques Charles links a gas's temperature and volume.

1812 German mineralogist Friedrich Mohs defines hardness scale.

1912 German physicist Max von Laue invents X-ray crystallography.

1928 English theoretical physicist Paul Dirac predicts antimatter existence.

1932 American physicist Carl Anderson detects antimatter.

PROPERTIES OF MATTER

DIFFERENT TYPES OF MATTER CAN BE IDENTIFIED

by their different properties. The main mechanical properties of matter include hardness, density, strength, and elasticity. Some of these properties are only possessed by certain states of matter – solids can have elasticity, but liquids and gases cannot. However other properties, such as density, are common to all states of matter. Different substances have very different values of these various properties; for example air can be about 1,000 times less dense than water. Manufacturers use standard tests for different properties when they develop new materials to help them understand how they will behave.

This overstretched spring can no longer return to its original shape.

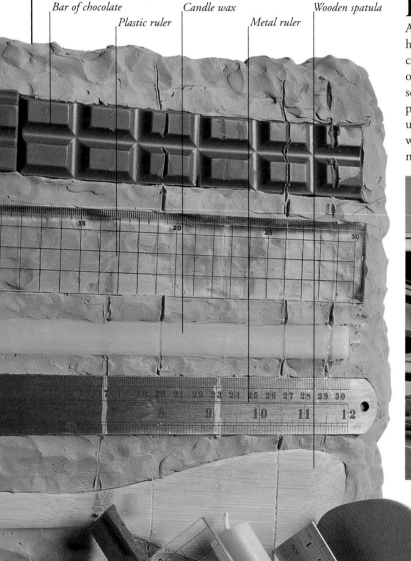

Bar of chocolate

Plastic ruler

Candle wax

Metal ruler

Wooden spatula

Each substance is used to test the comparative hardness of the others.

HARDNESS

A solid's resistance to being dented or scratched is known as its hardness. The hardest natural substance is diamond. Diamonds can scratch into all other solids – and other diamonds – so are often used in industry for cutting. This picture (left) shows how scratching can be used to compare hardness. Five substances were pressed into modeling clay, and then the same substances were used to scratch them. The metal ruler could scratch everything, whereas the chocolate was only able to scratch itself (and the modeling clay). Which was the hardest substance used?

STRENGTH

The amount of force, or stress, that a material can withstand before it crushes or breaks is known as its strength. Strength varies widely. The strength of some materials varies depending on what type of stress is applied to them. Concrete is strong when compressed, but much weaker when stretched. The concrete pillars supporting this overpass are compressed by the weight of the road above them.

Elasticity

If a solid object or material returns to its original shape and size after it has been stretched, we say it is elastic. If the force used to stretch any material is larger than its "elastic limit," the object will be left permanently stretched. This metal spring has been stretched beyond its elastic limit.

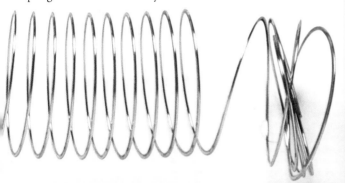

LET'S EXPERIMENT
MEASURING DENSITY

DENSITY IS THE amount of matter contained in a specific volume. A block of wood is less dense than a block of iron the same size. This experiment shows how to figure out the density of an object. **You will need**: an adult to help you; kitchen scales; plastic soft-drink bottle; plastic straw; modeling clay; measuring cup; solid objects for testing.

1 Use the scales to weigh each object to be tested. This value is the mass. Mass is the amount of matter in an object, while weight is the force exerted on it by gravity. Weight changes as gravity changes – in space for example – but mass remains constant.

2 Ask an adult to cut off the top of the bottle and make a hole in the side of the bottle near the top edge. Make a spout by putting the straw into the hole with clay. The clay seals the edge, making it watertight.

3 Place the measuring cup below the spout, then fill the bottle with water. The spout keeps an even water level in the bottle by letting any extra water drip out. Empty the excess water from the measuring cup.

4 Place the object to be tested into the water and watch as the water shoots down the spout. Measure the amount of water displaced into the cup. This is the object's volume. To obtain its density, divide the mass of the object by its volume.

Brittleness

When certain solids such as the hard candy shown above are hit, they shatter. They are termed brittle because they hardly bend or squash before they break. By contrast, ductile materials are much softer and tend to deform before breaking. A china tea cup will smash when dropped because it is brittle, but a metal automobile body is ductile and tends to deform when hit.

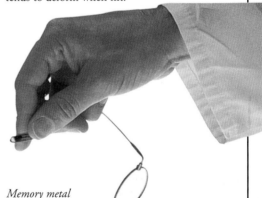

Memory metal glasses being twisted.

Smart materials

Materials that can react in a certain way to changes in their surroundings are called "smart" materials. These memory metal glasses frames will return to their original shape even after being bent. There are many different types of smart materials. Some have sensors embedded in them that can warn engineers they are about to break. Others can change their properties under different circumstances.

SOLIDS

THE ATOMS IN SOLIDS VIBRATE LESS THAN THE ATOMS IN
liquids or gases. This means that the atoms in solids
remain in the same place, so solids stay the same size
and shape. Heating a solid to its melting point causes
the order of the atoms to break down. The result is
that the solid melts and becomes a liquid. There are
many different types of solids. They range from
rocks, metals, and plastics, through bricks and
concrete, to nylon and rubber. All of these solids have
very different values of properties, such as hardness,
strength, and elasticity. The type of order of the atoms
gives a solid some of its properties.

*A rock climber
scales the vertical
face of a cliff. Most
of the Earth is made
from solid rock.*

METALS

Metals have a vast range of uses. They
are sometimes used inside the human
body. The flower shape (right) is an
artificial hip joint made from metal.
Most elements are metals. Metals look
shiny and are good conductors of
electricity and heat. We tend to think
of them as being very hard, but in fact
pure metals are often quite soft and
can easily be hammered or pulled into
different shapes. Some rare metals like
gold can be found on their own, but
most are found combined with other
elements, in rocks called ores.
Melting is used to separate these
metals from the other elements.

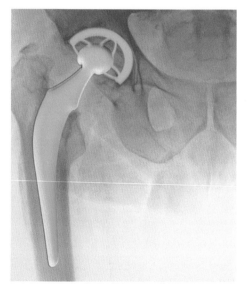

*This bicycle frame is made
from chrome
molybdenum,
a steel alloy.*

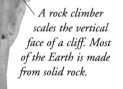

‹ POLYMERS ›

Some solids can be artificially created. Polymers, which
are made up from long chains of molecules, can either
occur naturally, such as rubber, or be made artificially,
such as plastics and nylon. We use a lot of polymers
every day. Food and drinks containers, and many
household objects are made from plastic. `56` ➤

Alloys

Mixtures of metals, such as bronze made from copper and tin,
or mixtures of metals and nonmetallic elements, such as steel
made from iron and carbon, are known as alloys. Alloys
combine substances in order to combine their properties.
Alloys can therefore be custom-made for specific applications.

Composites
Solid materials that are made by combining substances with different useful properties are known as composites. Reinforced concrete (shown in the picture) is a building material that has steel rods embedded in it to make it much stronger when it is under tension.

MELTING

The atoms in solids vibrate all the time, but when solids are heated they vibrate much more. If the solid is hot enough, the atoms or molecules move around so much that they can't stay in one place any more. At this temperature, known as the melting point, the solid becomes a liquid. The heat from this flame (right) has turned the wax into a liquid. Different substances have different melting points. For example, ice melts at 32°F (0°C), while gold melts at 1,949°F (1,065°C).

DEMONSTRATING
MELTING POINTS

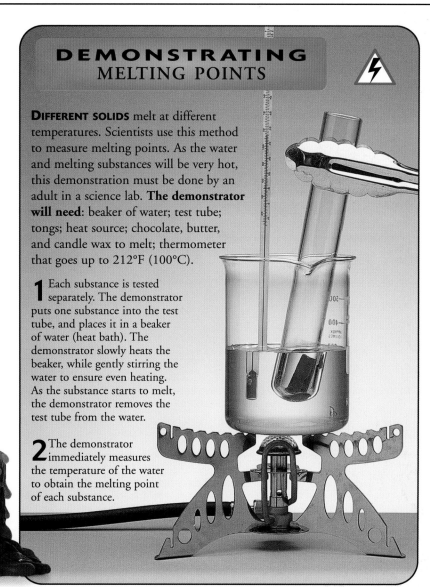

DIFFERENT SOLIDS melt at different temperatures. Scientists use this method to measure melting points. As the water and melting substances will be very hot, this demonstration must be done by an adult in a science lab. **The demonstrator will need**: beaker of water; test tube; tongs; heat source; chocolate, butter, and candle wax to melt; thermometer that goes up to 212°F (100°C).

1 Each substance is tested separately. The demonstrator puts one substance into the test tube, and places it in a beaker of water (heat bath). The demonstrator slowly heats the beaker, while gently stirring the water to ensure even heating. As the substance starts to melt, the demonstrator removes the test tube from the water.

2 The demonstrator immediately measures the temperature of the water to obtain the melting point of each substance.

LET'S EXPERIMENT
ICE CUTTING

NORMALLY, ICE stays frozen below 32°F (0°C), but pressure can cause it to melt. For example, there is often a thin layer of water under glaciers due to pressure melting. You can observe the effects of pressure on ice in this experiment. **You will need**: an ice cube; a bottle; a copper wire; two weights.

1 Tie the weights to each end of the copper wire. Place the ice cube on top of the open bottle and hang the weighted wire over the top of the ice cube.

2 Pressure from the wire melts the ice below it, allowing the wire to pass through the ice cube. As the wire drops, the water above it refreezes because it is no longer under pressure.

15

CRYSTALS

MANY SOLIDS ARE CRYSTALLINE, WHICH MEANS THAT their atoms are arranged in a repeated pattern. If a crystal is particularly well formed, it will reveal this regular internal pattern by its outward shape. Crystals are often brightly colored, and we use some as gemstones, particularly rare and beautiful types like diamond and emerald. Not all crystalline substances look like crystals, though. Rocks are made from minerals, most of which are crystalline, and solid metals can be crystalline, too. There are even tiny crystals inside our bodies. Bones contain crystals of a mineral called apatite, and our inner ears contain tiny crystals which help us to know which way is up.

X-ray crystallography

To learn more about crystals, scientists need to know how the atoms are arranged inside. They often use a technique called X-ray crystallography, which was invented in 1912 by the German physicist Max von Laue. This involves shooting X-rays at a crystal and analyzing the patterns produced on photographic film as the atoms scatter the X-rays. The arrangement of atoms inside each type of crystal is different and shows up as a different pattern. In 1953, this method was used to reveal the structure of the DNA molecule.

X-ray diffraction pattern obtained from a crystal of the plant enzyme, Rubisco.

CRYSTAL FORMATIONS

Every type of crystal has its atoms arranged in a particular pattern that repeats over and over to form the whole solid. The patterns, and numbers of atoms in them, differ depending on the crystalline substance. However, there are only seven basic geometric shapes – known as crystal systems – that these patterns can have. The shapes are cubic, orthorhombic, hexagonal, tetragonal, trigonal, monoclinic, and triclinic. The crystals pictured around the edge of these pages are examples of each of the seven crystal systems.

This yellow baryte crystal is orthorhombic. Baryte is also found in several other colors.

Crystal glass

We often see glasses and vases labeled "crystal." This actually means that they are made from a particularly clear type of glass called crystal glass, although glass is not crystalline at all. Instead of having a regularly repeating pattern of atoms like a real crystal, glass is amorphous, which means that its atoms are much more randomly arranged than those in crystals.

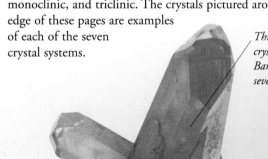

Pyrite crystals are cubic and are sometimes known as "fool's gold," since they can be mistaken for gold.

A CRYSTAL CAN be grown from a solution of copper sulfate. This demonstration must be done by an adult in a science lab, as copper sulfate is poisonous. It is important to wash hands after handling copper sulfate. **The demonstrator will need**: water; copper sulfate; shallow dish; cotton thread; cardboard; glass jar.

The crystal after three weeks

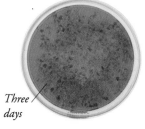

Three days

Five days

1 Copper sulfate is dissolved in water to make a strong solution. A small amount of this solution is poured into a shallow dish and left to evaporate.

2 As the water evaporates, the solution reaches the point of saturation. The solution can no longer hold the copper sulfate, so small crystals start to grow.

3 In a few days, crystals cover the dish. The largest crystal is removed. Cotton is tied around it and it is suspended from the cardboard in a jar of the remaining copper sulfate solution. This crystal is a "seed" for further crystallization, and will continue to grow. You can grow salt crystals using this same method with a salt solution.

Although attractive, axinite crystals are too brittle to be used as gemstones. Their structure is triclinic in shape.

LIQUID CRYSTALS

Most calculators have a liquid crystal display (LCD). Liquid crystal pours like a liquid but has a structure similar to a crystal. It is sandwiched between two thin pieces of glass in an LCD. When light passes through an LCD, it reflects off the mirror behind it and makes the display look light. The top piece of glass has a conductive coating. Any electricity flowing through it changes the arrangement of the liquid crystal molecules directly beneath it, and stops light from reflecting back, making that section of the display look dark.

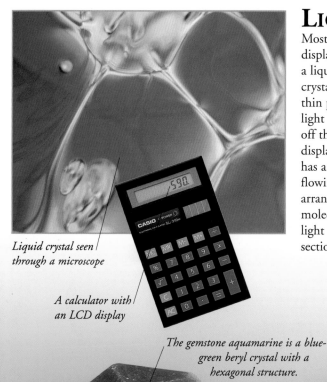

Liquid crystal seen through a microscope

A calculator with an LCD display

These gypsum crystals are an example of the monoclinic crystal system. They are "twinned," which means they are joined along one edge.

Purple-colored quartz is known as amethyst. This trigonal crystal is used as a gemstone.

Zircon is a gemstone with a tetragonal structure. It is found in various different colors.

The gemstone aquamarine is a blue-green beryl crystal with a hexagonal structure.

LIQUIDS

IF YOU POUR MILK INTO A CUP,
it takes the shape of the cup. Pour it into a
wine glass and it takes the shape of the glass.
All liquids are fluids – they flow, or pour, and
take the shape of any container they are put
in. Like all matter, liquids are made of particles,
or molecules. In solids, these particles attract one
another strongly and form a rigid structure. In
liquids, the particles are less strongly attracted and
can move around, usually in bundles. If conditions
change, liquids can change state. They can freeze and
become solids, or they can evaporate and become gases.

*Liquid chocolate is poured into a
mold. The chocolate will freeze
solid in the shape of the mold.*

DEMONSTRATING
BOILING POINTS

HOW DO LIQUIDS EVAPORATE? When some of the molecules near the
surface move fast enough, they escape into the air. As the temperature
rises, more surface molecules escape. At a certain temperature, all of the
molecules move fast enough to escape, and the liquid boils. Boiling liquids
are very hot, so this experiment must be done by an adult in a science lab.

**The demonstrator will
need**: heat-proof container;
heat source (such as a
Bunsen burner); selection
of liquids; thermometer
that goes up to 680°F
(360°C); heat-proof gloves
and tongs.

1 A small amount of liquid
is heated in the heat-proof
container. Using gloves and
tongs, the thermometer is
dipped into the liquid. The
temperature starts to rise.

2 Soon the liquid will
bubble. The temperature
stops rising and remains
constant. The liquid has now
reached its boiling point. This
temperature is recorded. The
procedure is repeated with
other liquids and the results
compared. It is clear that the
boiling point is different for
different liquids.

*Orange
juice*

FREEZING SOLID

In a liquid, the molecules are free to move around.
But the lower the temperature, the slower they
move and the more they attract one another. At
a certain temperature, the molecules attract one
another so strongly that they move very little,
and the liquid turns into a solid. We say the
liquid freezes. Every liquid becomes solid at
a different temperature – its freezing point.

Evaporation and condensation
When water evaporates into the air, it forms water vapor
(a gas). As the vapor rises into cooler air, the molecules
in the vapor slow down. Eventually, they start strongly
attracting one another, and the vapor turns into droplets of
liquid water. This process, called condensation,
creates clouds and then rain.

TEST THE VISCOSITY OF different liquids by dropping marbles into them. The longer a marble takes to fall, the higher the liquid's viscosity. **You will need**: identical glasses or jars; a selection of liquids (see examples below); marbles of the same size and weight.

1 Pour the liquids into identical glasses or jars, filling them to the same level. Drop marbles into two of them at the same time and from the same height. The first marble to hit the bottom is in the least viscous liquid.

2 Compare the viscosity of all the liquids by noting which marble hits the bottom first each time. Make a list of the liquids in order of their viscosity. You could also try gently warming the liquids to see how this affects viscosity.

Corn syrup

Vegetable oil

Red wine vinegar

Bubble bath

VISCOSITY

When you pour water into a glass, it flows easily and fills the glass quickly. If you try the same thing with corn syrup, it flows much more slowly. Corn syrup is a thicker liquid than water and has a higher viscosity. Viscosity is a measure of a liquid's resistance to flow. It is a kind of internal friction. Viscosity in liquids is put to good use to make lubricants, such as engine oil. The oil helps separate the moving metal parts of engines to stop them from rubbing together. Gases have viscosity too, though much less than liquids.

Corn syrup forms coils as it pours due to its high viscosity.

‹ **TAKING SHAPE** ›

Liquids take the shape of their container. But what shape do they take when they are on their own? A good place to find out is on a spacecraft in microgravity (almost zero gravity), where water forms a sphere. A force between its molecules called surface tension makes it form this shape. But a water drop on a leaf forms a teardrop shape because gravity tugs at it. 26, 70 ▶

Gravity distorts the shape of the water drop.

WATER

THE MOST COMMON SUBSTANCE ON THE FACE OF THE Earth is water; it covers nearly three-quarters of our planet. Water is vital to the survival of life on Earth. It is unlike most other substances because it exists in all three states of matter – solid, liquid, and gas. Water is usually found as a liquid, for example, in our vast oceans. However, water also exists as a solid in the form of ice and snow, and as a gas in the form of water vapor in the air. Another unusual property of water is its ability to dissolve many other substances. Water is one of the best solvents we know. The substances that do not dissolve in water can often be filtered out to make cleaner water.

THE WATER CYCLE

Water constantly circulates between the Earth's surface and the atmosphere. This is called the water cycle. As the Sun heats the water molecules on the surface, these molecules evaporate, turning to vapor. The water vapor rises and cools, condensing into droplets which form clouds. When the drops get big enough, they fall back to the surface as rain, or snow if the air is cold enough.

Water as a liquid
The Earth's average temperature is ideal for water to exist as a liquid. It is not so hot that the water evaporates quickly, nor is it so cold that the water freezes. As in all liquids, the molecules in water tend to gather together in bundles. These bundles have the ability to slide over each another, allowing liquid water to flow easily.

Water as a gas
At most temperatures, molecules gradually escape from the surface of liquid water to form a gas, or vapor. This process of evaporation becomes quicker as the temperature rises. At sea level, water boils at 212°F (100°C), causing rapid evaporation. What we call mist forms when the hot vapor cools in the air to make a cloud of water drops.

Molecules in motion
The chemical formula of water is H_2O. This shows that a molecule of water is made up of two hydrogen atoms (H) and one oxygen atom (O). The oxygen atom is much bigger than the two hydrogen atoms. This computer graphic shows the molecules in liquid water. They are much closer together than they are in water vapor and they move more slowly.

Water as a solid
As liquid water cools, the bundles of molecules move closer together. However, when water cools to 32°F (0°C), a strange thing happens. The molecules move farther apart and freeze into the solid structure that is ice. In other words, when water freezes, it expands and becomes lighter. That is why ice floats on water.

LET'S EXPERIMENT
FILTERING WATER

THE WATER FROM our faucets looks crystal clear, but it didn't start out that way. Originally, it came from rivers, lakes, or reservoirs, and it contained bits of dirt and other matter. This experiment shows how to remove dirt from water by filtering. **You will need:** an adult to help you; two beakers or jars; clear plastic soft-drink bottle; knife; dirty water (tap water mixed with a combination of bagged potting soil, rice, flour, tea leaves, coffee grounds); large dish; filter paper (such as that used in coffeemakers); charcoal; sand; gravel.

1 Ask an adult to cut off the top of the bottle, and make a hole in the bottom of it. Line the bottom of the bottle with filter paper.

2 Stand the bottle in the dish. Fill it with a layer of charcoal at the bottom, then a layer of sand, and finally a layer of gravel at the top. Pour the dirty water into the top of the bottle.

3 As the water seeps through the bottle, the layers filter out smaller and smaller particles of dirt. The gravel traps the coarsest particles, while the filter paper traps the finest particles. The result is cleaner water. However, there are still invisible chemicals and germs in the water, so do not drink it!

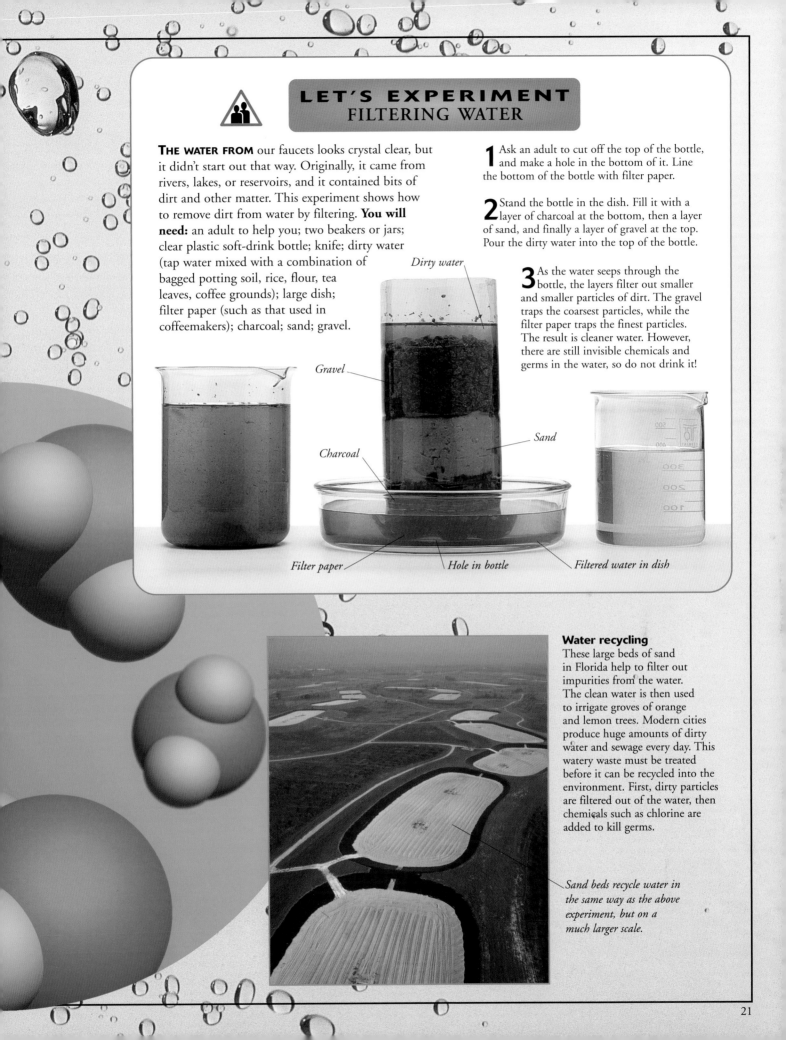

Dirty water

Gravel

Charcoal

Filter paper

Sand

Hole in bottle

Filtered water in dish

Water recycling

These large beds of sand in Florida help to filter out impurities from the water. The clean water is then used to irrigate groves of orange and lemon trees. Modern cities produce huge amounts of dirty water and sewage every day. This watery waste must be treated before it can be recycled into the environment. First, dirty particles are filtered out of the water, then chemicals such as chlorine are added to kill germs.

Sand beds recycle water in the same way as the above experiment, but on a much larger scale.

LIQUID DENSITY

DENSITY IS THE AMOUNT OF MASS
in a certain volume. Compare a
substance of large, closely-packed
molecules with a second substance of
small, well-spaced molecules. The first
substance will have a greater mass per
volume, and will therefore be denser
than the second substance. Liquid metal
mercury, for example, is much denser
than water. In general, solids are denser
than liquids, and liquids denser than
gases. However, density can change, for
instance, by heating or cooling a liquid.

Cooking oil

Water

Corn syrup

*Different liquids
separate according
to their densities.*

LIQUID LAYERS

Liquids with different densities
float on top of each other in
layers. You can demonstrate this
with oil, water, and corn syrup.
First, pour some corn syrup into
a glass. Then pour in some
cooking oil. Because the oil is
less dense, it floats on top of the
corn syrup. Now pour in some
water. The water forms a layer
between the other two liquids
because it is denser than the oil,
but less dense than the corn syrup.

*An oil slick floating
on the sea can cause
serious damage to
the environment.*

Oil and water
Oil is made up of tangled strings of
molecules that are more spaced out than
water molecules. As a result, oil has a lower
density and can float on water (as shown
above). In our everyday world, this property
of oil can have serious consequences. Oil
slicks float on the surface of the sea, causing
harmful pollution. The oil can kill seabirds
and other marine life, and contaminate
beaches. Oil fires are another problem.
They cannot be extinguished with water
because the burning oil floats on top of
the water. Oil fires must be tackled
with special foam.

‹ ROADSIDE RAINBOWS ›

Have you noticed the rainbow colors in puddles at the
side of the road? They are caused by drops of oil spilled
by passing traffic. The oil floats on the water in the
puddles and spreads out as a thin film. When light hits
the puddles, it is reflected both from the film of oil and
from the water underneath. The two beams interfere with
each other and some of the wavelengths, or colors, in the
light cancel each other out. The result is a constantly
changing pattern of rainbow colors. 118▶

*Oily puddles create
rainbow effects.*

The colored hot water rises because it is less dense than the surrounding cold water.

MAKE AN UNDERWATER volcano to see how heat lowers the density of water.
You will need: a large jar; a small bottle that will fit inside the jar; a long piece of string; cold tap water; hot tap water; food coloring.

1 Fill the jar three-quarters full with cold water. Loop the string firmly around the neck of the bottle to act as a handle. Fill the bottle with hot tap water and add food coloring to the hot water.

2 Carefully, lower the bottle of hot water into the jar using the string handle. Watch as the hot, colored water rises out of the bottle, like lava from an erupting volcano. Heat gives the water molecules energy, causing them to move farther apart and take up more space. In other words, the hot water is less dense than the cold water, so it rises to the top of the jar.

3 After a while, the molecules of hot and cold water will mix, causing the water temperature throughout the jar to even out.

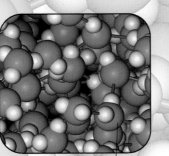

Cold water molecules are closely packed together. They do not have enough energy to move very far.

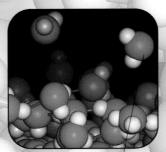

As water heats up, the molecules gain energy. If enough heat is applied, they will fly off to become water vapor.

The spacious, fixed pattern of molecules in ice means that ice is less dense than liquid water.

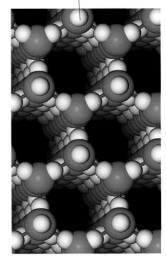

Unusual ice
When most liquids freeze into solids, the molecules squeeze more closely together and the density increases. Water is different. Its solid form (ice) is less dense than its liquid form. This is why ice floats on water. The molecules in liquid water are packed together but can still move around. The molecules in ice are fixed in a rigid lattice pattern, with space between them. They take up more room than molecules in the liquid form, making ice less dense. This unusual property of water is vital to underwater life. Ice floating on the surface acts as a barrier to stop the water underneath from freezing.

SALTWATER
When substances dissolve in a liquid, the density of the liquid increases. The dissolving molecules mix with the liquid molecules, so each drop of liquid now has more molecules in it. Seawater has salt and other substances dissolved in it that makes it more dense than freshwater. The Dead Sea, on the borders of Israel and Jordan, is the world's saltiest and densest body of water. Nearly 25 percent of the water is dissolved salts – more than six times the amount in ordinary seawater. Due to the hot climate, any water that flows into the Dead Sea evaporates quickly, leaving the salt behind. The concentration of salt in the water is so high that the only living things that can make their home there are bacteria.

People can float effortlessly in the Dead Sea because their bodies are less dense than the salty water.

FLOATING AND SINKING

AN OBJECT THAT IS LESS DENSE THAN WATER, SUCH AS A
log, can float in water. An object that is more dense, such
as a rock, will sink. More than 2,000 years ago, a Greek
scientist named Archimedes (c. 278–212 BC) found that an
object weighs less in water than in air because the upward
force of the water, called upthrust or buoyancy, partly
supports the object. If an object is less dense than the
water beneath it, the upthrust will support its entire weight
and the object will float. Notice that an object in water
displaces some of that water, pushing it aside. The amount
of upthrust exerted on the object equals
the weight of this displaced water.

Eureka!
Archimedes' principle states that the weight
of an object is equal to the weight of the liquid
that the object displaces. He is said to have made
his discovery when he stepped into his bathtub
and noticed the water in the tub rising. Excited,
Archimedes rushed naked into the street, crying
"Eureka!" meaning "I've got it!" He used his
findings to prove that King Hieron's
crown was not pure gold.

FLOATING STEEL

Huge ships, like the *Queen Elizabeth 2*, are made
from steel plates that weigh tens of thousands of
tons. How do such heavy ships float? The secret
is in the structure. The hull of a large ship takes up
a great deal of volume, but its overall density is less
than the density of water. The weight of the water
that it displaces equals the weight of the ship. In
other words, the displaced
water creates an upward
force (upthrust) that
exactly balances
the downward
force of the
ship's weight.

LET'S EXPERIMENT
MAKING THINGS FLOAT

IF YOU DROP a glass marble
into some water, it sinks to the
bottom because glass is denser
than water. The weight of the
marble causes a downward force
that is greater than the upthrust
of the water being displaced.
Modeling clay is also denser than
water. However, you can make
the modeling clay to float by
changing the shape to increase its
volume and decrease its density.
You will need: a ball of modeling
clay; a glass or container
of water; some marbles.

1 Drop the clay ball into the glass of
water. It sinks to the bottom because
modeling clay is denser than water.

2 Now shape the modeling clay into
a boat with a wide bottom and high
sides. Place it in the water and watch it
float. Its bigger shape displaces a
larger volume of water which is
heavy enough to balance the
weight of the modeling
clay. You may find that
the clay boat will even
hold marbles.

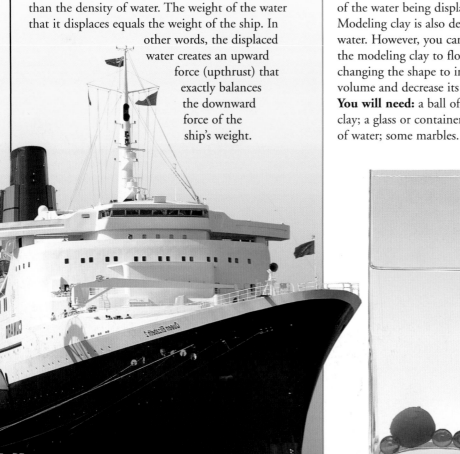

BUOYANCY

Our bodies are lighter than water, allowing us to float on the water's surface. However, this natural buoyancy makes it harder to swim underwater, because the water's upthrust tries to push the body up to the surface. This causes a particular problem for deep-sea divers, who spend long periods of time underwater. To resist buoyancy, divers wear belts with heavy lead weights attached. Their total weight acting downward balances the upthrust. In this state of neutral buoyancy, divers are in effect weightless, somewhat like an astronaut in orbit.

Diver's belt containing weights

◄ LOAD LINES ►

Boats ride high in dense water because they have to displace less water in order to float. Salty seawater is denser than freshwater, and cold seawater is densest of all. A boat fully loaded in cold seas may sink if it sails into warm seas or into a river. To prevent this, boats have Plimsoll lines to indicate maximum load level in different waters.

These fishing boats are unloaded, so they have less density and sit high in the water. 22 ►

LET'S EXPERIMENT
DEEP-SEA DIVER

MAKE A TOY DIVER that dives and surfaces according to Archimedes' principle. **You will need:** modeling clay; plastic pen cap; glass; water; paper clips; plastic soft-drink bottle with lid.

1 Attach a lump of modeling clay to the end of a plastic pen cap. Adjust the amount of clay until the top just floats above the surface in a glass of water. A bubble of air trapped inside the cap makes it light enough to float.

Seal any holes in the tip of the pen cap with modeling clay.

2 Use paper clips to make a hook and weights. Now put your diver into a full bottle of water and screw on the lid.

3 Gently squeeze the bottle. The diver sinks as extra water pushes into the pen cap, forcing the air bubble to shrink. The diver is now too heavy to float.

4 Release the bottle. The diver rises as the extra water leaves the cap, making it light enough to float again. Experiment with the number of paper clips to see how the extra weight affects your diver.

SUBMARINES

A submarine works in a similar way to the toy diver above. Special chambers called ballast tanks are filled with either air or water. On the surface, the tanks are full of air. The submarine's weight balances the upthrust of the water, so it floats. To dive, water is let into the tanks, making the submarine heavier. The submarine's weight is now greater than the upthrust, so it sinks. To surface, compressed air is blown into the tanks to force out the water and make the submarine lighter again.

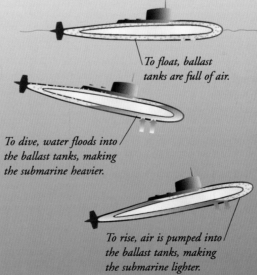

To float, ballast tanks are full of air.

To dive, water floods into the ballast tanks, making the submarine heavier.

To rise, air is pumped into the ballast tanks, making the submarine lighter.

SURFACE TENSION

CAREFULLY PLACE A STEEL PAPER CLIP IN A GLASS
of water so that it floats on the surface. Steel is denser
(heavier) than water, so how does the paper clip float?
Water and many other liquids behave as if they
have a skin on the surface. It is this "skin" that
supports the paper clip. The "skin" on liquids
is caused by the inward pull on molecules
at the surface. The effect is called surface
tension, and it explains how insects
can walk on water, why the dew on
a spider's web forms tiny, round
drops, and why water alone
cannot "wet" greasy plates.

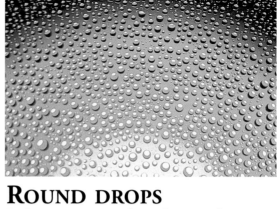

ROUND DROPS

Surface tension causes drops of water to form
a spherical shape. In the middle of a drop, the
molecules are attracted equally in all directions by
the molecules around them. At the surface, there
are no molecules above to pull outward, leaving
only an inward attraction. This inward force
pulls the surface into a shape with as small a
surface area as possible – a sphere.

Leakproof fabric

Secure a gauze bandage
over the end of a bottle
of water. Turn the bottle
upside-down – the water
will not pour out. It is
held inside by the surface
tension of the water in
the holes between
the gauze threads.
Fabric tents stop
rain from getting
through in a
similar way.

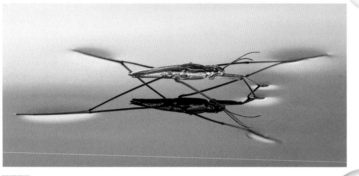

WALKING ON WATER

A pond skater skims quickly over the "springy" skin
formed by surface tension on the water. The pond skater
distributes its weight over a large area by spreading out its
legs. The skin stretches slightly under the weight
of the tiny insect, but is strong
enough to support it.

*Secure the gauze bandage
over the end of the open
bottle with a rubber band.*

BUBBLE POWER

Dip a circle of wire or plastic into a mixture
of dishwashing liquid, glycerine, and water. Surface
tension causes a skin of soapy water to form across
the circle. Blow against the skin, and it stretches to
form spherical bubbles. The glycerine makes the
solution thicker so the bubbles don't burst as easily.

Adhesion and cohesion

A contained liquid often has a curved surface, which is called the meniscus. Water in a glass tube (left) has a meniscus that curves up at the edges because water molecules are more attracted to glass molecules than to one another. We call this force adhesion. Mercury in a glass tube (right) has a meniscus that curves down at the edges. Its molecules attract one another more than they attract the glass molecules. This force is called cohesion.

Capillary action

Place a narrow tube in certain liquids and the liquid rises inside the tube. This is called capillary action. It occurs when the liquid molecules are more attracted to the molecules of the tube than they are to one another. Towels dry by means of capillary action in their fibers.

LET'S EXPERIMENT
SURFACE TENSION

CERTAIN SUBSTANCES CAN break down surface tension in a liquid. In this experiment, the surface tension of the milk initially holds the drops of food coloring in place. However, what will happen to the drops of food coloring when you add dishwashing liquid to the dish? **You will need:** shallow dish; milk; two eye-droppers; food coloring; dishwashing liquid.

2 Using a different dropper, squeeze some dishwashing liquid onto the milk. Watch the colors spread as the flexible skin on the milk starts to break down where the drops of dishwashing liquid fall. The stronger surface tension around the edge of the dish then pulls the milk and food coloring outward.

1 Pour milk into a shallow dish and leave it to warm up to room temperature. Using an eye-dropper, carefully squeeze a few drops of different food colorings onto the surface. Notice that the drops of food coloring form separate circles on the surface. The food coloring does not break the surface tension of the milk.

The food coloring and the milk swirl into one another.

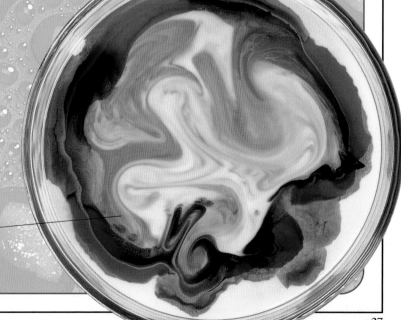

GASES

WE CAN'T USUALLY SEE OR FEEL THEM, BUT GASES

are just as real as the other two states of matter –
solids and liquids. It's just that the molecules
in gases are much farther apart. We live at
the bottom of a vast layer of gas – the
air in our atmosphere. Air is not just
one gas but a mixture of several,
the main ones being nitrogen and
oxygen – the gas we must breathe
to stay alive. Air is typically
colorless and odorless. But
other gases are colored, such
as the yellowish-green chlorine.
Some smell, such as hydrogen
sulfide, which stinks
of rotten eggs!

GAS ON THE MOVE

The molecules in gases are in constant motion,
and they travel very fast. For example, at room
temperature, air molecules travel at speeds of about
1,000 miles (1,600 km) an hour. Because they move so
fast, gases quickly fill any container they are put in. And
because their molecules are far apart, gases have a much lower
density than solids and liquids. A liter of a typical gas at room
temperature and pressure weighs less than one ounce (one gram). A liter
of water under the same conditions weighs over two pounds (one kilogram).

*Gas molecules
travel swiftly
and in all
directions.*

THE GAS LAWS

The properties of gases are
different from those of solids
and liquids. Solids have a
definite volume and shape.
Liquids have a definite volume
and no definite shape. But
gases have no definite volume
or shape. They take the
volume of their container, and
can be squeezed into a smaller
volume by pressure. Increasing
the temperature of gases can
increase their volume or their
pressure. Thus, the volume,
pressure, and temperature of
gases are all related, and are
described by three gas laws.

Boyle's law
English chemist Robert Boyle
first stated this law in 1662.
It says that if the temperature
of a gas is constant, its pressure
(P) increases as its volume (V)
decreases. Mathematically,
$P \times V$ = constant.

Pressure law
This law states that if the
volume of a gas is constant,
its pressure (P) increases as
its temperature (T) goes up.
Mathematically,
P/T = constant. This law
follows from the other laws.

Charles' law
French scientist Jacques
Charles first stated this law
in about 1787. It says that
if the pressure of a gas is
constant, its volume (V)
increases as its temperature (T)
goes up. Mathematically,
V/T = constant.

Volume

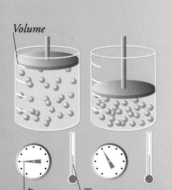

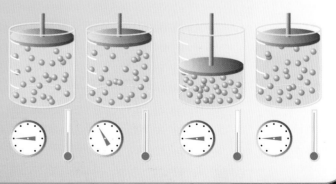

Pressure *Temperature*

GAS DIFFUSION

Because gases travel very fast, they mix rapidly and completely with each other. This process is called diffusion. We can smell a flower because its scent molecules diffuse through the air into our noses. Gases can also diffuse into and out of liquids. This happens in our lungs, where oxygen diffuses from the air into the blood, and carbon dioxide diffuses out of the blood and into the air. Gases diffuse into solids, too. This is often done during the production of microchips (p. 145), in a process called doping, in which pure silicon is impregnated with different elements.

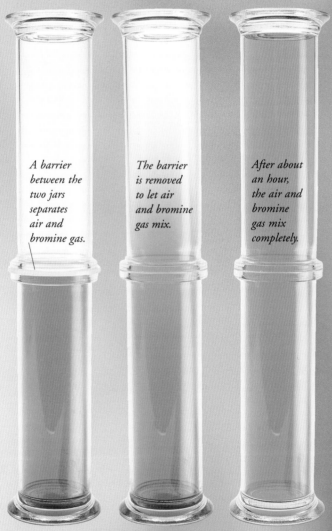

A barrier between the two jars separates air and bromine gas.

The barrier is removed to let air and bromine gas mix.

After about an hour, the air and bromine gas mix completely.

Bromine gas diffusing in air

LET'S EXPERIMENT
CREATE A GAS

WHEN YOU FIRST UNSCREW the cap of a carbonated drink bottle, gas bubbles rush out of the liquid. This gas is carbon dioxide. In this experiment, we make carbon dioxide using a simple chemical reaction.
You will need: an adult present; narrow-necked bottle; funnel; small uninflated balloon; vinegar; small amount of baking soda.

1 Pour vinegar into the bottle until it is about one-quarter full. Using the funnel, fill the uninflated balloon with baking soda. Carefully stretch the neck of the balloon over the neck of the bottle, making sure no baking soda falls in.

2 Quickly upend the balloon so that the baking soda falls into the vinegar. The vinegar, which is an acid, attacks the baking soda, releasing carbon dioxide gas. The mixture starts fizzing, and the balloon begins to inflate with the gas. Turn your face away from the balloon in case it pops.

Carbon dioxide gas inflates the balloon.

Balloon filled with baking soda

Vinegar

Vinegar and baking soda mix, producing carbon dioxide gas.

Sublimation

Most solid substances, such as metals, melt (turn into a liquid) if they are heated enough. And with more heating, the liquid eventually turns into gas. But some substances are different. For example, when iodine (below) is heated, it turns directly into a purple gas without melting into a liquid first. This process is called sublimation. Dry ice (frozen carbon dioxide) does the same, turning directly into gas as it warms up.

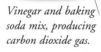

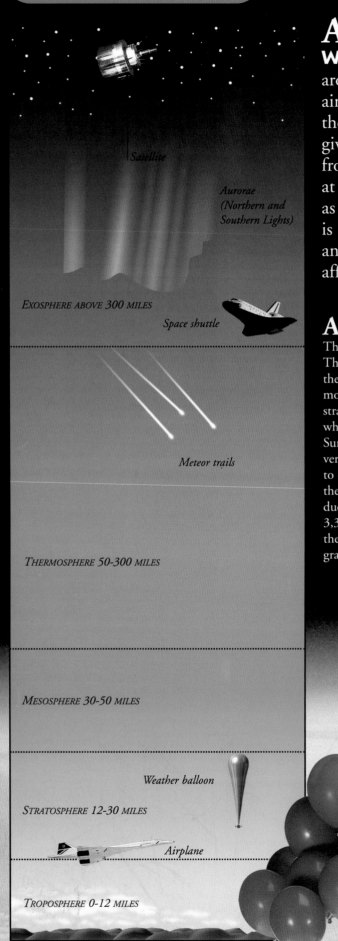

Satellite

Aurorae
(Northern and
Southern Lights)

EXOSPHERE ABOVE 300 MILES

Space shuttle

Meteor trails

THERMOSPHERE 50-300 MILES

MESOSPHERE 30-50 MILES

Weather balloon

STRATOSPHERE 12-30 MILES

Airplane

TROPOSPHERE 0-12 MILES

AIR

WE CAN'T SEE IT OR TASTE IT, BUT AIR IS ALL

around us. We live at the bottom of a great ocean of
air called the atmosphere. Without the atmosphere,
there would be no life on Earth. The atmosphere
gives us oxygen to breathe, filters out dangerous rays
from the Sun, and acts like a blanket to keep Earth
at a habitable temperature. By burning fuels, such
as gasoline in cars, more and more carbon dioxide
is released into the atmosphere, making it trap more
and more heat. This global warming seems to be
affecting weather patterns around the world.

ATMOSPHERE

The atmosphere has five layers.
The troposphere is the nearest to
the Earth's surface. This is also where
most of our weather takes place. The
stratosphere contains the ozone layer,
which filters out deadly rays from the
Sun. Above this, the mesosphere is
very cold, with temperatures dropping
to -148°F (-100°C). In the
thermosphere, temperatures rise again
due to the Sun's energy, reaching
3,300°F (1,800°C). The top layer is
the exosphere, where the atmosphere
gradually merges into space.

Hot air
Hot-air balloons rise into the
morning sky. Burning gas heats
the air inside a balloon. As the air
in the balloon gets hotter, it also
expands and becomes lighter (less
dense) than the cold air outside,
causing the balloon to rise.

GASES IN THE AIR

Air is a mixture of gases, but only nitrogen and oxygen
exist in large amounts. Air comprises 78 percent nitrogen,
21 percent oxygen, and only one percent other gases.
These balloons show the proportion of different gases
in the air. Blue represents nitrogen, red represents
oxygen, and white represents all other
gases. Humans and other
animals breathe in oxygen
from the dense air in the
troposphere. The one
percent of other gases
includes carbon dioxide
and water vapor, which
are both vital for life on
Earth. Plants take in
carbon dioxide to make
food, while water vapor
controls the weather.

ALL OF THE GASES IN AIR have different properties. Carbon dioxide, for example, is denser than air and does not support combustion, meaning that things can't burn in carbon dioxide like they can in oxygen. These two properties make carbon dioxide an ideal material for a fire extinguisher. **You will need:** an adult present; small candle; shallow bowl; match; bottle; baking soda; vinegar.

1 Place a small candle into a shallow bowl and carefully light the wick. Pour baking soda into a bottle, followed by some vinegar. The mixture fizzes and gives off an invisible gas. This is carbon dioxide. Cover the bottle with your thumb to hold in the carbon dioxide gas.

2 Carefully, bring the open end of the bottle over the burning candle and remove your thumb. The dense carbon dioxide gas sweeps away the oxygen, putting out the flame.

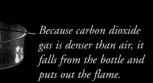

Because carbon dioxide gas is denser than air, it falls from the bottle and puts out the flame.

Make sure not to spill any liquid.

FIRST ATMOSPHERE

More than four billion years ago, erupting volcanoes created Earth's original atmosphere. Volcanoes spewed out gases such as nitrogen, carbon dioxide, and water vapor. As Earth cooled, most of the water vapor condensed out of the atmosphere to form oceans. Volcanoes, such as Popocateptl in Mexico (above), still emit dust, carbon dioxide, and water vapor into the atmosphere.

WHAT HAPPENS WHEN FIRE is starved of oxygen? How can we estimate the amount of oxygen contained in air? Many scientists have used this experiment to find out more about air. **You will need:** an adult present; candle; adhesive putty; shallow bowl of water; match; jar with wide opening.

1 Stick a piece of adhesive putty into the middle of the shallow bowl. Now stick the candle on the adhesive putty, making sure that the candle stands securely. Pour water into the bowl so it is about two-thirds full. Light the candle. Carefully place the jar upside-down over the candle to close off the air supply. Take note of the water level in the jar.

2 Notice the water level in the jar rises as the candle burns. The flame uses up the oxygen inside the jar, causing extra water to fill the available space.

3 Soon, the flame goes out because it has used up all of the oxygen in the jar. Note the water level again. The water in the jar has risen to take the place of the used-up oxygen.

The flame burns in oxygen.

Note the water level in the jar.

The flame goes out when the oxygen is used up.

The water level in the jar rises to take the place of the oxygen.

FLUID PRESSURE

DID YOU KNOW THAT YOU ARE CARRYING A
16.5 ton (15 tonne) weight? This is the force
caused by the air in the atmosphere pressing
on the outside of your body. You can't feel
this pressure because the air inside your
body is pressing back with the same
force. The large weight of air above our
heads gives air its pressure. All fluids –
gases and liquids – exert pressure in
a similar way. In science, pressure has
a precise meaning. It means the force
pressing down on a certain area, and
is measured in units of pounds per
square inch or newtons per square
meter (pascals).

RESISTING THE PRESSURE

The pressure at any point in a fluid depends on the
weight of fluid above it. Pressures are much greater in
liquids than in gases because they are denser and weigh
more. In water, the pressure 33 ft (10 m) beneath the
surface is twice atmospheric pressure – the pressure
at the surface. Some 98 ft (30 m) down, the pressure is
four times atmospheric pressure. Divers who descend
deep into the sea experience even greater pressure
that could crush their bodies. To avoid this, they
wear special metal suits built to withstand high
pressures, like this Newtsuit (right).

The deepest depths
The deepest parts of the oceans can be explored only by
special submarines with pressure-resistant hulls. The Deep
Submergence Vehicle (DSV) *Alvin* (below) can reach depths
of 14,800 ft (4,500 m). The deepest-diving craft are called
bathyscaphes. *Trieste* was one that descended to a record
depth of nearly 7 miles (11 km) in 1960.

WATER ENERGY
Engineers harness water pressure
to produce electric power. We call
it hydroelectric ("water-electric")
power. It provides about a quarter
of the world's electricity. Most
hydroelectric power plants are built
at the foot of dams, which hold
back reservoirs (stores) of water.
Water is piped from the bottom of
a reservoir through the dam to the
power plant. There it flows through
turbines and spins them around.
The turbines in turn spin generators
to make electricity. Since water is
piped from the bottom of the
reservoir, it is at high pressure.

*The Glen Canyon Dam and
hydroelectric plant on the
Colorado River in Arizona.*

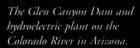

AIR PRESSURE IN THE atmosphere is always changing as warm air rises (low pressure) and cold air sinks (high pressure). By measuring the pressure in different places, scientists can tell how the weather is changing. They measure air pressure with barometers. You can make a simple one at home. **You will need:** glass or mug; balloon; rubber bands; double-sided tape; straw; wooden board; cardboard; scissors.

1 Carefully stretch a balloon over the top of an empty glass. Hold it in place with strong rubber bands. Tape the glass to the wooden board. Cut the end of the straw to a point. Tape the uncut end to the balloon. Make a scale with cardboard.

2 Attach the scale to the board so that the straw pointer reaches the scale. When the air pressure outside rises, the air inside the glass contracts (gets smaller), causing the balloon to dip and the end of the straw to move up.

3 When the air pressure outside drops, the air inside the glass expands, pushing the balloon up and the straw downward.

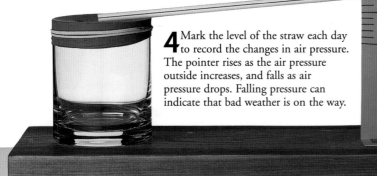

Air pressing against the bottom of the cardboard stops the water from falling out.

4 Mark the level of the straw each day to record the changes in air pressure. The pointer rises as the air pressure outside increases, and falls as air pressure drops. Falling pressure can indicate that bad weather is on the way.

AIR PRESSURE
The air in the atmosphere presses down on our bodies with a force of about 14.7 pounds on every square inch (100 kilopascals or 1 kg/sq. cm). This is called atmospheric pressure. The air doesn't just press down – it presses in all directions, including upward. This can be shown with a little trick. Fill a glass right to the brim with water and put a piece of cardboard on top. Pressing your hand against the cardboard, turn the glass upside down. Now take your hand away. The cardboard will stay where it is, held up by air pressure alone.

Compressed air
When you pump up the tires of your bike, you are forcing more air into the same space. You are compressing the air, or increasing its pressure. Compressed air is a useful source of power for driving machines, including pneumatic ("worked by air") drills for breaking up roads (above).

THE FOOT BRAKES of cars and the arms of diggers use hydraulic, or liquid-pressure, systems to transmit power. In a hydraulic system, one piston forces liquid through a pipe to push against another piston, as in this experiment. Never hold the syringes near your face, as they could pop out suddenly under the pressure. **You will need:** 2 syringes; plastic tubing; water.

1 Fill a syringe with water and pump it into a plastic tube. Half-fill a second syringe with water and connect it to the other end of the tube.

2 Press one of the plungers in, and the other one will be forced out. The water carries the pressure from one piston to the other.

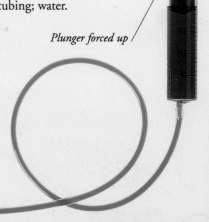

Plunger forced up

Plunger pressed down

FLUID FLOW

THE LARGEST JET AIRLINERS WEIGH

hundreds of tons, yet they can climb into the air and fly. They can do this because of forces set up by the air flowing around the wings. The science concerning the flow of fluids – liquids and gases – is known as hydrodynamics. It is important in many fields. For example, it governs the design of aircraft, cars, and even bridges and skyscrapers, which are all affected by the air flowing over them. Similarly, the way water flows affects the design of pipelines, ships, and submarines, and explains why fish and other water creatures are shaped the way they are.

Thrust of engines acts forward.

HOW FLIGHT WORKS

Aerodynamics is the science concerned with the forces acting on bodies moving through the air. It is the science that explains how airplanes can fly. The secret of flight lies in a plane's wings, which create the necessary lifting force to support it in the air. The three other main forces that act on a flying plane are its weight, the thrust, which is the propelling force of its engines, and the air resistance, also known as drag. In steady flight, lift equals weight, and thrust equals drag.

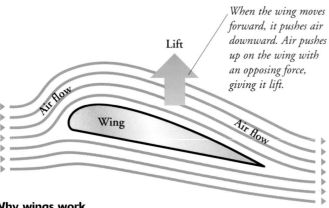

Lift

When the wing moves forward, it pushes air downward. Air pushes up on the wing with an opposing force, giving it lift.

Air flow

Wing

Air flow

Why wings work

Wings are designed with a special shape called an airfoil. When air flows past this shape, it is accelerated downward. The force of this air movement acting downward is accompanied by an equal and opposite force upward, which follows from Newton's third law of motion (pp. 64–65). This upward force is called lift. If the air flows fast enough over the wing, there will be enough lift to support it in the air.

A dolphin uses its front flippers for steering itself through the water.

Smooth, hairless skin helps with streamlining.

Upside down

Today's race cars are so light and travel so fast that they almost fly! To stop this from happening, they have upside-down airfoils attached front and rear. These foils produce a downward force that keeps the car firmly on the track.

Upside-down airfoil

Upside-down airfoil

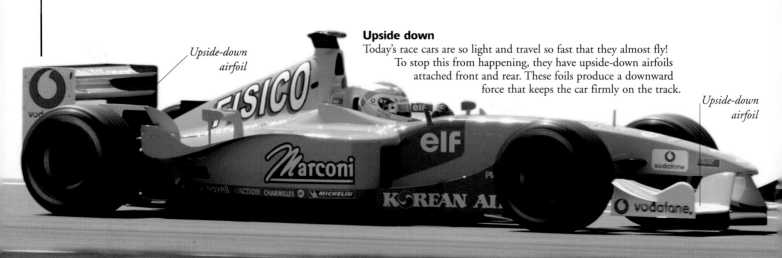

When the wing moves forward, it pushes air downward. An opposite force pushes upward, giving it lift.

Drag of air acts backward.

Weight of plane acts downward.

STREAMLINING

When objects travel through fluids, they meet resistance because of friction (pp. 66–67), and this slows them down. Planes experience a lot of air resistance, or drag, and are carefully designed to reduce it to a minimum. First, all the external surfaces are made as smooth as possible. Second, they are streamlined, which means they are shaped so that the air flows smoothly around them. To find the best shape, model planes are tested in wind tunnels, where air is blown past them. Many other objects are now tested in wind tunnels to help streamlining, including ski equipment (right).

Natural streamlining
Dolphins are among the ocean's fastest swimmers, perfectly at home in their underwater world. Their bodies are smooth and streamlined so that they slip through the water with the least resistance. They propel themselves with the tail and steer with the front flippers.

Underwater wings
Ordinary boats travel relatively slowly because of the resistance of the water on the hull. Hydrofoil boats, such as the one pictured above, can travel much faster because the hull lifts out of the water. The hull is mounted on "underwater wings," or hydrofoils, which develop lift as they travel through the water.

LET'S EXPERIMENT
AIRSTREAMS

ANOTHER ASPECT OF FLUID FLOW is that the pressure in a fluid drops as it moves faster. This is known as the Bernoulli effect, named after the Swiss mathematician Daniel Bernoulli (1700–82). We can use this theory to explain how we are able to make a table tennis ball hover in the air. **You will need:** a hairdryer set to "cool"; a table tennis ball.

1 Hold a hairdryer so that it points upward. Place the table tennis ball in the middle of the airstream.

2 You'll find that the ball will stay put. In the middle, the air flows faster (less pressure) than it does at the edges (higher pressure). The higher pressure always pushes the ball back.

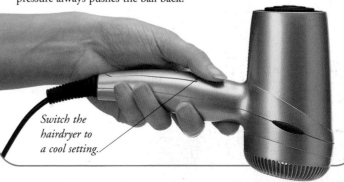

Switch the hairdryer to a cool setting.

MIXTURES AND SOLUTIONS

WHEN YOU ADD SALT TO SAND AND STIR

them together, you get a mixture. If you taste a little of this mixture, you'll still find it's salty and gritty. In general, the properties of a mixture are a combination of the properties of the substances mixed together. Mixtures are not the same as compounds. Compounds are substances in which elements are combined chemically with one another. The substances in mixtures aren't combined chemically, and so can usually be easily separated. Solutions are special kinds of mixtures.

Panning for gold.

Heavy gold particles remain in the pan.

MANY MIXTURES

Most of the substances we come across in our everyday lives are mixtures. Food is a mixture of substances like carbohydrates, fats, and proteins. Most rocks are solid mixtures of minerals. Oil is a liquid mixture of many hydrocarbons. The air we breathe is a mixture of gases, like nitrogen and oxygen. The substances in mixtures can usually be separated because of differences in their properties. Salt can be separated from sand because it dissolves in water and sand doesn't. Gold can be separated from gravel because it is much heavier. Prospectors (gold-panners) use this property when they pan for gold.

SOME LIQUIDS MIX together, others don't. Alcohol and water mix readily together – they are described as miscible. Oil and water don't mix – they are immiscible. An experiment can show this. **You will need:** cooking oil; water; food coloring; jar; dropper.

1 Pour the oil on top of the water in a jar. They form separate layers because they are immiscible. With an eyedropper, carefully place a drop of food coloring in the oil.

2 The food coloring stays as a drop because it is also immiscible with oil. Now, push the drop down into the water. It colors the water because it is miscible with water.

Fat globules suspended in milk

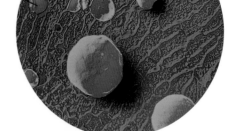

In suspension
Smoke and fog are a mixture of particles suspended in air. They are called aerosols. Suspending particles of coloring in a liquid makes most paint suspensions. Milk contains tiny globules (drops) of fat suspended in a liquid. Because the particles aren't solids, milk is called an emulsion.

Lifeblood

Blood looks like a simple red solution. In fact it is both a solution and a mixture. If you put blood in a centrifuge (a machine that separates particles) and whirl it around very fast, it separates into two parts. The clear part is a solution, called plasma. The dark part consists of tiny solid blood cells.

Plasma contains dissolved salts, foodstuffs, and gases.

Red blood cells carry oxygen. White blood cells fight infection.

IN SOLUTION

When river water flows over chalk rocks, some of the chalk mixes with the water and disappears – it dissolves and forms a chalk solution. What happens is that the chalk molecules mix completely with the water molecules. This always happens when one substance (the solute) dissolves in another (the solvent) to form a solution. Chalk comes out of solution in caves to form stalactites (on the roof) and stalagmites (on the floor). The mineral-rich water that drips into the caves evaporates. The chalk is deposited and builds up to form the icicle-like shapes.

Dissolved oxygen

Underwater life in rivers and oceans is made possible because oxygen from the air dissolves in the water. Fish and other water creatures extract the oxygen by means of their gills. This strange creature, called an axolotl, is unusual because its gills (red) are outside the body.

LET'S EXPERIMENT
DISTILLING WATER

IF YOU WERE SHIPWRECKED on a desert island with no freshwater to drink, how would you survive? You couldn't drink seawater because it's too salty. What you would have to do is remove the salt from the water (distill). This experiment shows how water can be distilled. **You will need:** an adult present; water; salt; a small saucepan; a large pan lid; a dish; a heat source. Make sure you let all equipment cool down before putting it away.

1 Make up a salt solution by dissolving one tablespoon of salt into two cupfuls of water. Pour into a saucepan and cover with a large lid. Tilt the lid as shown in the picture, and place a dish under the lower end. Ask an adult to help you heat the saucepan on the stove.

2 As the saltwater heats up, it evaporates, or turns to vapor. When the water vapor meets the cool lid, it condenses, or turns back to liquid water, which drips into the dish. Taste this water – it shouldn't be salty. The salt stays behind in the pan.

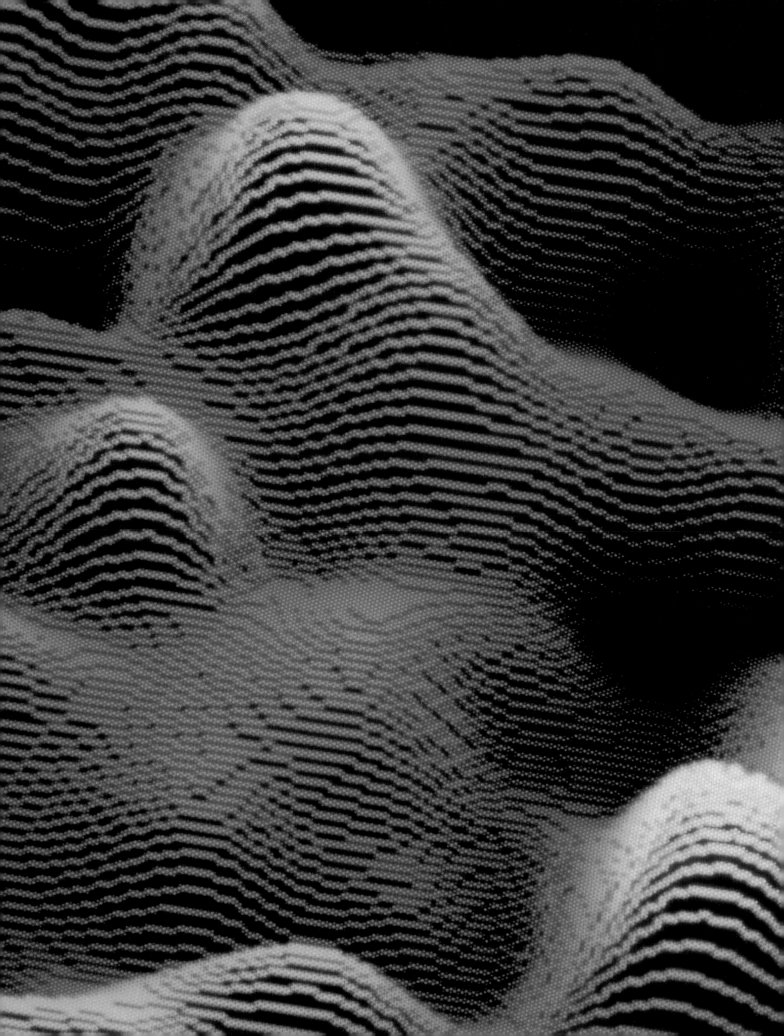

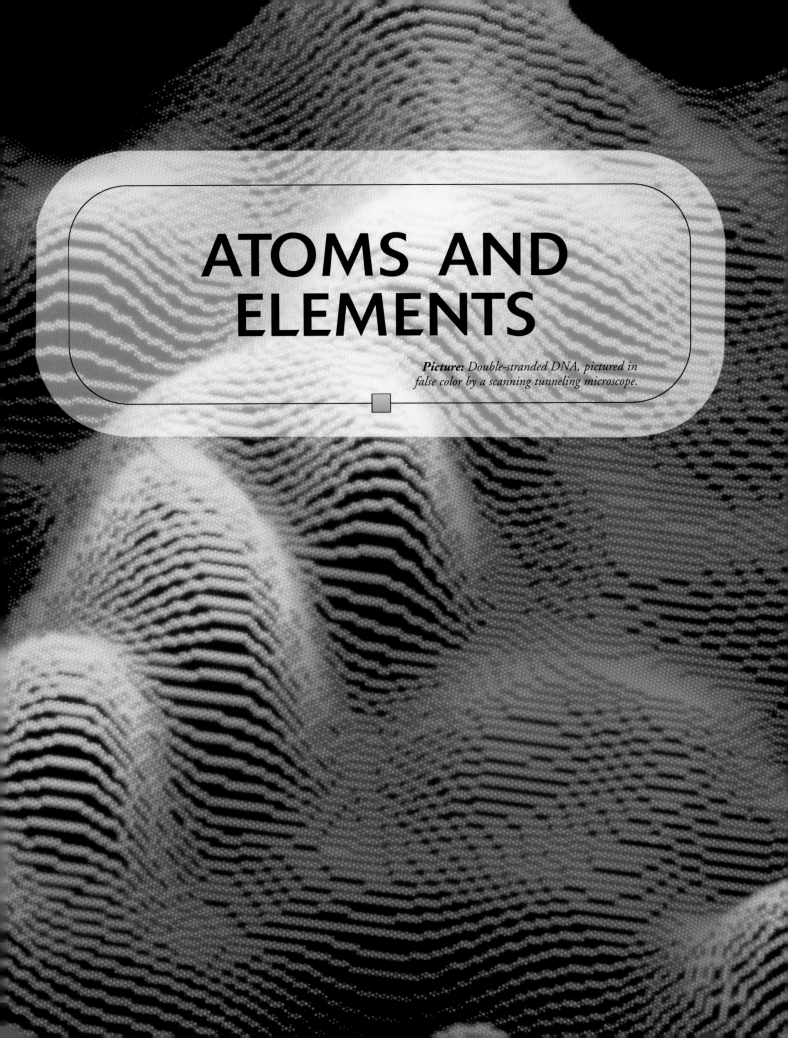

ATOMS AND ELEMENTS

Picture: *Double-stranded DNA, pictured in false color by a scanning tunneling microscope.*

LITTLE BITS OF MATTER

EVERY SUBSTANCE WE FIND IN THE WORLD AROUND US, SUCH as wood, rock, water, or air, is made up of stuff we call matter. There are millions of different kinds of matter, but they are formed from only about 90 basic substances. We call these substances the chemical elements. Gold is an element, for example, because you cannot break it down into simpler substances. In turn, the chemical elements are made up of tiny particles called atoms. All the atoms in each element are identical, and different elements have different kinds of atoms. These ideas form the basis of the atomic theory of matter.

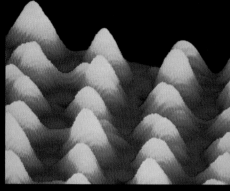

Scanning tunneling microscopes (STMs) can "see" atoms and the structures they form. This STM image shows the layered structure of a fatty acid. Fatty acids are essential ingredients of fats.

ATOMS AND MOLECULES

In most substances, the atoms are not found on their own. They are found linked to other atoms to form particles we call molecules. In certain elements, the molecules consist of combinations of the same atoms. In other substances, the molecules are combinations of different atoms. For example, water molecules consist of atoms of the elements hydrogen and oxygen linked together. It is the properties of the molecules that determine what a substance is like. The science that deals with the properties of all the different elements and other substances is called chemistry. Chemists investigate the changes that take place when substances react together. Using chemical reactions, scientists are able to change substances and make new materials.

SMASHING ATOMS

Scientists once thought that atoms were the smallest particles of matter. But they were wrong. Atoms are made up of even tinier particles, known as subatomic (smaller than the atom) particles. Most of them carry an electric charge. The electron was the first subatomic particle to be discovered, followed by the proton and the neutron. These three are by far the most important. Protons and neutrons are found together in the solid center (nucleus) of the atom. Much tinier electrons surround the nucleus. More than 200 other subatomic particles have been discovered in experiments in which scientists use beams of accelerated (speeded up) particles

to bombard atoms. The machines they use to do this are called particle accelerators, popularly known as atom-smashers.

RADIOACTIVE

The atoms of some elements do not need to be smashed before they split up. They are unstable and break down naturally. As they do, they give off streams of radiation. We call these elements radioactive. Fortunately there are not many elements in the world that are radioactive. This is a good thing because the radiation they give out can be harmful. It can damage and kill the body cells and alter the genes, affecting future generations. Of the three kinds of radiation – alpha, beta, and gamma – gamma is the highest energy. Gamma radiation can penetrate most materials.

NUCLEAR FISSION

The best-known radioactive element is uranium. Its atoms not only break down naturally – they can be made to split apart artificially. Since it is the nucleus of the

Electrically charged particles produced in nuclear experiments are detected in a bubble chamber. The particles leave a trail of hydrogen bubbles behind as they travel through the chamber.

400s BC Greek philosopher Democritus suggests that all matter is made up of indivisible particles that he calls atoms.

c. 350 BC Greek philosopher Aristotle believes matter is made up of four "elements" – earth, air, fire, and water.

1661 Irish scientist Robert Boyle states that matter is made up of "primary particles," anticipating the chemical elements.

1772 French chemist Antoine Lavoisier begins systematic experiments that lay the foundations of chemistry.

1808 English chemist John Dalton proposes that the elements are made up of atoms, and that different elements have different atoms.

Timeline

atom that splits, this process is called nuclear fission (splitting). The fission of a uranium atom releases a great deal of energy. Under the right conditions, the fission of one atom can trigger off the fission of others in a so-called chain reaction. When this happens, fantastic amounts of energy are released. When the chain reaction gets out of control, the

reaction, called fusion, which still produces fantastic amounts of energy, but no radioactivity. In nuclear fusion, atoms are made to fuse (join) together, the opposite of fission. It could be said that fusion powers the Universe, because it is the process that stars use to produce their energy. Scientists around the world are trying to harness fusion energy by combining atoms of hydrogen at lower temperatures than stars use. If they finally succeed, the world will have another clean energy source.

Nuclear scientists produce swarms of subatomic particles by smashing together beams of particles, such as protons, at high speed. To do this they use machines called colliders.

Heat is extracted by circulating a coolant through the reactor, then the heat is used to boil water into steam. The steam drives turbine generators to produce electricity, as in other power stations.

ENERGY FOREVER?

One reason nuclear power stations are not used as widely as they might is because they produce dangerous radioactive waste. Another reason is the danger that radioactivity can escape in an accident. However, there is another kind of nuclear

result is a devastating explosion. This is what happens in an atomic bomb. But when the chain reaction is brought under control, it can provide a steady source of energy. This controlled energy is harnessed at nuclear power stations in a nuclear reactor, which is where fission takes place.

A mushroom cloud of radioactive dust and gas rises over Bikini Atoll in the Pacific after an atomic bomb test in 1946. Nuclear fission produces the energy that caused the devastating explosion.

1896 French physicist Antoine Becquerel discovers radioactivity.

1897 English physicist J.J. Thomson discovers the electron.

1911 New Zealand/English scientist Ernest Rutherford discovers that atoms have a nucleus. Two years later Niels Bohr discovers electron shells.

1932 English physicist James Chadwick discovers the neutron.

1939 German chemists Otto Hahn and Fritz Strassman and Austrian physicist Lise Meitner discover nuclear fission.

1942 Italian-born American physicist Enrico Fermi builds the first nuclear reactor.

INSIDE THE ATOM

ATOMS ARE THE TINY PARTICLES THAT MAKE up all matter. But just how small are they? They are smaller than you could ever imagine – it would take millions of them side by side to measure 1 in (2.5 cm). Every atom has a central core called a nucleus, with tiny electrons circling around it at high speed. The nucleus takes up only a tiny space, since it is only about one ten-thousandth the size of the atom. If the nucleus were the size of a golf ball, the diameter of an atom would be bigger than the height of the Empire State Building in New York. Most of an atom is actually empty space!

STRUCTURE OF AN ATOM

Most of an atom's mass rests in the nucleus at the center. The nucleus contains the two heaviest nuclear particles – protons and neutrons. Much lighter electrons circle around the nucleus, with different groups circling in different layers, or shells. There are as many electrons in an atom as there are protons. The carbon atom, for example, has six protons in the nucleus and six electrons circling around it. Two electrons circle in an inner shell, four electrons in an outer shell.

LET'S EXPERIMENT
THE SIZE OF AN ATOM

IT IS VERY HARD TO imagine how tiny an atom is. You can gain an idea of its smallness by cutting up a strip of paper. **You will need:** a strip of paper 11 in (28 cm) long; scissors.

1 Cut the strip in half (cut 1). Discard one half. Now cut the other half in two (cut 2). Continue cutting the strip into halves, discarding one half, as many times as you can. Always cut parallel to the previous cut.

2 How many cuts did you make before the paper became too small to cut in half again? Probably only about eight. If you wanted to cut the paper until it was as small as an atom, you would have to cut it 30 times!

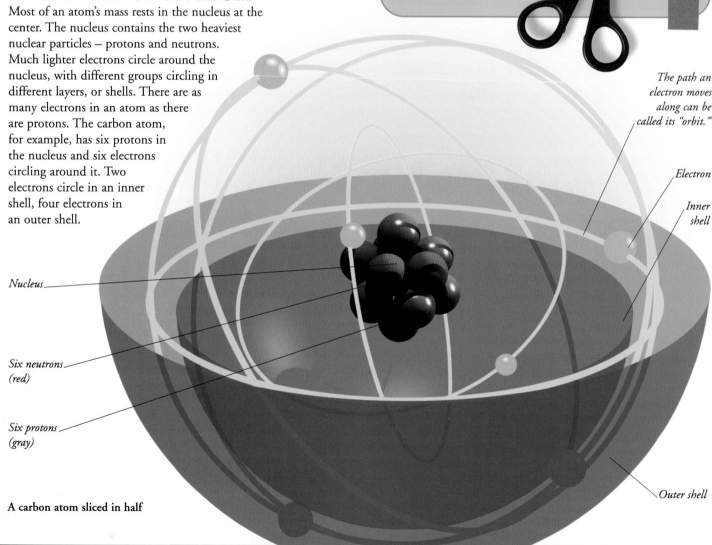

The path an electron moves along can be called its "orbit."

Electron

Inner shell

Nucleus

Six neutrons (red)

Six protons (gray)

Outer shell

A carbon atom sliced in half

*A neutron
sliced in half*

*A neutron is made
up of three quarks.*

*The tunnels housing the large accelerators
are marked on the photograph.*

*The three quarks
are held together
by particles
called gluons.*

THE MAIN PARTICLES

Protons, neutrons, and electrons are the
main particles found in atoms. Protons and
neutrons are much bigger – they are more
than 1,800 times heavier than electrons.
Protons have a tiny positive electric
charge. Neutrons have no charge – they
are neutral. Electrons have a tiny negative
electric charge. The atom is held together
by the attraction between the positive
and negative charges. Because they have
equal numbers of protons and electrons,
atoms are electrically neutral. Electrons are
true basic, or fundamental, atomic particles.
But protons and neutrons are not. They are
each made up of three particles called quarks,
which are true fundamental particles.

Particle physics
Physicists divide the 200 or
so known subatomic particles
into a number of families,
which includes quarks, baryons,
mesons, and leptons. Protons
and neutrons are baryons.
Electrons are leptons. Mesons
are found in cosmic rays.
Machines called accelerators
are used to produce and study
these particles. The largest is
found in a circular tunnel near
Geneva, Switzerland. It is
17 miles (27 km) in diameter.

Ernest Rutherford
(1871–1937)
Born in New Zealand,
Ernest Rutherford
made fundamental
discoveries in nuclear
science. In 1902, he
explained the nature
of radioactivity in his
"theory of atomic transmutation," which
won him the Nobel prize for chemistry
in 1908. Three years later, he proposed
his revolutionary atomic theory that saw
the atom as a kind of solar system, with
a heavy nucleus at the center and electrons
circling around it. In 1919, Rutherford
carried out the first artificial atomic
transmutation – changing one element
(nitrogen) into another (oxygen). In
this and subsequent transmutations,
Rutherford found that positively charged
hydrogen atoms were always given off,
So he concluded that they must be
common to the nuclei of all atoms.
Rutherford called these particles protons.

ISOTOPES

All the atoms in an element
contain the same number
of protons, but the
number of neutrons may
vary. Iron, for example, is
made up of four kinds of
atoms, or isotopes, each
with different numbers
of neutrons. Altogether in
nature there are about 320
different isotopes. Most of
them are stable and never
change. But some are unstable.
We call them radioisotopes because they
are radioactive and break down into other elements. Living
things contain traces of a carbon radioisotope, carbon-14
(most of our carbon is carbon-12). Archaeologists can date
ancient remains by the amount of carbon-14 left in them.

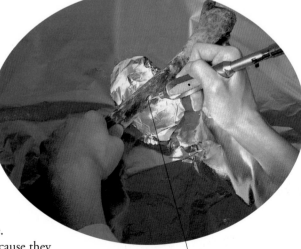

*Samples being taken
from an ancient
bone prior to
radiocarbon dating*

Deadly waste
Radioactive isotopes
give off three kinds
of dangerous radiation.
Alpha rays penetrate
the least and are easily
blocked. Beta rays are
more penetrating, and
gamma rays more
penetrating still. The
fuel elements from
nuclear reactors are
highly radioactive and
are stored in deep pools
of water. The radiation
makes the water
particles glow blue.

ELEMENTS AND COMPOUNDS

THE CHEMICAL ELEMENTS ARE THE BUILDING BLOCKS from which all matter is put together. About 90 elements are found in nature, but we come across only a few on their own. One is graphite, a form of carbon found in pencils. Another is gold, found in its pure state in 24-carat jewelry. Most elements are found combined with other elements as compounds – water is a compound of hydrogen and oxygen, for example. In a compound, the elements are not just mixed together. They are linked to each other by strong bonds and cannot simply be separated like mixtures.

Dalton's atomic theory
Around 400 BC, a Greek philosopher named Democritus suggested that matter was made up of tiny particles he called atoms. However, his idea didn't catch on. It was not until 1808 that this theory of matter was revived. In that year, the English chemist John Dalton put forward his atomic theory, based on years of experimental work. He said that all elements are made up of atoms that cannot be destroyed or split. All the atoms in the same element are similar, and elements are different because they have different atoms.

John Dalton (1766–1844)

BIRTH OF THE ELEMENTS

All the elements in our world came from the stars. Deep inside their cores, stars build up elements in nuclear fusion reactions. They use as their starting point hydrogen, the simplest and most common element in the Universe. First they make it into helium, then transform helium into carbon, and so on. Over time, many elements are produced. When the star dies, it may explode and scatter the elements throughout space, and make new elements in the explosion.

A star explodes as a supernova in 1987.

Galileo space probe carries batteries with plutonium.

Same but different
Ordinary oxygen gas is made up of molecules containing two oxygen atoms. But high in the atmosphere there is a layer of oxygen that contains three atoms in each molecule. We call this form of oxygen ozone. Ozone is an allotrope (another form) of oxygen. It is the same element, but put together differently.

A false-color image of the Earth's thinning ozone layer

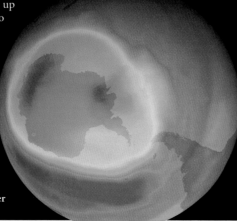

ARTIFICIAL ELEMENTS

Of the elements found in nature, uranium has the biggest atom, which contains 92 protons. In 1940, a team of US scientists led by Glenn Seaborg bombarded uranium with deuterons (the nuclei of a heavy isotope of hydrogen) and created a new element containing 94 protons. Called plutonium, it was the first artificial element made. Since then many have been produced, with more than 109 protons in the nucleus. They are known as transuranium elements and, like uranium, they are all radioactive.

BONDING

Most elements combine with other elements to form compounds. To form a compound, the atoms of one element form links, or bonds, with the atoms of others. Atoms form bonds in different ways, using the electrons in their outer shells. These electrons may be transferred or shared.

Ionic bonds

When sodium combines with chlorine to form sodium chloride, an electron from the sodium atom is transferred to the chlorine atom. The atoms become electrically charged ions, and the link between them is called an ionic bond.

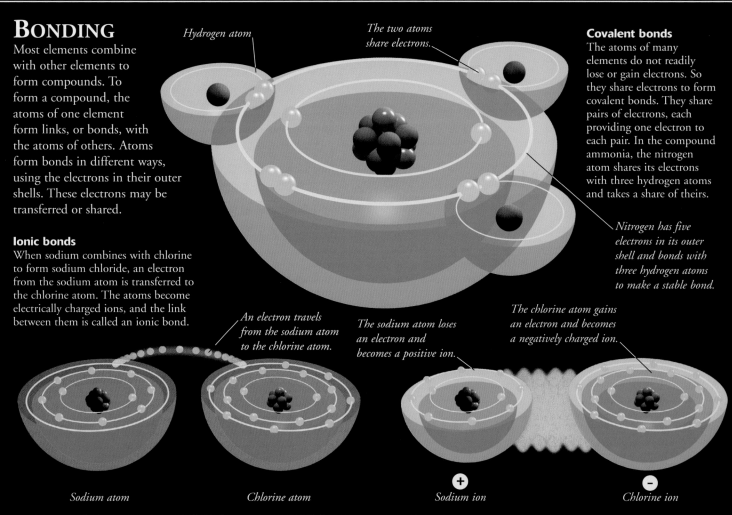

Hydrogen atom

The two atoms share electrons.

Covalent bonds

The atoms of many elements do not readily lose or gain electrons. So they share electrons to form covalent bonds. They share pairs of electrons, each providing one electron to each pair. In the compound ammonia, the nitrogen atom shares its electrons with three hydrogen atoms and takes a share of theirs.

Nitrogen has five electrons in its outer shell and bonds with three hydrogen atoms to make a stable bond.

An electron travels from the sodium atom to the chlorine atom.

The sodium atom loses an electron and becomes a positive ion.

The chlorine atom gains an electron and becomes a negatively charged ion.

Sodium atom

Chlorine atom

⊕ *Sodium ion*

⊖ *Chlorine ion*

MOLECULAR STRUCTURES

The smallest unit of a covalent compound that can exist on its own is the molecule. Ionic compounds do not form individual molecules. They are just collections of positive and negative ions. Chemists may make models of molecules, using balls for atoms and sticks for bonds. They use a chemical formula to describe the makeup of a molecule or compound, using symbols to represent the atoms.

Many forms

Carbon is found in nature in two very different forms, as graphite and diamond. Graphite is very soft, while diamond is the hardest substance there is. They are different because they have very different structures. We call substances that have different forms polymorphic, meaning "many shapes."

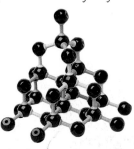

Graphite carbon atoms form flat sheets.

Hydrogen

Carbon

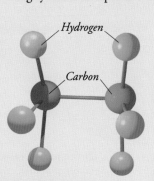

Oxygen

Carbon dioxide (CO₂)

In the molecule, the carbon atom shares pairs of electrons with each oxygen atom.

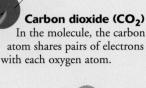

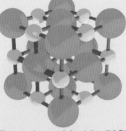

Ethane (C₂H₆)

In the molecule, each carbon atom shares a pair of electrons with three hydrogen atoms and also shares a pair of electrons with the other carbon atom.

Chlorine (Cl₂)

The molecule is made up of two chlorine atoms, sharing one pair of electrons.

Potassium chloride (KCl)

An ionic compound, made up of potassium and chlorine ions held in a lattice.

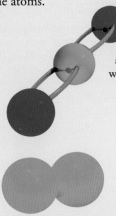

Diamond carbon atoms form a 3-D structure.

METALS AND NONMETALS

AMONG THE 90 OR SO ELEMENTS THAT OCCUR naturally in the world, nearly 70 are metals. They have very different properties from the remaining elements, which are called nonmetals and semimetals. Nonmetals include solid elements such as carbon and gaseous elements such as nitrogen. Most metals are shiny, strong, and have a high density and high melting point. They conduct heat and electricity well. In contrast, most nonmetals are dull, weak, and have a low density and low melting point. They don't conduct heat and electricity well. The semimetals (metalloids) have properties between metals and nonmetals.

Liquid metal
Mercury is unusual among metals because it is a liquid at room temperature. But it has all the other properties of a typical metal. It is silvery in color and conducts heat and electricity well.

GOOD CONDUCTORS
Metals have a number of properties that distinguish them from other elements. Most metals, for example, are hard and shiny. Gold is used to coat astronauts' visors (above) as it reflects bright sunlight well and doesn't corrode. Most metals are able to conduct, or pass on, heat and electricity. That is why we make pots and pans out of metal and use metal wires to carry electricity. In the atoms of a metal, the electrons are easily shared and drift readily from atom to atom. They can flow throughout the metal carrying heat or electricity.

A semiconductor wafer

SOFT SULFUR
Sulfur is a typical nonmetal. Yellow in color, it is a soft, light substance that melts easily and doesn't conduct heat or electricity. Sulfur behaves chemically much like oxygen – it is very reactive when it combines with other substances – and is found in the same group in the Periodic Table. On Earth, it is found in its natural state around the vents (openings) from volcanoes. It is also found on volcanoes on Jupiter's moon Io. Sulfur constantly flowing from Io's volcanoes has given the moon its vivid yellow-orange color.

Elements in between
Some elements are neither true metals nor true nonmetals, but have properties in between. They are often called semimetals or metalloids. In their pure state, the semimetals can hardly conduct electricity at all. But when certain elements are added to them, they start to conduct electricity a little. They become semiconductors. Silicon is the most common semiconductor, used to make microchips for computers and other electronic devices (pp. 144–145).

TOO REACTIVE

Magnesium metal burns rapidly in air with a dazzling white flame (right). It is a highly reactive element. This is the reason we don't find magnesium by itself in nature. We find it combined with other elements in compounds, such as magnesium sulfate (commonly known as Epsom salts). Most other elements are similarly too reactive to be found by themselves. Some exceptions are carbon, sulfur, some gases (such as oxygen), and the precious metals (such as gold). We call elements that can be found in nature native elements.

Dmitri Mendeleyev (1834–1907)

In the 1800s, chemists began trying to find ways of arranging the elements into some kind of order. Most successful was the Russian chemist Dmitri Mendeleyev. In 1869, he listed the 63 known elements in order of their atomic weights and arranged them into a table. (We now call atomic weight relative atomic mass. It's a way of comparing the masses of the atoms of the elements). He arranged the elements so that they showed a periodic change in properties. Since Mendeleyev created the table, every new element discovered has fit into the table.

The noble gases

The elements in the last group in the Periodic Table are gases. They are unusual because they don't combine readily with other elements. Only a few of their compounds have been prepared. Helium, used to fill airships, is one of the most useful of these so-called noble gases.

THE PERIODIC TABLE

The Periodic Table arranges the elements in a way that brings out their chemical relationships. It is organized into horizontal rows called periods and vertical columns called groups. The groups gather together elements with similar properties. Group I, for example, brings together highly reactive metals like sodium and potassium. Along a period, there is a gradual change in properties. In Period 3, for example, magnesium is less reactive than sodium, and aluminum less reactive than magnesium.

The atomic number shows the number of protons in the nucleus.

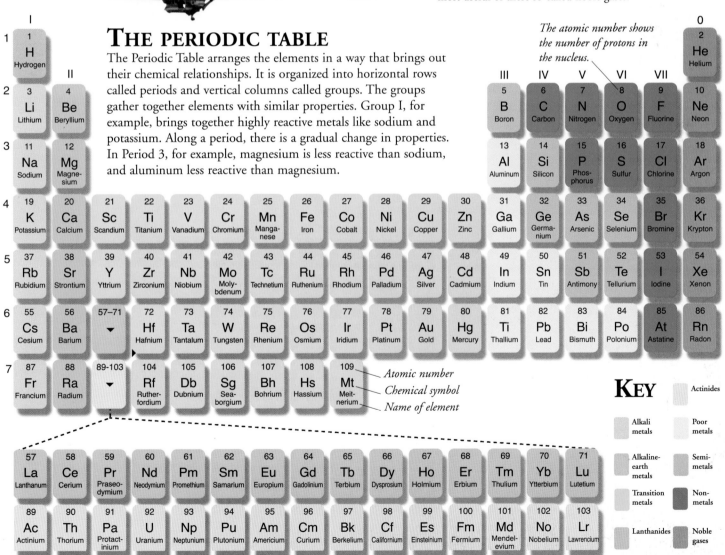

47

CHEMICAL REACTIONS

AROUND US, EVEN INSIDE US, ALL KINDS OF chemicals are constantly coming together and changing into different substances. We call these processes chemical reactions. Chemical reactions take place, for example, when wood burns on a fire, when nails turn rusty, and when you boil an egg. Inside our bodies, they help to keep us alive. Breathing and eating involve the chemical reaction of oxidation, in which oxygen combines with food to produce the energy we need. Oxidation is one of the most common chemical reactions. Burning and rusting involve oxidation too. Some reactions, such as rusting, take place slowly, whereas others, such as explosions, take place very quickly.

Oxidation and reduction

In an oxidation reaction, a substance can gain oxygen. It follows, therefore, that another substance has lost oxygen. That loss of oxygen is called reduction. Reactions in which oxidation and reduction go hand in hand are called redox reactions. Iron smelting is a redox reaction. In smelting, carbon is oxidized to carbon dioxide, and iron oxide ore is reduced to iron.

Iron is obtained from iron ore by a process known as smelting.

‹ PHYSICAL CHANGE ›

When iron metal rusts, it changes into another substance, iron oxide. It undergoes a chemical change, and you can't easily get the metal back. When an ice pop melts, it changes into a liquid. It only undergoes a physical change. It's still the same chemical substance (water) but in a different physical form. 14 ▶

Ice pops change their physical state when they melt.

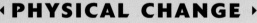

FAST FIRE

Combustion (burning) is a fast oxidation reaction. When substances burn, they combine with oxygen in the air and give out energy as heat and light (flames). Fuels such as coal and oil are substances that burn well and give out plenty of energy. They contain a lot of carbon, which combines with the oxygen in the air to form carbon dioxide gas. Reactions that give out energy, like combustion, are termed exothermic. Some reactions, however, take in heat and are known as endothermic. Instant cold packs use endothermic reactions.

SLOW BUT SURE

If shiny steel nails are left outside, they don't remain shiny for long. They become covered with a reddish-brown coating of rust. The iron in the nails gets attacked by oxygen and moisture in the air to form iron oxide. This process, rusting, is an example of a slow oxidation reaction. The rust layer on iron gradually flakes away, exposing more and more iron to attack. In time the whole metal corrodes and the nail is eaten away. Many metals corrode, but some, such as gold, resist corrosion. That is why gold can remain shiny for centuries.

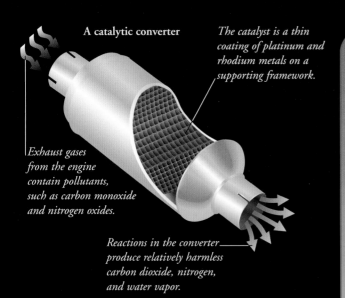

A catalytic converter

The catalyst is a thin coating of platinum and rhodium metals on a supporting framework.

Exhaust gases from the engine contain pollutants, such as carbon monoxide and nitrogen oxides.

Reactions in the converter produce relatively harmless carbon dioxide, nitrogen, and water vapor.

SPEEDING UP REACTIONS

Cars produce substances in their exhausts that cause pollution, including carbon monoxide, unburned fuel, and nitrogen oxides. To combat this problem, many are equipped with catalytic converters. These are so called because they convert the pollutants into less harmful gases with the help of a catalyst. A catalyst is a substance that helps bring about and speed up a chemical reaction, but doesn't get changed by the reaction. They reduce the energy needed for the reaction to take place. The reacting substances generally attach to the catalyst, react, and then let go.

LET'S EXPERIMENT
A FIZZY REACTION

CARBONATES ARE COMMON chemical compounds, in which a metal combines with carbon and oxygen. When acids, such as vinegar, attack carbonates, they release carbon dioxide gas. For this experiment, **you will need:** a glass and a dish; baking soda; detergent powder; vinegar; a spoon; red and blue food coloring.

1 Mix baking soda, detergent powder, blue coloring, and a bit of water in the glass and place it in a dish. Squeeze a few drops of red coloring into the vinegar and pour it into the glass.

2 The mixture may splutter, so turn your face away at first. The mixture fizzes vigorously, as the acid and carbonate react together, giving off carbon dioxide. The oozing froth looks like a mini volcanic eruption!

ELECTRIC REACTIONS

Chemical reactions need energy to work. In the atmosphere, lightning supplies the energy for reactions between nitrogen and oxygen, present in air, to form nitrogen oxide. This combines with moisture to form nitric acid, which rain then washes into the soil. The acid combines with other substances to form salts called nitrates, which are valuable nutrients for plants. Chemists also use electricity to bring about reactions. They use it to split up chemical compounds, in a process called electrolysis. Aluminum is extracted from its ore by electrolysis.

CHEMISTS AT WORK

USING THEIR KNOWLEDGE OF THE CHEMICAL elements and how they react together, chemists have developed countless useful products, such as plastics, new dyes, and new medicines. Chemists are scientists who study the properties and makeup of substances and the changes that take place in them. In two separate branches of chemistry, organic chemists study carbon and the compounds it forms, while inorganic chemists study all the other elements. Research into living things and the chemical changes that take place within them is the work of biochemists.

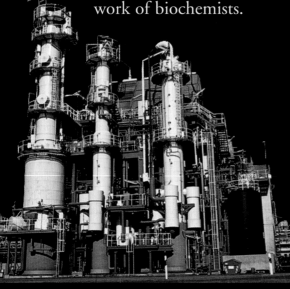

Chemical industry
Distillation – condensing vapors back into liquids – is a common factory process. This photograph (above) shows the distillation towers of a large chemical factory. The chemical industry produces millions of tons of chemicals every year, particularly acids, alkalis, and fertilizers, which are known as heavy chemicals. Chemical engineers design chemical factories and reproduce on a large scale the reactions that chemists carry out in their laboratories.

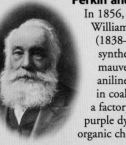

Perkin and synthetic dye
In 1856, the English chemist William Henry Perkin (1838–1907) made the first synthetic (artificial) dye, mauveine. He prepared it from aniline, an organic substance in coal tar. In 1857, he built a factory to produce the vivid purple dye, and launched the organic chemical industry.

FLAME TESTS

Chemists can use flame tests to identify the elements present in particular chemical samples. Because the tests involve hazardous chemicals, they are carried out under strictly controlled laboratory conditions. Scientists burn a little of each sample and note how it colors the flame. Different elements turn the flame different colors. Here, chemists burn salts (such as nitrates) of barium, copper, sodium, and lithium using methylated spirit. The salts are ground into a powder and put in separate glass dishes before methylated spirit is added and lit with a match. The color of the flame when it touches the salt indicates which element is present in the chemical sample.

Barium salts give the flame a greenish tinge.

TESTING TIMES

The analysis of chemical samples is an important part of a chemist's work. In qualitative analysis, chemists aim to find the nature of substances present in different samples. They may conduct simple tests, such as a flame test, and then carry out more systematic investigations using a range of standard chemicals and sophisticated apparatus. In quantitative analysis, chemists try to find the amounts of each substance present. They need to separate the various substances in the sample, then work out how much of each substance is present.

LET'S EXPERIMENT
CHROMATOGRAPHY

CHEMISTS OFTEN USE a technique called chromatography to separate substances from a mixture. Chromatography can be used to separate colored dyes and pigments. **You will need:** inks or food coloring; some glass jars; blotting paper; water; bulldog clips.

1 Mix together the inks (or food colors) in small jars, putting a different mixture into each one.

2 Place a drop of each mixture on separate strips of blotting paper. Put a little water in some clean jars, then attach a bulldog clip to each strip of blotting paper and dangle a strip into each jar so they just dip into the water.

3 As the water flows up through the paper, it carries the colors with it. Some colors travel faster than others, so the mixtures split into colored bands.

Methylated spirit by itself burns blue. This is the test flame.

Copper salts burn bright green.

Sodium salts burn a vivid yellow-orange.

Lithium salts burn bright red.

51

ACIDS AND BASES

WHEN YOU BITE INTO A LEMON, IT TASTES VERY SOUR.
If you drink stale milk, you find that this tastes sour, too. So does vinegar. They taste sour because they contain acids. The word acid means "sour" in Latin. The acids in lemons, sour milk, and vinegar are weak, but other acids are strong and dangerous. Car batteries contain sulfuric acid, which burns skin and attacks metals. Acids have chemical opposites, called bases. The bases that dissolve in water are called alkalis, and like acids, bases can be strong or weak. One of the strongest bases is caustic soda, a substance used in oven cleaners. It is termed caustic because it can burn flesh. Soap, on the other hand, is a weak base. Bases tend to feel soapy or slippery to the touch.

ACID ATTACK
Sulfuric acid is one of the most common acids. When concentrated, it can burn paper and human flesh. The acid dehydrates any substance it comes into contact with. It reacts with paper (above), which contains carbon, hydrogen, and oxygen, and leaves behind black carbon. In solution, the most common acids produce electrically charged particles of hydrogen, called hydrogen ions. Scientists give these ions the symbol H^+ because they have a positive electric charge.

Acid rain
When coal burns in power stations, it releases sulfur dioxide into the atmosphere. This combines with moisture in the air to form droplets of diluted sulfuric acid. When it rains, it rains acid, which can kill trees and pollute lakes and rivers.

Weak acids
The acid that gives lemons and other citrus fruits their sharp taste is citric acid. Apples and grapes contain a lot of tartaric acid. Sour milk contains lactic acid. These organic acids are much weaker than inorganic acids, such as sulfuric acid, because they don't let go of their hydrogen ions very easily.

ALKALIS
Lime is an alkali that can be used to treat acid in polluted water. A helicopter (left) is dropping lime onto a polluted lake in Sweden. Treating the lake with lime combats, or neutralizes, the acid in it. Lime is the compound calcium hydroxide. Like all alkalis, it produces hydroxide ions (OH^-) in solution. Acids can produce hydrogen ions (H^+). When an alkali and acid get together, the hydrogen ions and hydroxide ions combine to form water. If all the ions are used up, the final solution will be neutral – neither acidic nor alkaline.

Sting in the tail

Bee stings are very painful. The bee injects acid into a person's flesh with its barbed sting (shown magnified above). The person who has been stung can relieve the pain after the sting has been removed by washing the wound with soap. Soap is a mild alkali that neutralizes the acid. Ants and nettles also sting with acid.

Soothing the stomach

Sometimes when people eat very rich foods, acid builds up in their stomachs, which makes them feel uncomfortable. To relieve the symptoms of acid indigestion, sufferers can take antacid tablets. These contain a mild alkali, such as calcium carbonate, which reacts with the acid in the stomach and neutralizes it.

LET'S EXPERIMENT
ACID INDICATORS

CHEMISTS USE CHEMICAL solutions called indicators to find out whether a substance is an acid or an alkali, and also to see exactly how acidic or alkaline it is. Indicators work by changing color. A common indicator is litmus, made from certain plants called lichens. Litmus is red in acid solutions and blue in alkaline solutions. Indicators can also be made from other plant materials. In this experiment, red cabbage is used. **You will need:** an adult present; red cabbage; knife; saucepan; heat source; sieve; three jars; lemon juice; milk of magnesia (available from pharmacies); baking soda. Do not attempt to mix the test substances used in this experiment.

1 Chop up a red cabbage and slice it thinly. Next, heat a saucepan of clean water until it boils.

2 Carefully add the cabbage to the boiling water. Then take the pan off the heat. Leave it to cool.

3 Strain the cabbage through a sieve, catching the reddish-purple water in a jar. This is your indicator.

4 Pour a little of the indicator into jars. Add the substances you want to test, and note any change in color.

Lemon juice	Milk of magnesia	Baking soda

A weak acid turns the indicator red.

A fairly strong alkali turns the indicator green.

A weak alkali turns the indicator bluish-purple.

THE PH SCALE

How acidic or alkaline a solution is relates to the number of hydrogen ions (H^+) that are present. A solution with many such ions is strongly acidic. A solution with few ions is alkaline. Chemists can work out the amount of ions present using the pH scale. The letters pH stand for "power of hydrogen." On this scale, a solution with a pH of 1 is strongly acidic, and a solution with a pH of 14 is strongly alkaline. Neutral solutions, which are neither acidic nor alkaline, have a pH of 7.

Indicator paper turns pink in diluted hydrochloric acid, which has a pH of about 1.

Color changes in universal indicator paper

Hydrochloric acid / pH of about 1

Vinegar / pH of about 4

Tap water / pH of about 6

Liquid soap / pH of about 8–9

Household cleaner / pH of about 10

CARBON CHEMISTRY

CARBON IS ONE OF THE MOST COMMON ELEMENTS IN THE
world around us. Because carbon atoms link readily, both with
each other and with other elements, they can form millions of
different compounds. The variety of carbon substances found in
nature ranges from carbon dioxide in the air, to
diamonds, the hardest mineral on Earth.
Scientists once believed that all but the simplest
carbon compounds could only be produced by
living organisms. They used the term "organic" to
refer to carbon compounds, and the study of
carbon compounds was called organic
chemistry. We still use the term organic, even
though synthetic carbon compounds are
now commonplace.

ELEMENT OF LIFE

Carbon is vital to all living things.
For example, the sap from rubber
trees (above) contains a carbon
compound called isoprene (C_5H_8),
which forms a natural plastic. Like all
plants, the rubber tree absorbs carbon
dioxide (CO_2) from the air. Plants
combine carbon dioxide with water
to produce carbohydrates, which are
compounds of carbon, hydrogen, and
oxygen. Fossil fuels, such as oil, gas,
and coal, also release carbon dioxide
into the air when they burn. In fact,
fossil fuels are actually carbon
compounds created by decayed
plants and animals.

*Hydrogen atoms
linked to the
carbon chain*

*Carbon atoms
form the
backbone of
a polythene
polymer.*

Thermosets and thermoplastics
This old radio is made from Bakelite,
the first entirely synthetic plastic,
developed in 1907. Bakelite is an
example of a thermoset plastic,
which is set rigid after it hardens
and does not melt if reheated.
Polythene and nylon are
examples of thermoplastics,
which do melt if reheated. Plastics
are very useful, but can cause a
problem for the environment
because the molecules do not
break down and decay.

MOLECULE CHAINS

Most substances, such as water (H_2O)
and carbon dioxide (CO_2), have small
molecules that consist of a
few atoms. Many carbon
compounds have large
molecules with carbon
atoms linked together in
a long chain. Chemists use
the property of carbon atoms to link together
in chains to make plastics, a type of synthetic carbon
compound. Another name for plastics is polymers,
which means "many parts." Each basic repeated unit
of the chain is a monomer, which means "one part."

*The monomer
ethene (C_2H_4) forms
the basic unit of the
plastic polythene.*

Synthetic dyes
People have always liked to dye their
clothes, but were once limited in their
choice of colors. They had to extract
natural dyes from plants, snails, and
even insects. Today, we make most dyes
synthetically, using organic chemicals
from oil to produce an unlimited variety
of colors. Synthetic dyes
are generally brighter
and longer-lasting
than natural dyes.

Sting in the tail

Bee stings are very painful. The bee injects acid into a person's flesh with its barbed sting (shown magnified above). The person who has been stung can relieve the pain after the sting has been removed by washing the wound with soap. Soap is a mild alkali that neutralizes the acid. Ants and nettles also sting with acid.

Soothing the stomach

Sometimes when people eat very rich foods, acid builds up in their stomachs, which makes them feel uncomfortable. To relieve the symptoms of acid indigestion, sufferers can take antacid tablets. These contain a mild alkali, such as calcium carbonate, which reacts with the acid in the stomach and neutralizes it.

LET'S EXPERIMENT
ACID INDICATORS

CHEMISTS USE CHEMICAL solutions called indicators to find out whether a substance is an acid or an alkali, and also to see exactly how acidic or alkaline it is. Indicators work by changing color. A common indicator is litmus, made from certain plants called lichens. Litmus is red in acid solutions and blue in alkaline solutions. Indicators can also be made from other plant materials. In this experiment, red cabbage is used. **You will need:** an adult present; red cabbage; knife; saucepan; heat source; sieve; three jars; lemon juice; milk of magnesia (available from pharmacies); baking soda. Do not attempt to mix the test substances used in this experiment.

1 Chop up a red cabbage and slice it thinly. Next, heat a saucepan of clean water until it boils.

2 Carefully add the cabbage to the boiling water. Then take the pan off the heat. Leave it to cool.

3 Strain the cabbage through a sieve, catching the reddish-purple water in a jar. This is your indicator.

4 Pour a little of the indicator into jars. Add the substances you want to test, and note any change in color.

Lemon juice	Milk of magnesia	Baking soda

A weak acid turns the indicator red.	*A fairly strong alkali turns the indicator green.*	*A weak alkali turns the indicator bluish-purple.*

THE PH SCALE

How acidic or alkaline a solution is relates to the number of hydrogen ions (H^+) that are present. A solution with many such ions is strongly acidic. A solution with few ions is alkaline. Chemists can work out the amount of ions present using the pH scale. The letters pH stand for "power of hydrogen." On this scale, a solution with a pH of 1 is strongly acidic, and a solution with a pH of 14 is strongly alkaline. Neutral solutions, which are neither acidic nor alkaline, have a pH of 7.

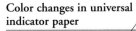

Indicator paper turns pink in diluted hydrochloric acid, which has a pH of about 1.

Color changes in universal indicator paper	Hydrochloric acid pH of about 1	Vinegar pH of about 4	Tap water pH of about 6	Liquid soap pH of about 8–9	Household cleaner pH of about 10

SALTS AND SOAPS

WHEN YOU GO SWIMMING IN THE OCEAN,
you will notice how salty the water is. This is
because the water is full of dissolved salts. The
main one is the chemical compound sodium
chloride, better known as common or table salt –
the ingredient we use to season our food. Salts are
formed when acids react with alkalis and other
bases, or when acids attack metals. Chlorides can
be produced from hydrochloric acid. Sulfates can
be made from sulfuric acid, and nitrates from
nitric acids. Soaps and detergents are special salts
that can remove grease and dirt.

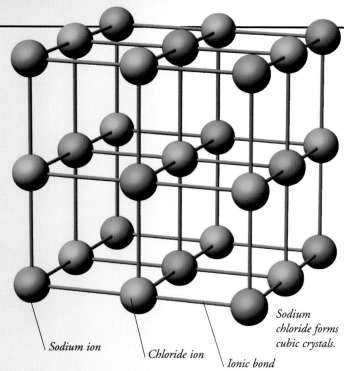

Sodium ion

Chloride ion

Ionic bond

Sodium chloride forms cubic crystals.

IONIC COMPOUNDS

Most salts are ionic compounds, made up of ions
(electrically charged atoms). Sodium chloride, for
example, is made up of positively charged sodium
ions and negatively charged chloride ions. In the solid
state, the ions in salt arrange themselves into a rigid
structure called a lattice. The electrical attraction
between the negative and positive charges makes a
bond between the ions. In water, most salts dissolve
easily because the ions attract the water molecules.

Adding fluoride
Fluorine is one of
the many minerals the
human body needs to stay
healthy. It helps make stronger
bones and teeth. In some areas,
fluoride salts are added to the
drinking water to help prevent tooth
decay. Fluorides are added to some
toothpastes for the same reason.

Panning for salts
Every quart of seawater holds
about 1 oz (25 g) of salt. In hot
climates, salt is "mined" straight
from the ocean. This is done by
channeling seawater into shallow
basins. As heat from the Sun
slowly evaporates the water, the
salt comes out of solution and
solidifies. Elsewhere, salt is
produced by mining deposits of
the mineral halite (rock salt).

‹ SILVER SALTS ›

Certain salts of silver have the unusual property of
being sensitive to light. This makes them useful in
photography. The light-sensitive coating, or
emulsion, on film contains silver bromide. When
light falls on it, the bromide changes invisibly.
Developing the film with chemicals produces a
visible image. Unchanged silver bromide is then
removed in a process called fixing. 114 ▶

*Here, hypo (sodium thiosulfate) is dissolving silver bromide.
This process is often used in photographic processing for fixing.*

This chalky limescale is deposited on a heating element in a hard-water area.

HARD WATER

When rain falls through the air, it absorbs carbon dioxide and other gases. These make the rain slightly acidic. On the ground, the acidic water dissolves rocks, especially soft rocks such as limestone. This produces salt solutions of magnesium and calcium hydrogen carbonates, which make water "hard." Hard water doesn't easily form a lather with soap. We can remove these salts from water by boiling, when they are precipitated (come out of solution) as a chalky deposit. We can also remove salts by using special water softeners.

SOAPS AND DETERGENTS

Soap is one of the oldest types of cleaning substances. It is made by boiling animal fats or plant oils with alkalis, such as caustic soda. This produces special salts that can attack grease and dirt. The trouble is that soap reacts with the dissolved salts in hard water to form a messy scum – something often seen left in a ring around the bathtub after washing. Modern detergents are also salts, often made from petroleum chemicals and sulfuric acid. They don't form scum and have other chemicals added to improve the cleaning action.

LET'S EXPERIMENT
WATER HARDNESS

FIND OUT HOW HARD your tap water is by comparing it with distilled (soft) water. Soft waters contain different salts from hard waters; some soft waters contain no salts at all. **You will need**: liquid soap; distilled water; tap water; two jars with lids; an eye-dropper.

1 Mix equal amounts of liquid soap and distilled water to make a soap solution. Half-fill the jars, one with distilled water, the other with tap water.

2 Using an eye-dropper, add soap solution to the distilled water drop by drop. Put on the lid and shake after each drop. Note how many drops are needed to make a good bubbly lather.

3 Now add soap solution to the tap water drop by drop. Shake the jar between drops. How many drops do you need to make a good lather in the tap water as compared to the distilled water? The extra number of drops you need is a guide to the water's hardness.

HOW SOAP WORKS

Soaps and detergents can lift greasy dirt from objects because they have special kinds of molecules, which have a head and a tail. The head is attracted to water – it is hydrophilic (water-loving). The tail is attracted to grease, but not to water – it is hydrophobic (water-fearing). The tails attach to the greasy dirt, surrounding it. The heads are attracted to the water and float the dirt away.

Long, water-fearing tails of the detergent molecules are attracted to the grease on the spoon.

Grease particles are surrounded by detergent tails. The water-loving heads outside now pull the particles into the water.

CARBON CHEMISTRY

CARBON IS ONE OF THE MOST COMMON ELEMENTS IN THE world around us. Because carbon atoms link readily, both with each other and with other elements, they can form millions of different compounds. The variety of carbon substances found in nature ranges from carbon dioxide in the air, to diamonds, the hardest mineral on Earth. Scientists once believed that all but the simplest carbon compounds could only be produced by living organisms. They used the term "organic" to refer to carbon compounds, and the study of carbon compounds was called organic chemistry. We still use the term organic, even though synthetic carbon compounds are now commonplace.

Carbon atoms form the backbone of a polythene polymer.

Hydrogen atoms linked to the carbon chain

Thermosets and thermoplastics
This old radio is made from Bakelite, the first entirely synthetic plastic, developed in 1907. Bakelite is an example of a thermoset plastic, which is set rigid after it hardens and does not melt if reheated. Polythene and nylon are examples of thermoplastics, which do melt if reheated. Plastics are very useful, but can cause a problem for the environment because the molecules do not break down and decay.

ELEMENT OF LIFE

Carbon is vital to all living things. For example, the sap from rubber trees (above) contains a carbon compound called isoprene (C_5H_8), which forms a natural plastic. Like all plants, the rubber tree absorbs carbon dioxide (CO_2) from the air. Plants combine carbon dioxide with water to produce carbohydrates, which are compounds of carbon, hydrogen, and oxygen. Fossil fuels, such as oil, gas, and coal, also release carbon dioxide into the air when they burn. In fact, fossil fuels are actually carbon compounds created by decayed plants and animals.

MOLECULE CHAINS

Most substances, such as water (H_2O) and carbon dioxide (CO_2), have small molecules that consist of a few atoms. Many carbon compounds have large molecules with carbon atoms linked together in a long chain. Chemists use the property of carbon atoms to link together in chains to make plastics, a type of synthetic carbon compound. Another name for plastics is polymers, which means "many parts." Each basic repeated unit of the chain is a monomer, which means "one part."

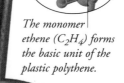

The monomer ethene (C_2H_4) forms the basic unit of the plastic polythene.

Synthetic dyes
People have always liked to dye their clothes, but were once limited in their choice of colors. They had to extract natural dyes from plants, snails, and even insects. Today, we make most dyes synthetically, using organic chemicals from oil to produce an unlimited variety of colors. Synthetic dyes are generally brighter and longer-lasting than natural dyes.

Composites

As this pole-vaulter springs into the air, his pole bends but does not break. The pole is made of fiberglass, a type of plastic called a composite. Fiberglass contains long glass fibers that reinforce the plastic, making it particularly strong and flexible, while also being fairly light in weight. Other composites use carbon fibers for extra strength and flexibility.

Heat-resistant carbon

Carbon has a very high melting point of 6,300°F (3,500°C), making it an ideal refractory (heat-resistant) material. In industry, carbon is used to make containers to hold molten metals. The nose and wings of the space shuttle are tipped with carbon to resist the high temperatures experienced during reentry into the Earth's atmosphere.

Carbon protects the most vulnerable parts of the space shuttle from extreme heat.

LET'S EXPERIMENT
MAKING A POLYMER SLIME

IN THERMOPLASTICS like PVA (polyvinyl acetate), cross-linking agents are sometimes added to bind the polymers together. In this experiment, we use a cross-linking agent to turn PVA into a gooey slime. PVA's main use is in emulsion paints, in which it forms the protective film. It is also used to make glue, like the glue in this experiment. The agent we use to make the PVA cross-link is borax, used in laundry softeners. **You will need:** an adult present; PVA glue; borax powder (available from pharmacies and grocery stores); bowl; jar; tablespoon; water. Be careful – borax is a skin and eye irritant. Always wash your hands after handling the slime. This slime is not edible!

1 In a bowl, mix together equal amounts of the PVA glue and water. Stir well. Pour some water into a separate jar and stir a tablespoon of borax powder into the water. Keep adding the borax until no more will dissolve. You now have a saturated solution.

2 Add two tablespoons of the borax solution to the PVA mixture. Stir the new mixture quickly to combine all of the substances. The mixture should become thicker as the borax begins working as a cross-linking agent. The borax binds together the long-chain polymers of the PVA, thickening the liquid mixture and turning it into wonderful slime!

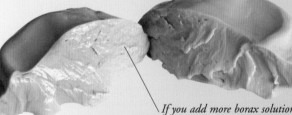

If you add more borax solution to the PVA mixture, it will become more solid, like putty.

The synthesis of urea

Friedrich Wöhler (1800–82)

In 1828, a German chemist named Friedrich Wöhler produced a synthetic substance that had previously only been found in living things. He boiled a solution of ammonia and a cyanide salt to make urea, the main substance in animal urine. It was the first organic compound created artificially from inorganic chemicals. Since Wöhler's discovery, scientists have synthesized many carbon compounds, including paints, dyes, plastics, flavorings, detergents, and drugs.

THE SCIENCE OF LIFE

OUR PLANET TEEMS WITH LIFE. WE KNOW OF MILLIONS of different species (kinds) of plants, animals, and other living things, such as bacteria and fungi. All these organisms have certain things in common. They take in (eat) raw materials, they obtain energy from the raw materials, they get rid of the waste, and they reproduce (produce offspring similar to themselves). All life is made up of cells – from the smallest insect to the largest tree. Cells are the building blocks of living things and are like tiny chemical factories, producing the substances that make living things work.

HOW LIFE BEGAN

No one really knows how life on Earth began. Many scientists believe that life began in a "soup" of organic chemicals in the oceans, produced by reactions between gases in the early atmosphere. Later, other reactions in the oceans produced more complex molecules that could reproduce themselves. However, some astronomers believe that comets like Hale-Bopp (below) may have carried the simple organic compounds to Earth. Traces of such organic matter have already been detected in comets.

SINGLE CELL LIFE

The simplest life-forms consist of organisms with single cells. The plantlike organisms called algae are made up of single cells with nuclei (centers). Like plants, algae contain green chlorophyll, a vital substance that allows them to make their food by photosynthesis. The microscopic algae known as *Volvox* (below) are made up of loose colonies of simple cells. Hundreds of identical simple cells are arranged on the outside of round balls.

Cells and tissues

More complex animals are made up of many different kinds of cells – a human body contains over 200 kinds. Human nerve cells (above left) are cablelike structures which link all the body parts to the brain and the spinal cord. Cells group together to form different kinds of tissues, depending on their function.

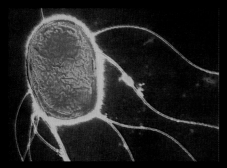

Bacteria

This highly magnified salmonella bacterium can cause food poisoning. Bacteria are by far the most common life-form on Earth – there are billions in your body alone. They are a very simple life form, usually consisting of just one single cell, with no nucleus.

DEMONSTRATING
HOW PLANTS MAKE FOOD

PHOTOSYNTHESIS IS THE PROCESS by which green plants use the energy in sunlight to make their food from water and carbon dioxide. Food is stored in their leaves as starch. This demonstration shows how plants need light to make their food, using iodine to test for starch. It must be done by an adult in a lab, as methylated spirit is highly flammable.
The demonstrator will need: a plant; methylated spirit; hot plate; pan; iodine solution; dropper; heat-resistant beaker; scissors; black plastic; tape; petri dish; tweezers.

1 Some of the plant's leaves are wrapped in black plastic and left in the light for 2 days. Two leaves are then picked: one that has been covered and one that hasn't.

2 3.4 fl.oz (100ml) methylated spirit is placed in a heatproof beaker. This is stood in a pan of water and heated until the spirit boils. The pan and beaker are removed from the heat. Using tweezers, each leaf is carefully dropped into the boiling water for 1 minute, and then into the beaker of methylated spirits, and left until they are almost white.

3 Each leaf is placed on a petri dish and a few drops of iodine added. The leaf exposed to light will turn dark – it contains starch as photosynthesis has taken place. The covered-up leaf will not turn dark because it contains no starch – no light reached it so photosynthesis didn't take place.

Normal leaf   *Leaf kept in dark*   *Leaf in light*

A model of a short section of human DNA

DNA

Inside the nucleus of your cells is a very important molecule. It is known as DNA, which is short for deoxyribonucleic acid. DNA carries all the chemical instructions that tell cells how to work, for example how to make the proteins that keep the body alive and growing. DNA is found in long, threadlike packages called chromosomes. Humans normally have 23 pairs of chromosomes. They carry all the characteristics, or genes, that make you different from everybody else on Earth.

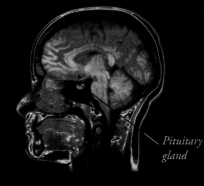

Pituitary gland

Human chemistry

Chemical reactions take place in our bodies all the time. Oxidation takes place in our cells as the oxygen in the air we breathe combines with carbon in the food we eat. This produces the energy we need to live. In digestion, chemical enzymes help break down foods for the body to absorb. Our glands produce hormones, which are chemical messengers that help control the body. The pituitary gland is the hormone "headquarters" of the body. Hormones released from here are able to instruct other hormone-making glands what to do.

FORCES AND ENERGY

Picture: The cue ball slams into a pack of pool balls, transferring its energy to them.

FORCES AND ENERGY

ENERGY IS ALL AROUND US – IT POURS down onto Earth from the Sun as heat and light. It is stored in our fuels and released when they burn. We use many different forms of energy in many different ways – for example, to heat our homes, drive our machines, and send space probes to alien worlds. Whenever energy is used to make something happen, forces come into play. We can think of forces as being the means by which energy is applied. They are the pushes and pulls that get things moving. Without energy and forces, nothing would happen in our world or indeed in the Universe.

The chemical energy rockets bursts out as sound, and heat ener this fireworks display

ENERGY SOURCES

Three main substances provide us with energy in our everyday lives – oil, natural gas, and coal. They are fuels, which we burn to produce energy. We call them fossil fuels because they are the remains of ancient plants and animals. These

Nuclear power stations, such as this one in France, harness the energy locked up in atoms.

organisms grew by harnessing the energy from the Sun, and when they died, this energy remained stored inside them. Today, we are beginning to harness solar energy directly, with solar heating panels and solar cells. Solar energy is a source of energy that will never run out. We call it a renewable resource. Scientists and engineers are developing other renewable resources to keep the world supplied with energy when the fossil fuels run out. They include wind, water, and wave power.

ENERGY CONVERSIONS

Energy can be converted from one form to another. The energy in fuels is stored within the chemicals they contain. When we burn them, we break down the

chemicals and rele the stored energy as The chemical energy converted into heat en We can use the heat en boil water into steam, and use the steam to spin turbines. heat energy is converted into mechan energy – the energy of motion. In tu can use the turbine to spin a generate

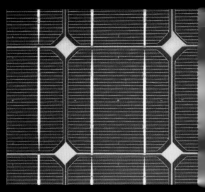

The cells on this solar panel convert the ene sunlight into electricity.

---

c. 370 BC Greek philosopher Aristotle notices that falling bodies accelerate, but thinks heavy bodies fall faster than light ones.

c. 250 BC Greek mathematician Archimedes studies simple machines, such as the lever and screw.

c. 100 BC Roman engineer Vitruvius develops the waterwheel for power production.

1590 Italian scientist Galileo proves all falling bodies accelerate at the same rate and later investigates pendulum laws.

1687 English physicist and mathematician Isaac Newton publishes the *Principia*, describing the laws of and the nature o

which makes electricity. The mechanical energy is converted into electrical energy. We can now convert electricity back into other forms of energy – into mechanical energy to drive machines; into heat in an electric fire; or into light in a light bulb.

ENERGY CONSERVATION

Almost every form of energy can be changed into other forms in a similar way. But whenever one form of energy changes into another, the total amount of energy remains the same. There is the same amount of energy after a change as there was before. No energy has been created or destroyed. This leads us to one of nature's basic laws, the law of the conservation of energy. This states that energy can be neither created nor destroyed, only changed in form. Strictly speaking, this law doesn't seem to apply to nuclear reactions, when vast amounts of energy appear to be created. But this happens because some matter changes into energy. The equivalence of mass and energy – that they are two aspects of the same thing – is explained by Einstein's Special Theory of Relativity.

FORCES AND MOTION

Energy, in its many different forms, is used to make things happen in our world – to drive a machine, to spin a pinwheel, to kick a ball. Whenever energy is used, forces are involved. Forces get things moving and change the way they move. The science of how forces affect movement is described by three laws of motion. These laws form the basis of a branch of physics called mechanics, which deals with the way objects move and interact with each other. The laws of motion generally account for the behavior of all moving bodies in our everyday world, from the collisions of billiard balls to the acceleration of space rockets against the pull of the Earth's gravity. But these laws break down when dealing with atoms.

Powered by the force of gravity, a roller coaster gathers speed as it descends.

FUNDAMENTAL FORCES

Gravity is not just something that happens on the Earth. It happens all over the Universe. The Sun and other stars have gravity, and the galaxies have gravity. Anything with mass has gravity. In fact gravity is a fundamental (basic) force of the Universe, which acts over vast distances. It is one of four fundamental forces, or interactions, in nature. The others are the electromagnetic force, strong force, and weak force. These three

forces act only over short distances. The electromagnetic force accounts for the electric and magnetic interaction between bodies. For example, it causes opposite electric charges or opposite magnetic poles to attract one another. The other two forces act only within the nucleus of an atom. The strong force acts between the nuclear particles and binds them together. There is also a weak force, which allows nuclear particles to change and helps explain how an atom can become radioactive.

QUANTUM MECHANICS

Inside atoms, the everyday rules of mechanics don't apply. The particles interact with each other and move around in very different ways from, say, the balls shooting around on a pool table. The science that seeks to describe how particles behave within atoms is known as quantum mechanics. It takes as its starting point the fact that energy at the atomic level comes in the form of little "packets," or quanta (singular "quantum"). And it considers that particles sometimes behave as waves.

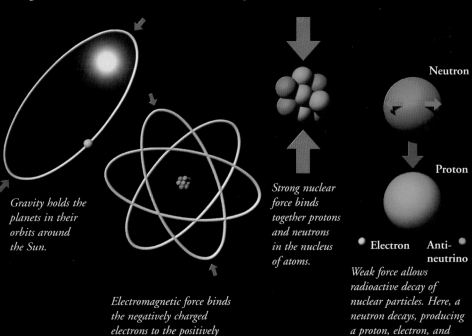

Gravity holds the planets in their orbits around the Sun.

Electromagnetic force binds the negatively charged electrons to the positively charged nucleus in an atom.

Strong nuclear force binds together protons and neutrons in the nucleus of atoms.

Neutron

Proton

Electron   Anti-neutrino

Weak force allows radioactive decay of nuclear particles. Here, a neutron decays, producing a proton, electron, and an antineutrino.

1843 English physicist James Joule establishes that heat is a form of energy.

1859 American railroad conductor Edwin Drake launches the oil industry when he drills a well near Titusville, Pennsylvania.

1900 German physicist Max Planck develops the quantum theory: objects radiate energy in tiny "packets," or quanta.

1905 In his *Special Theory of Relativity*, German physicist Albert Einstein says that mass can be converted into energy.

1991 European scientists control nuclear fusion in JET (Joint European Torus) to produce energy.

FORCES AND MOTION

WHEN YOU PUT A BALL ON LEVEL GROUND AND leave it, the ball will stay where it is. Only when you apply a force, such as a kick, will the ball start to move. It will then keep moving until another force acts upon it, for example when it hits a wall. The way that the ball behaves is the result of one of the most important laws of physics, first described by the English scientist Isaac Newton more than 300 years ago. Newton summed up his ideas about forces and movement in his three laws of motion. The first law is sometimes called the law of inertia. Inertia is the property of matter that makes a body – in this case a ball – resist a change in motion.

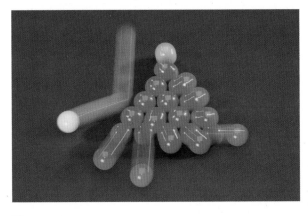

INERTIA

At the beginning of a game of snooker or pool, the balls are placed together in the shape of a triangle. If they are left alone, they will not move because their inertia keeps them where they are. They stay put until the cue ball hits them and provides the force to make them move. The cue ball travels in a straight line until it is acted on by a force – the force of hitting another ball.

MASS AND MOMENTUM

Once a body is set moving, it has kinetic energy, which is the energy of motion. A measure of its energy is its momentum, which equals mass multiplied by speed. The more massive (heavy) a body is and the greater its speed, the greater is its momentum. A moving car has great momentum, and when it hits something, its momentum tries to keep it moving. A powerful force is created that can crumple the steel body and throw the passengers forward in the crash. This is why the occupants must wear seat belts.

Isaac Newton 1642–1727

Newton's laws of motion

Put simply, Newton's first law says that an object speeds up or slows down only when a force acts on it. According to the second law, the amount by which an object changes speed (acceleration) depends on its mass and how big the force is. The third law states that whenever a force acts, an equal force acts in the opposite direction.

LET'S EXPERIMENT
INERTIA

WITH A LITTLE HELP FROM INERTIA, you can remove a cloth from a table without touching the objects on top of it. **You will need:** an adult present; cloth without a hem; plastic tableware. Do not use the best china!

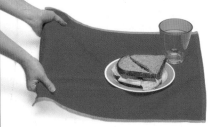

1 Lay the cloth on the table and place the objects on it. Hold the end of the cloth with both hands and give a really sharp horizontal tug.

2 With practice, you should be able to whisk away the cloth and leave the objects where they were. Their inertia stops them from moving with the cloth.

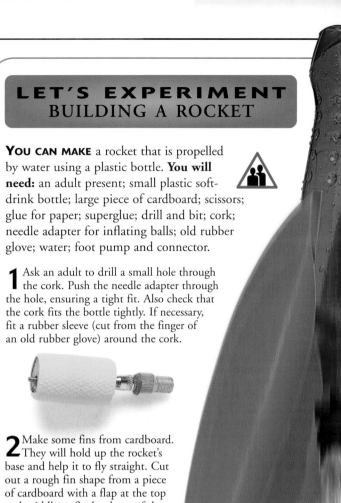

ACTION AND REACTION

Rocket engines like those of the *Saturn V* Moon rocket (above) work on the principle of Newton's third law of motion. Fuel burns inside a rocket's combustion (burning) chamber to produce hot gases, and these gases shoot backward out of the engine nozzle at high speed. The action (force) of them shooting backward sets up a reaction (equal force in the opposite direction) that propels the rocket forward. New rocket engines are coming into use that are propelled by ions (charged particles) instead of hot gases. Such engines also work according to Newton's third law of motion regarding action and reaction.

YOU CAN MAKE a rocket that is propelled by water using a plastic bottle. **You will need:** an adult present; small plastic soft-drink bottle; large piece of cardboard; scissors; glue for paper; superglue; drill and bit; cork; needle adapter for inflating balls; old rubber glove; water; foot pump and connector.

1 Ask an adult to drill a small hole through the cork. Push the needle adapter through the hole, ensuring a tight fit. Also check that the cork fits the bottle tightly. If necessary, fit a rubber sleeve (cut from the finger of an old rubber glove) around the cork.

2 Make some fins from cardboard. They will hold up the rocket's base and help it to fly straight. Cut out a rough fin shape from a piece of cardboard with a flap at the top and middle to fit the shape of the upturned bottle. Use this fin as a template to make two more. To strengthen the fins, cut smaller fin shapes, fold, and then glue them to the fins. Ask an adult to superglue the three fins at equal distances around the bottle.

Blast off! The rocket lifts off, propelled by a jet of water and air.

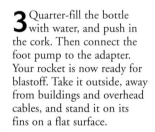

3 Quarter-fill the bottle with water, and push in the cork. Then connect the foot pump to the adapter. Your rocket is now ready for blastoff. Take it outside, away from buildings and overhead cables, and stand it on its fins on a flat surface.

4 Keeping your distance, start slowly pumping air into the bottle using the foot pump. The air pressure inside the bottle will build up until the cork pops out (the connector might backlash). The water and air shoot out at high speed, propelling the rocket into the air. The action of the water and air escaping backward creates a reaction in the opposite direction, which propels the rocket upward. This demonstrates Newton's third law of motion.

The fins support the rocket and keep it steady on the launch pad.

FRICTION

IF YOU PLACE A BLOCK OF WOOD ON THE GROUND AND GIVE IT A push, it doesn't move very far before it stops. Some kind of force must have stopped it, otherwise it would have continued moving forever. The block's movement was stopped by friction, a force that acts between any two surfaces rubbing together. The rougher the surfaces, the greater the friction, because the raised pieces on rough surfaces keep catching on one another. The friction, or rubbing between surfaces, produces energy in the form of heat. That is why we rub our hands together on cold days to make them warm up.

HOT STUFF

When you strike a match against a rough surface, the friction produces heat. The heat triggers off chemical reactions in the substances that coat the match head, which cause the match to burst into flame. "Strike-anywhere" matches ignite when struck on any surface. Safety matches ignite only when struck on a special surface.

ON YOUR BIKE!

The bicycle is one of the most efficient machines ever invented. It evolved into its modern form in 1885, when Englishman John Starley built his safety bicycle. It had two equal-sized wheels, central cranks and pedals, and a chain driving the rear wheel. Friction governs the working of a bicycle. Without friction, the wheels wouldn't grip the road and the rider's feet wouldn't grip the pedals. The rider would have no means of stopping because brakes rely on friction to work. In the moving parts, however, friction needs to be reduced so that they can move more easily. Oil and grease provide the answer. They help keep the moving metal surfaces apart.

Oil lubricates the chain and reduces friction.

Friction between tire and road allows the wheel to roll over the ground without sliding.

LET'S EXPERIMENT
MAKING A MINI HOVERCRAFT

HOVERCRAFT REST ON A "CUSHION" OF AIR. This reduces friction, enabling high speeds. In this experiment, a glass becomes a hovercraft. The air cushion is formed by warm air escaping from the glass. **You will need:** a glass; dishwashing liquid; hot tap water; a smooth surface (such as a tray).

1 Wash a glass in hot soapy water and place it upside-down on a wet, smooth surface.

2 Give the glass a little push. It will slide easily as the warm air escapes beneath it.

Hovercraft

In a hovercraft, a powerful fan pumps air under the hull to create an air cushion. A flexible "skirt" around the bottom helps keep the air in. The craft is driven by spinning propellers at the rear. It is steered by moving flaps in the air stream coming from the propellers.

Perpetual motion machines
For centuries, people tried to make machines that would continue moving indefinitely once they had started. But such machines are impossible because friction eventually stops them from moving. In this 1834 machine, the movement of the balls outward was supposed to keep the wheel turning.

Brakes force pads against the wheel rim, creating friction that slows down the wheel.

Grease reduces friction in the wheel bearings and allows the wheel to turn more smoothly.

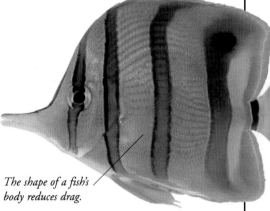

The shape of a fish's body reduces drag.

STREAMLINING

Fluids (liquids and gases) cause friction too. Boats traveling through the water experience resistance, or drag, caused by water molecules rubbing against the hull. Planes experience drag because of friction with air molecules. Drag is reduced if the moving body has a smooth surface and is correctly shaped, or streamlined. Fish are beautifully streamlined and travel through water with the least resistance.

Tread allows water to escape beneath the tire. A layer of water reduces friction, but makes it more difficult for the tire to grip the road.

SPEED AND ACCELERATION

IF YOU WALK BRISKLY, YOU MIGHT BE ABLE TO COVER a distance of about 2.5 miles (4 km) in an hour. During this time you would have been moving at a speed of 2.5 mph (4 kmh). Speed is the distance traveled divided by the time taken. Often, in science, we talk about velocity rather than speed. Velocity is speed in a particular direction. So even if the speed stays constant, if the direction changes, so does the velocity. However, speeds are rarely kept constant – things are always speeding up or slowing down. When something speeds up, we say it accelerates. When it slows down, we say it decelerates.

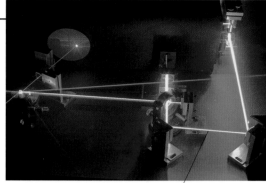

Laser light being used to carry signals in a laboratory experiment

SPEED OF LIGHT

During a storm, lightning and thunder happen at nearly the same time, but the lightning flash is seen seconds before the thunder is heard. This is because light travels faster than sound. Scientists have found that light travels at the incredible speed of about 186,000 miles (300,000 km) a second, or more than 600 million mph (1 billion kmh). They tell us that this is the highest speed anything can ever reach.

SPEED OF SOUND

When a rifle fires a bullet, a loud bang is heard. It is the noise of the shock waves made by the bullet traveling faster than the speed of sound. Sound travels through the air at a speed of about 750 mph (1,200 kmh). Bullets travel at more than twice this speed. Sound travels much faster in solid objects than it does in air. In steel, it travels at a speed of over 10,000 mph (16,000 kmh). But sound has zero speed in a vacuum. It can't travel where there are no molecules of matter to carry it.

Speedometers

A speedometer displays a car's speed. It is usually driven by a cable from the car's gearbox. Inside the speedometer, the cable turns a magnet, which drags with it a metal cap attached to the pointer. A spring opposes the cap's movement and makes the pointer stop at a certain position. This position corresponds to the car's speed and is read by the driver in either miles or kilometres per hour.

G-force acceleration

When you get into an elevator and it starts to rise, you feel your feet pressing harder against the floor. It's as though you have suddenly become heavier or that gravity has suddenly increased. What you are experiencing is what astronauts call a G-force. It is an extra gravity-like force on your body brought about by the acceleration of the elevator upward. Space shuttle astronauts experience forces of up to 4 Gs (four times normal gravity) when they are launched, accelerating from 0 to over 17,500 mph (28,000 kmh) in less than nine minutes.

Increasing G-forces push the astronaut back in his seat as he accelerates.

When the astronaut suddenly stops, even bigger G-forces throw him forward.

In training, astronauts experience G-forces in a centrifuge. They are whirled around at high speed in a gondola on the end of a long arm.

Dragster deceleration

Dragsters reach high speeds, but they don't have very good brakes! They often use parachutes to help them slow down, or decelerate. The parachutes are deployed (opened) at the rear. As they billow out, they catch the air and force the dragster to slow down. Note the short wings, or airfoils, at the front and back of this car. They are angled into the airstream to produce forces that press down on the car to help stop it from lifting.

BUILT FOR ACCELERATION

Drag racing is one of the most exciting types of auto racing. Two long cars, called dragsters, with huge exposed engines, battle it out on a traditional quarter-mile track to see which can accelerate the fastest. Some dragsters can cover the distance in less than 5 seconds, reaching speeds of over 290 mph (460 kmh). The powerful engines drive the big, broad, rear wheels. The spinning of these wheels tends to make the front of the dragster lift, so it is built with a long body to counter this effect. In the dragster below, the central position of the engines helps too.

GRAVITY, MASS, AND WEIGHT

WHEN YOU DROP SOMETHING, IT FALLS BECAUSE AN invisible force is pulling it – the force of gravity, or rather Earth's gravity. Gravity is a basic property of all matter, from atoms to planets. The more mass a body has, the stronger its gravity. The English scientist Isaac Newton was the first to understand the nature of gravity in the 1660s. It is said that watching apples falling triggered his ideas. Gravity gives bodies their weight. Weight is the force a body experiences because of its mass in the presence of gravity.

FALLING BODIES

Gravity acts between bodies and pulls them together. If the bodies are different masses, the uneven pull makes the smaller mass fall toward the larger mass. We notice this on Earth when objects fall downward – toward the massive planet. About 400 years ago, the Italian scientist Galileo (p. 72) decided to experiment with falling bodies. He found that gravity causes everything to fall at the same rate. Light bodies fall as quickly as heavy bodies. So in a vacuum (to avoid air resistance), a feather falls as fast as an apple (right).

Free fall

To start with, gravity pulls free-fall parachutists toward the Earth at ever-increasing speeds. But the faster they fall, the more air resistance they experience. When they reach about 190 mph (300 kmh), air resistance becomes so high that it balances the pull of gravity. They then continue to fall steadily at this speed, which is called the terminal velocity.

Zero-g

Astronauts in orbit around the Earth feel as if their bodies have no weight. It seems as if gravity no longer exists. We call this peculiar state weightlessness or zero-G. But the proper name for it is continuous free fall. Gravity does still exist in orbit (it's only five percent less than on the Earth's surface) and is making them fall to Earth. Because their space shuttle is traveling forward so fast, the amount they fall toward the Earth in any time equals the amount the Earth's surface curves away beneath them. Therefore they stay at the same height above the Earth, even though they are falling.

Moon and tides

The Moon has a much smaller mass than Earth, and its gravity is only one-sixth as strong. Nevertheless, its pull still affects our planet. As it orbits Earth, it tugs at the water in the oceans and creates high and low tides. Some land masses, such as the one below, are joined to the mainland at low tide, but become islands at high tide.

Mont St. Michel, France

GRAVITY GONE MAD

When a large star dies, it blasts itself apart as a supernova, the biggest explosion in the Universe. The matter in its core (center) collapses so rapidly that it releases a huge amount of energy, causing the blast. What's left of the core gets crushed smaller and smaller. The smaller and denser the core gets, the stronger its gravity becomes. Eventually, the core is crushed almost to nothing, leaving only a region of space with enormous gravity. We call this region a black hole because we can never see it – not even light rays escape from its gravitational grip.

LET'S EXPERIMENT
CENTER OF GRAVITY

IN ANY OBJECT, all the weight appears to be concentrated at one point. We call it the center of gravity (or center of mass). As you will see in this experiment, if you support an object beneath its center of gravity, it will balance. **You will need:** pencil; piece of cardboard; scissors; pin; a board (such as a cork board, in a vertical position); cotton thread; a weight.

Make the weight heavy enough to pull the thread taut.

1 Draw an outline of your hand on the cardboard and cut it out. Pin it to the board by the tip of one finger so that the hand swings freely. Hang a weighted thread from the pin and draw along the line of the thread on the card. Repeat using the rest of the fingers. Be careful not to prick yourself with the pin.

Balance the hand on a pencil.

2 You should find that all the lines you drew on the hand meet at one point. This is the center of gravity. Place the end of the pencil beneath the point, and you should find that the hand balances.

SWINGING AND SPINNING

A PLAYGROUND IS THE PERFECT PLACE TO
investigate swinging and spinning. The swings show
pendulum laws, and the merry-go-round shows
circular motion. Time how long it takes to swing back
and forth on both huge and tiny swings. Surprisingly,
you'll find that the swing always moves back and
forth in more or less the same time. The Italian
scientist Galileo Galilei (1564–1642) noticed this
in the 1580s when he experimented with
pendulums. He found that pendulums of the same
length always have the same period (time of swing).
Try also spinning on a merry-go-round. A force
acting inward keeps you traveling in a circle. The
faster you spin, the stronger the
force pulls you toward its center.

*This pendulum clock
was built in 1883
to Galileo's design.*

PENDULUMS

Galileo realized that the
constant period of swing
of a pendulum could be
used to regulate clocks. But
he died before his design
could be built. The first
pendulum clock was built
in 1657 by the Dutch
scientist Christiaan
Huygens. In this, each
swing released an escape
wheel, tooth by tooth,
which drove the
clockwork mechanism.
Grandfather, or long-
case, clocks have a
"seconds" pendulum
3 ft 3 in (1 m) long,
which swings from
one side to the other
in exactly one second.

LET'S EXPERIMENT
PENDULUM SWINGS

PENDULUMS HANG FROM A FIXED POINT and swing under the action
of gravity. Below are some pendulum investigations for you to try.
You will need: string; two vertical supports (such as clamp stands or
chairs); a ruler; scissors; 6 identical weights (such as nuts or lumps of
modeling clay); a stopwatch.

1 Secure each end of a 3 ft 3 in (1 m)
length of string to vertical supports.
Stretch the string taut. Your
pendulums will hang from this.

2 Cut three different lengths of
string. Attach a weight to each
and hang them from the taut string.
Set one swinging. Time 20 complete
swings (back and forth) and divide
by 20 to get an accurate time for one
swing. Repeat with the other two
pendulums. You should find that the
different lengths have different swing
times. Try adding extra weights to
the pendulums and timing them.
Compare your results. Do the
weights affect the swing times?

3 Now make your three
pendulums the same length,
and hang one weight from each.
Set one swinging. You'll find that
the others start swinging too.
This effect is called resonance and
occurs when identical objects all
vibrate at their natural frequency.

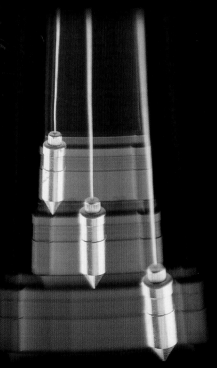

Out of balance

When designing structures, engineers must
ensure that all the forces balance. The Leaning
Tower of Pisa, in Italy, started leaning soon after
building began. The ground began to sink on
one side, creating an unbalanced force. Its center
of gravity has so far stayed within its base. At
present it is being stabilised at an angle 5 degrees
out of vertical. If the center of gravity moves
outside its base, a turning
force will be
created and
the tower
will topple
over.

The Leaning Tower of Pisa, begun in 1174

CIRCLING AND SPINNING

On some fairground rides, you are whirled around in circles. Your body wants to shoot off in a straight line, but is held back by a force acting inward toward the center of the circle. We call it centripetal force. When satellites orbit the Earth, gravity provides the centripetal force to keep them circling. Like everything that moves, spinning objects have momentum to keep them in motion. With spinning objects, it is called angular momentum.

Conserving momentum
Skaters often perform spectacular spins. They start spinning with their arms outstretched. This gives them a larger spin diameter and more angular momentum. By suddenly pulling in their arms, they reduce their diameter. To conserve angular momentum, their bodies automatically spin faster.

Spinning rotor

Outer gimbal

Supporting frame

Gyroscopes
Gyroscopes are amazing things. They can balance on a piece of string or on the tip of a pencil, and if you push them, they don't fall over. They have these unusual properties because of their rapidly spinning wheel, or rotor, which spins inside pivoting frames, or gimbals. When the rotor spins quickly, its angular momentum, which acts along the rotor axis, tries to keep it pointing in the same direction.

LET'S EXPERIMENT
CENTRIPETAL FORCE

CAN YOU TURN A BUCKET of water upside-down without the water falling out? You can with the help of centripetal force.
You will need: an adult present; strong string; scissors; light plastic bucket; water; pitcher; glove (optional).

1 Tie one end of the string to the handle of the bucket. Quarter-fill the bucket with water. Any more water will make the bucket too heavy.

2 Take the bucket outdoors. For comfort perhaps wear a glove, then wind the string around your hand. Start swinging the bucket in a circle around your hand. Once the bucket is circling, centripetal force will hold the water inside.

INVESTIGATING ENERGY

WHEN A RUBBER BAND IS STRETCHED, THEN RELEASED, IT shoots through the air. Stretching it builds up energy inside the rubber band. This energy is called potential energy. When the rubber band is released, it moves. Its potential energy is converted into the energy of movement, or kinetic energy. Potential and kinetic are the two main forms of energy. Potential energy is the energy stored in something because of its position or state. Gravitational energy, chemical energy, nuclear energy, and electrical energy are all forms of potential energy. Kinetic energy is the energy of motion. Every moving body has kinetic energy.

Towers at an oil refinery venting off waste gases

FUEL AND POWER

Most of the energy we use comes from burning fossil fuels, such as oil (below), coal, and natural gas. These fuels have formed naturally over millions of years, but are being used up very quickly – oil will probably run out later this century. Burning fossil fuels also causes air pollution. Our other main energy sources are hydroelectricity (water power) and nuclear power. Nuclear power stations currently produce energy by fission, or splitting atoms. The problem is this produces lots of harmful radioactive waste.

Renewable resources
Some energy sources will never run out. These everlasting, or renewable, resources include flowing water and the wind. We harness flowing water in hydroelectric plants, and harness the wind with windmills. Modern windmills, called wind turbines, are now being used to generate electricity. Solar energy and geothermal energy are two other useful renewable resources now being exploited. Geothermal energy is the heat found in underground rocks, particularly in volcanic regions.

A wind farm in California

Energy without end
A machine called JET (Joint European Torus) creates a ring of searing hot gas called plasma during experiments into nuclear fusion. Unlike fission, this kind of nuclear reaction doesn't produce deadly radiation. It is the process that stars use to make their energy. If fusion can be controlled, the world will have plenty of energy because the oceans are full of the "fuel" it uses, deuterium (a heavy form of hydrogen).

LET'S EXPERIMENT
ENERGY CONVERSION

LIFTING AN OBJECT GIVES IT MORE gravitational potential energy. In letting it go, the "potential" energy is converted into kinetic energy as it falls under the pull of gravity. This is how a roller coaster works. See for yourself by making a mini roller coaster.

You will need: foam pipe lagging (wide enough for a marble to slide down easily); marbles; scissors; all-purpose glue; tape; two vertical supports (such as chairs); adhesive putty; pins.

1 Cut the lagging in half lengthwise with some scissors, parallel to its existing slit. Glue or tape the two pieces together end to end. Bend the track as shown in the picture. Rest it on a surface, propping it up against two vertical supports. Hold it in place by pinning it to mounds of adhesive putty.

2 Place a marble on the steep drop of the track and let it go. Find the best starting height through trial and error. If too high, the marble will have too much kinetic energy and fly off the track. If too low, it won't have enough energy to roll over the hump.

A roller coaster ride
On a roller coaster, the cars climb to the highest point under power, and are then let loose to descend under gravity. They gain increasing kinetic energy as they fall, which takes them up and over a series of lower humps.

"The Big One" roller coaster in Blackpool, England.

CHAINS OF ENERGY

Logs burn vigorously on a bonfire, giving out energy in the form of light (seen as flames) and heat. Energy can't be made or destroyed, it can only be converted from one form to another. So where did all this energy come from? It was chemical energy, stored in the molecules of the wood. This chemical energy was converted from the energy in sunlight. The leaves of the tree used sunlight, in a process called photosynthesis, to manufacture the materials needed for the tree to grow.

Einstein's famous formula
Early last century, Albert Einstein realized that mass and energy are related. Mass can be changed into energy, according to his famous equation $E=mc^2$. E is the energy produced when a mass m is converted into energy, and c is the speed of light. Squaring c (multiplying it by itself) gives a huge number, so a tiny amount of mass can be converted into a huge amount of energy.

$$E = mc^2$$

SAVING ENERGY

The industrialized world uses vast amounts of energy in industry, transportation, and in the home. But much of it is wasted. For example, much of the energy we use for home heating is wasted when heat escapes through the roof, walls, and windows. As our fuel supplies dwindle, we should be saving more energy. One example would be to improve insulation in our houses. Another way to save energy is by reusing, or recycling materials, like metals and glass. Recycling requires much less energy than extracting substances from raw materials.

Tin cans ready for recycling

ENERGY AND WORK

SCIENTISTS DEFINE ENERGY AS THE ABILITY TO DO WORK.
But they don't mean work in the everyday meaning of the word. Instead they say work is done whenever a force moves an object. The work done is calculated by multiplying the distance the object has moved by the force needed to move it. So moving a heavy object a short distance could involve the same amount of work, and use the same energy, as moving a lighter object a longer distance. This relationship is used by machines to make work easier to perform.

As the wedge slices down, its widening shape creates a large sideways force that splits the wood.

This mountain road is an inclined plane. Cars travel a longer distance, but with less effort than climbing straight up the mountain.

The screw thread is like an inclined plane wrapped around the screw. The path is longer so the effort is reduced.

At the wheel's axle (center), a large force turns a short distance. This gives the rim a small force to turn a long distance.

SIMPLE MACHINES
Any device that performs work is called a machine. They can often be very simple. A crowbar, for example, is a type of machine called a lever. Other simple machines include the inclined plane, wedge, screw, wheel and axle, and pulley. Most machines magnify the force applied to them (the effort) to shift a larger force (the load). When they magnify a force, they give what is called a mechanical advantage. But to get this advantage, the effort must move a long distance to shift the load a little.

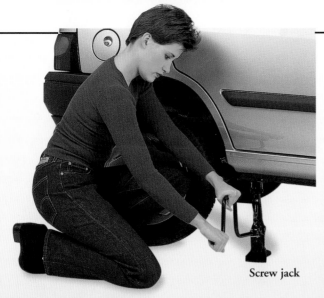

Screw jack

What's the advantage?

Can you lift a car on your own? You can with a screw jack. This is a lifting device that uses the principles of the screw and the lever. By turning the jack handle a long way (lots of leverage), you make the screw move upward a short way, lifting the weight of the car. The jack produces a big force for a small effort – it has a large mechanical advantage.

LET'S EXPERIMENT WITH LEVERS

THE LIDS OF PAINT CANS fit tightly to prevent spills. They can be opened with a lever, using the edge of the can as a fulcrum (pivot). **You will need:** a can of paint (ask permission); a coin; an old teaspoon; an old tablespoon; a screwdriver; old newspaper.

1 Rest the paint can on some old newspaper (in case the paint spills). Try to lever off the lid with a coin. Because the coin is so short, you can't get much leverage to magnify the effort you apply. However hard you try, you can't overcome the force that keeps the lid shut.

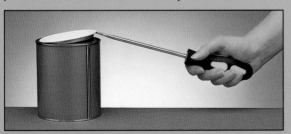

2 Now try opening the lid with the teaspoon, the tablespoon, and the screwdriver. You'll find that the longer the lever is, the easier it is to open the can. You apply less effort, but your hand has to move much further to produce enough force to lift the lid.

LAWS OF THE LEVER

The Greek scientist Archimedes worked out the laws of the lever more than 2,000 years ago. For a simple lever resting on a fulcrum (pivot), the lifting effort multiplied by its distance to the fulcrum equals the load multiplied by its distance to the fulcrum. So a small effort applied a long way from the fulcrum can lift a large load that is close to the fulcrum. This setup produces a large mechanical advantage – it gives you good leverage. Said Archimedes: "Give me a leverage point and I will move the world."

First-class lever

A simple lever like a seesaw is known as a first-class lever. It has a fulcrum in the middle, the effort is applied on one side, and the load is lifted on the other. Pliers are another first-class lever. They have a mechanical advantage because the handles are longer than the jaws.

Effort

Load

Effort

Fulcrum

Second-class lever

A second-class lever has the load positioned between the effort and the fulcrum. Because the effort is further from the fulcrum than the load, mechanical advantage is achieved. A nutcracker is a second-class lever, and so is a wheelbarrow.

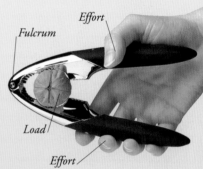

Fulcrum

Effort

Load

Effort

Third-class lever

In a third-class lever, the effort is applied between the fulcrum and the load. The effort is closer to the fulcrum than the load, so there is no mechanical advantage here. Instead, third-class levers are used whenever a delicate grip is required, for example when using chopsticks.

Effort

Fulcrum

Load

Effort

Prime movers

All machines need energy to perform work. Some machines convert energy directly into mechanical motion. We call them prime movers. Gasoline engines and steam locomotives are examples; they harness the energy in gasoline and steam. Prime movers are not very efficient – they supply much less energy than they take in. Gas engines produce only 25 percent of the energy in their fuel; the rest is lost as heat.

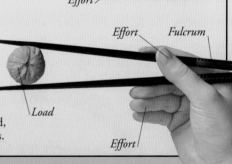

GEARS AND PULLEYS

WHEN YOU RIDE YOUR BIKE, A SET OF GEARS
transmits the motion of the pedals to the rear wheel.
In a car (or other motorized vehicle), gears transmit
power from the engine to the wheels to make the
car go. Most gears take the form of wheels with
teeth cut around the edge. Gears not only transmit
motion, they can also change it. Using the gears
on your bike, you can change speed while still
pedaling at the same rate, thereby gaining a
mechanical advantage. A pulley can also
give a mechanical advantage. Both gears
and pulleys reduce the effort required.

*Shaft of
worm gear
with screw
thread*

*Toothed
wheel of
worm
gear*

LET'S EXPERIMENT
CHANGING GEARS

FIND OUT HOW CHANGING gear makes a
bike go slower or faster. **You will need:** an
adult to help; bike with multiple gears (such
as a mountain bike); gloves; colored tape.

1 A bike with multiple gears has different-sized chainwheels,
to which the cranks and pedals are attached, and different-
sized sprockets (gears) on the rear wheel. Ask an adult to turn the
bike upside-down and to hold the frame steady. Wear gloves to
protect your fingers. Slowly, turn the pedals until one of the
cranks is vertical. Mark a point on the rear tire with colored tape.

Low gear
Rear tire
Crank
Pedal

High gear

Chain

Rear sprocket hub
Chainwheels *The rear wheel powers
the bicycle. The front
wheel controls steering.*

2 In low gear, the chain
connects a small
chainwheel and a large
rear sprocket. Slowly, turn
the crank once. Watch the
tape mark. How many
times does the rear wheel
turn? How much force is
needed to turn the pedals?

3 In high gear, the chain
connects a large
chainwheel to a small
sprocket. Turn the crank
again. How many times
does the rear wheel turn?
How much force is
needed on the pedals?

4 In high gear, you
need more force on
the pedals, but the rear
wheel turns faster. In low
gear, you need less force
and the wheel turns
slower – helpful when
riding your bike uphill!

*Turning the
handle of this
eggbeater sets the
bevel gear in
motion, which
turns the beater.*

*Bevel
gear*

GEARING UP

On a bike, a chain connects the
toothed gears on the chainwheel
and rear wheel hub. In most
gear systems, sets of gears mesh (link)
directly with their teeth, so when one gear
turns, the other turns with it. A worm gear
(above) transmits motion at right angles as the
toothed wheel meshes with the screw thread on
the shaft. Bevel gears (left) have slanting teeth
that also mesh at right angles. Gears with
straight teeth that mesh together are called
spur gears. They transmit motion between
parallel toothed shafts, as in a car gearbox.

Gear ratios

In machines, meshing gears usually
change the speed of motion. A small
gear with few teeth will drive a large
one with many teeth more slowly.
A gear with 12 teeth, for instance,
will drive another with 24 teeth
at only half the speed. The
12-tooth gear must turn
twice in order to turn the
24-tooth gear just once.
Therefore, the gear
ratio is two to one
(2:1). Mechanical
clocks and watches use
a train of meshing gears
with precise gear ratios to
turn the hands at the correct
speed for accurate timekeeping.

*A series, or train, of gears drives
the hands of this watch.*

PULLEYS AND CRANES

The simplest kind of pulley is a rope running over a grooved wheel. The wheel is attached to a support, while one end of the rope carries the load. The load can be lifted by applying force, or pulling, the other end of the rope. While a single pulley doesn't give a mechanical advantage, it does make lifting easier by changing the direction of force required. Adding other pulleys increases the force applied, which means less effort is required – a mechanical advantage. A building crane gets much of its lifting power from a multiple pulley system called a block and tackle, which is positioned at the lifting end of the rope.

Block and tackle pulley system

Brunelleschi's dome
The Italian architect Filippo Brunelleschi (1377–1446) is believed to have invented a crane called a swiveling jib for use in building the huge dome of this famous cathedral in Florence, Italy. It was one of "the many machines invented by his divine genius," as his epitaph in the cathedral says. Building on the cathedral began in 1296. The dome itself was built between 1420–1436.

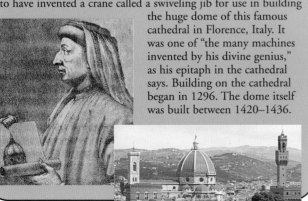

FIND OUT HOW a set of pulleys (a block and tackle) can help you to lift loads more easily. **You will need**: an adult to help you; two blocks of wood; nail or gimlet; two screw hooks; four screw eyelets (with closed metal rings); two lengths of strong string; candle; firm support (such as a rail attached to the wall); a load to be lifted (such as a bag of oranges).

1 Ask an adult to make small starter holes in the two blocks of wood with a nail or gimlet – one hole in the middle of one side of each block and two holes evenly spaced in the opposite side. In each block, screw a hook into the single hole and screw two eyelets into the holes on the opposite side. Using a length of string, hang one block of wood from the support by its hook. Rub the other string with the edge of the candle. The wax will reduce the friction between the string and the pulleys.

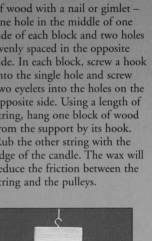

2 Thread the waxed string through the rings of the wooden blocks in a zigzag pattern to make the pulleys. Attach a load to the bottom hook, then pull on the free end of the string. You will find that you need less effort to lift the load with the pulley than if you picked it up directly. Try threading the string in different ways to compare the effort needed to lift the load.

String attached to support

Pulleys

Waxed string

Secure the end of the string around the first ring.

Pulley

Pull this end of the string

Load

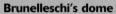

TIME AND MOTION

WE'RE AWARE THAT TIME IS PASSING WHEN WE
see the hands of a clock going around, or when we look older each year. We tend to think of time flowing forward at a steady pace, but the German physicist Albert Einstein (1879–1955) showed that the pace of time depends on how fast we're moving. Time is measured in seconds, minutes, hours, days, months, and years. A year is the length of time it takes the Earth to orbit once around the Sun, while a day is how long it takes the Earth to spin once on its axis. In order to coordinate time, the Earth is divided into 24 time zones by lines running from pole to pole, called lines of longitude. Time in each zone is measured from the 0° line of longitude that runs through Greenwich, UK.

Digital watch

CLOCKS AND WATCHES

In order to keep time, clocks and watches are controlled by a mechanism with a constantly repeating motion. Early clocks used a swinging pendulum to keep time. Modern pendulum clocks may gain or lose up to 0.01 of a second in a day. Many smaller clocks and watches use a balance wheel that rocks to and fro at a steady rate. More accurate clocks are controlled by the vibrations of a quartz crystal. Quartz clocks are much more accurate than even the best pendulum clocks.

There are 24 hours in a day.

There are 60 minutes in an hour.

There are 60 seconds in a minute.

ATOMIC CLOCKS

When scientists measure time they need to be very accurate. Ordinary clocks just won't do the job. Instead they use a special type of clock known as an atomic clock, which is kept regular by the vibrations of atoms or molecules. In fact, an atomic clock is so accurate that it is used to define the standard second. All atoms can absorb and emit electromagnetic radiation, and the standard second is measured by counting 9,192,631,770 vibrations of the radio waves that cesium atoms can absorb. This picture (left) shows the first cesium atomic clock. It was built at the UK's National Physical Laboratory in 1955.

11:00 12:00 13:00 14:00 15:00 16:00 17:00 18:00 19:00 20:00 21:00

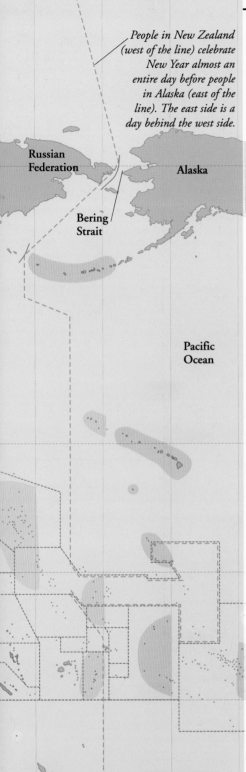

People in New Zealand (west of the line) celebrate New Year almost an entire day before people in Alaska (east of the line). The east side is a day behind the west side.

Russian Federation

Alaska

Bering Strait

Pacific Ocean

The date line moves off the course of the 180° longitude line so that groups of islands and distant ends of countries can have the same calendar date.

New Zealand

DATE LINE

In time zones to the east of the Greenwich 0° line, time is ahead of Greenwich Mean Time (GMT). Zones west of Greenwich are behind GMT. Exactly halfway around the globe from Greenwich is the International Date Line (left). At 12 noon GMT, the day is ending on the west side of this line, and the same day is just beginning on the east side. There is a time difference of a day between either side.

Time travel

According to Einstein, time travel into the future is possible. His Special Theory of Relativity, published in 1905, states that time speeds up or slows down depending on how fast you are traveling. If, for example, you went on a year-long trip around the Universe in a spaceship, traveling one per cent slower than the speed of light, time, for you, would slow down. In fact, it would go so slow that although your onboard clock would tell you that you've been traveling for one year, seven years will have passed for people on Earth. So when you return home, you will have traveled six years into the future. No-one knows whether time travel into the past is possible. But because time and space are linked, some scientists believe that traveling through wormholes (tunnels connecting two points in "spacetime") could lead to the past.

Internal clock

Many of the processes of living organisms, such as people sleeping, animals migrating, and plants sprouting, happen at regular intervals. These intervals are timed by an "internal clock," which, in animals, is thought to be in the brain. We become aware of our internal clocks if we fly across several time zones. If you were to leave New York in the evening and fly to London, UK, you would arrive during the UK's morning. You would feel like sleeping in the day, and be awake during the night. The tiredness and other effects you feel, as your internal clock adjusts to the time zone, are called jet lag.

Star time

In solar time, one day equals the time it takes the Earth to spin once on its axis in relation to the sun. Because the Earth is orbiting the Sun as well as spinning, the stars appear in a different place in the sky at the same time each night. To locate stars, astronomers use sidereal time (time relating to stars) rather than solar time. A sidereal day is how long it takes the Earth to rotate once in relation to a particular star. The rotation of the Earth is the reason the stars appear to move in circles, as this long-exposure photo shows.

3:00 | 00:00 | 01:00 | 02:00

03:00 | 04:00 | 05:00 | 06:00 | 07:00 | 08:00 | 09:00 | 10:00

HEAT AND SOUND

Picture: *Shock waves form around a model plane when air reaches the speed of sound.*

MOLECULES IN MOTION

WHEN YOU LIE ON THE BEACH SUNBATHING,

listening to the waves crashing onto the shore, you are
being bombarded with energy. The heat of the Sun
and the sound of the waves are forms of energy that
can be sensed; heat is felt and sound is heard. Both
heat and sound involve the movement of molecules.
Heat is the energy that moving molecules possess. It is
often called internal energy and thermal energy. Sound
is also a traveling vibration. It vibrates the molecules it
travels through and can be picked up by our ears.

*Exploding
firecrackers give out
heat, light, and sound.*

HEAT SOURCES

The Sun is the Earth's main source of heat.
It makes our world a warm enough home
for millions of different types of plants and
animals. But we can only use a little of this

*This Cassini space probe contains a generator
powered by thermoelectricity.*

heat directly, for example, in solar power
programs. We get most of the heat we use
in our homes and industry by burning
fuels, such as oil and natural gas. Fuels give
off heat when they are burned. This heat
may be converted into other forms of
energy, such as electricity. In turn, the
electricity can be turned back into heat
again, in electric fireplaces.

HEAT ENGINES

The engines that power cars, buses, ships,
and planes all burn fuel and harness the
fuel's heat. That is why we call them heat
engines. Most of the fuels we use come
from petroleum, or crude oil. Petroleum is
converted to gasoline for car engines, diesel
for bus and ship engines, and kerosene for
jet plane engines. Heat engines are not very
efficient at harnessing the heat in their
fuels. A gasoline engine uses only about a
quarter of the energy in its fuel. The rest is
lost as heat in the exhaust gases, and
friction among the moving parts.

TEMPERATURE

We measure how hot something is by its
temperature. But temperature is not the
same as heat. Temperature measures the
kinetic energy of molecules. Heat measures

the total internal
energy, kinetic and
potential, of the entire
substance. To understand
the difference, compare
a sparkler with a cup
of hot coffee. A spark
from the sparkler has
a much higher
temperature than the
coffee, but the coffee
has more heat overall.
The spark's molecules
are faster but fewer
than in the cup of
coffee. So when all the
molecular energies are
added together to find
the amount of heat,
the coffee has
more heat
because it has
many more
molecules.

*Lab samples
are preserved
at very low
temperatures.*

1592 Italian scientist Galileo
invents the thermometer,
calling it a thermoscope.

1658 Irish scientist Robert
Boyle proves sound
can't travel in a vacuum.

1698 English engineer
Thomas Savery invents a
steam pump – the first
practical steam engine.

1714 German physicist Daniel
Gabriel Fahrenheit
makes a thermometer
with a Fahrenheit scale.

1824 French engineer Sadi
Carnot investigates
thermodynamics.

1842 Austrian physicist
Christian Doppler
explains the effects of
moving sound.

MOVING
HEAT

If you go outside without a coat on a cold day, heat escapes from your warm body into the cold air. Back inside, heat from a hot fire travels to your cold body to warm you up. Whenever heat moves, it always travels from a warmer object to a cooler one. This is a basic law of thermodynamics, the study of heat and energy movement. There are three ways in which heat can travel, or be transferred – conduction, convection, and radiation. In conduction and convection, molecules pass on the heat. In radiation, no medium is needed. It can take place in a vacuum.

With their large ears, fennec foxes can pick up the faintest sounds.

Heat radiates from a red-hot horseshoe.

SOUND WAVES

One thing that can't travel through a vacuum is sound. Sound is carried by waves made by vibrating molecules. In a vacuum, there are no molecules and therefore no sound. Our world is full of sound because it is surrounded by air. But the Moon is silent since it has no air. We tend to think about sound traveling only through air. But sound travels though any material. If you place a ticking clock on a table, then put your ear to the table, you'll hear the ticking loud and clear. The sound travels through the molecules in the table.

EARS AND VOICES

People hear sounds when vibrations, traveling through the air or another material, reach their ears. Most animals pick up sounds in a similar way, with ears in their heads. But some animals are different. The cricket, for example, has ears on its legs; the mosquito picks up sounds with its antennae. Of course, sounds are not only heard, they are also made – with voices. Vibrations again hold the key to making sounds. When we speak, we make bands of tissue in our throat vibrate. These set up vibrations in the air as we breathe out.

Voice patterns are made visible on an oscilloscope.

NOISE AND MUSIC

Our world is full of sound – of people talking, music playing, traffic honking, and so on. High levels of sound can damage the ears. Some of these sounds are pleasant, others are considered unpleasant – they are noise. The difference between pleasant sounds, such as music, and noise often lies in the nature of the vibrations. Music is made up of regular vibrations at regular intervals, which the brain can sort out. Noise tends to be made up of irregular vibrations at irregular intervals, which the brain finds harder to cope with.

Xylophone players make music by hammering.

1847 English physicist James Joule measures mechanical equivalence of heat.

1877 American inventor Thomas Edison's phonograph makes the first sound recording.

1895 German engineer Carl von Linde launches cryogenics.

1911 Dutch physicist Kamerlingh Onnes finds superconductivity.

1947 American Captain Charles (Chuck) Yeager breaks sound barrier in a Bell X-1 rocket plane.

1997 Thrust SSC Supersonic car breaks sound barrier on land, reaching 763 mph (1,228 kmh).

HEAT AND TEMPERATURE

HEAT IS A FORM OF ENERGY – AND IT IS all around us. Heat is found in the air, in the sea, in the rocks, in our bodies, and even in ice and snow. All these things possess heat, or internal energy, because their molecules are moving. However, in each of these substances, the molecules are moving at different speeds. They move faster in our bodies than they do in snow, for example, which means our bodies are warmer than snow. The temperature scale – a measure of heat energy – is used to tell us how hot or cold things are.

HIDDEN HEAT

On hot days, we sweat a lot. Our bodies give off little beads of water, which evaporate into the air. To evaporate, water has to take in heat. So it takes in heat from our skin, which helps cool us. This heat is called latent heat. Latent heat is the heat taken in or given out when any substance changes its state. Most changes of state, such as melting and boiling, take place at a fixed temperature.

‹ EARTH HEAT ›

Deep inside the Earth, the rocks are hot. In volcanic regions, hot rocks are found near the surface. When water drains into a deep hole down among the hot rocks, it boils into steam. When the steam pressure is high enough, it forces water back up the hole and into the air as a geyser. In some areas, engineers are harnessing this geothermal ("Earth-heat") energy to produce electricity. 74 ▶

The geyser Pohutu ("Big Splash") erupts. It is the biggest geyser in New Zealand.

MEASURING TEMPERATURE

We measure temperature with a thermometer. Common thermometers work on the principle that liquids expand when the temperature rises. They consist of a liquid (usually mercury or colored alcohol) in a narrow glass tube. When the temperature increases, the liquid expands and rises in the tube. Press-on strip thermometers use special liquid crystals that change color as the temperature changes. In science, temperatures are usually measured in degrees on the Celsius scale. On this scale, water freezes at 0° and boils at 100°. Normal body temperature is 37°.

Taking a child's temperature with a strip thermometer

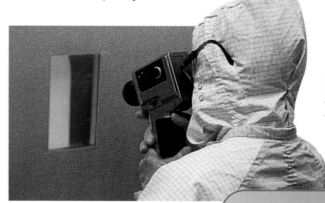

Taking the temperature of a furnace with a pyrometer

Hot stuff
Ordinary thermometers are no use for measuring very high temperatures, such as those of furnaces or red-hot lava. Instruments called pyrometers ("fire-measurers") are used instead. A common type matches the color of a glowing electric filament (wire) with the color of the hot object. When the colors match, the temperatures are the same. The temperature of the filament is calculated from the current passing through it.

FAHRENHEIT'S SCALE
The German physicist Daniel Gabriel Fahrenheit (1686–1736) made the first mercury thermometer in 1714 and devised the temperature scale named after him. On this scale, water freezes at 32° and boils at 212°. Normal body temperature is 98.6°.

°F
190
180
170
160
150
140
130
120

LET'S EXPERIMENT
MAKING A THERMOMETER

YOU CAN MAKE A simple thermometer using water, which will expand and contract as the temperature changes. Allow plenty of time for it to reach the temperature of its surroundings. **You will need:** small bottle; modeling clay; long plastic tube (such as a drinking straw); ink; water; cardboard; tape; pen; ruler; refrigerator; warm closet; thermometer that ranges 32–122°F (0–50°C).

1 Fill a bottle to the brim with water colored with ink. Using modeling clay, make a stopper-shape to fit in the opening of the bottle. Push the plastic tubing through the clay, making sure it is airtight. Push the clay and the straw into the neck of the bottle, and the liquid will rise in the tube. Tape a piece of cardboard to the tube for a scale.

Setting up

2 Now you need to calibrate your thermometer to show temperature levels. Place it in a refrigerator with the other thermometer. After about half an hour, take out your thermometer. Mark on the scale where the water level comes to. Write next to it the temperature shown by the other thermometer.

In the refrigerator

3 Now place your thermometer in a warm closet, again with the other thermometer. (If you don't have a warm closet, immerse the bottle and thermometer in a cup of warm tap water.) After about half an hour, take out and mark where the water level comes to. Write down the temperature shown on the other thermometer.

In a warm closet

4 You now need to complete your scale by dividing up the distance between the two points you have marked into equal parts. If your low temperature was 40°F (4°C) and your high was 110°F (44°C), you will need to divide the distance between them into 70 parts. When you have done this, your thermometer will be ready to use.

Calibrated

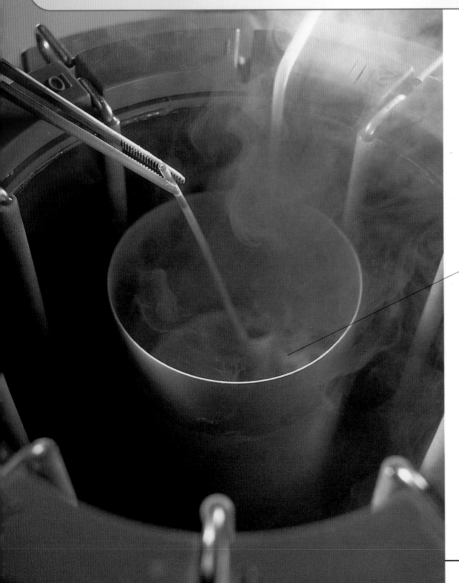

COLD SCIENCE

The Antarctic is the coldest place on Earth, where temperatures fall as low as -128°F (-89°C). Scientists can produce even lower temperatures that can make gases turn to liquids and even freeze. The study of very low temperatures is called cryogenics. The lowest theoretical temperature that can be reached is absolute zero (-459.67°F, -273.15°C), when all molecular motion ceases. It is the starting point for the Kelvin temperature scale, widely used in science. The units on this scale are called kelvins (K). Absolute zero is 0K, the freezing point of water just over 273K.

A lab sample preserved in a tank of liquid nitrogen (about -321°F, -196°C, 77K).

Super materials
At temperatures of about 20K (-423°F, -253°C) and below, some metals and alloys become superconductors, which can pass electricity without any resistance. At about 4K (-452°F, -269°C), liquid helium becomes a superfluid and can flow without friction.

Liquid helium cools instruments on infrared satellites.

HEAT ENERGY AND ENGINES

WHEN WE LIGHT A FIRE TO KEEP WARM, THE
heat given out comes from a chemical reaction.
This reaction is combustion (burning). When fuels
burn, they combine chemically with the oxygen in
the air, and as a result of this process, energy is given
off as heat. We call this kind of reaction exothermic,
which means "heat out." Some chemical reactions,
however, take in heat and are called endothermic,
which means "heat in." The heat from the
combustion of fuels is the power source for all
common engines, which drive our cars, buses, ships,
and planes. That is why we call them heat engines.

James Joule
In the 1840s, English
physicist James Joule was
one of the first to realize
that heat is a form of
energy. He therefore
devised a system for
measuring the heat
produced by mechanical
energy. The unit of
energy, the joule (J),
is named after him.

James Joule
(1818–89)

CHEMICAL HEAT

When magnesium metal and copper oxide are heated together, they
react, forming new chemicals and giving off even more heat (right).
This additional heat is a result of a rearrangement of the chemical
bonds between the reacting elements. Heating breaks the bonds
between the elements in the original chemicals, and energy is
absorbed. Then the elements form new bonds with each other
to make new chemicals, and heat energy is given out. But the
energy released in making new bonds is much greater than
the energy absorbed in breaking the old ones, so overall
energy is given out. The reaction is exothermic.

*The exothermic reaction of magnesium metal
and copper oxide produces a white-hot flame.*

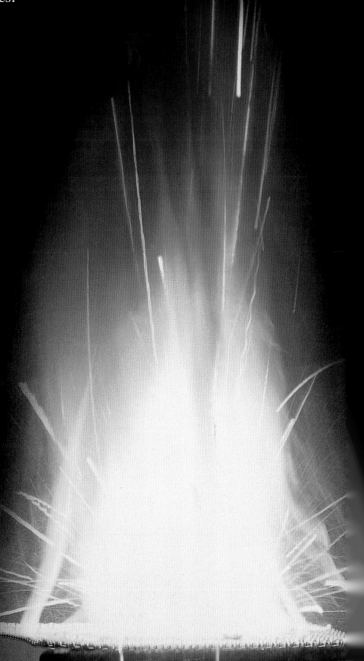

SHOOTING STARS

When two objects are rubbed
together, they become warm.
The rubbing between the
surfaces in contact (friction)
generates heat. The faster you
rub and the rougher the
surfaces, the more heat is
generated. When specks of
rock from outer space fall
into Earth's atmosphere, they
are traveling at speeds of
40,000 mph (60,000 kmh)
or more. Friction with the air
molecules is so great that the
specks become red-hot or
white-hot and then burn up.
We see the fiery trails these
specks make in the night sky
as meteors, popularly called
shooting or falling stars.

HEAT ENGINES

Just as mechanical energy can be converted into heat (as Joule proved), so heat can be converted into mechanical energy. We call the machines that do this heat engines. The first engines harnessed the heat energy of steam. The modern version of the steam engine is the steam turbine. It is called an external combustion engine because its fuel is burned outside the engine. In most other engines, such as gasoline, diesel, and jet engines, fuel is burned inside, so they are called internal combustion engines.

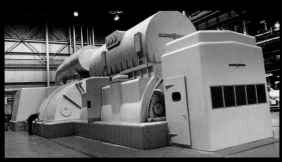

Burning outside
Steam turbines power this generator in a coal-fired power station. The heat from the burning coal turns water to steam in a boiler. The steam is fed into the turbines and expands through a series of turbine wheels, causing them to spin around and generate electricity.

Induction – fuel mixture is taken in.　　*Intake valve*

Compression – fuel mixture is compressed.

Spark plug　　*Exhaust – burned gases are forced out.*

Burning inside
Gasoline engines power most cars. The pistons in the cylinders produce power according to a regular cycle of four strokes (movements up or down). In each cylinder, a mixture of gasoline and air is taken in, compressed, then set alight by an electric spark. The hot gases produced expand and push against the piston to produce power. Finally, the burned gases are removed and released through the exhaust.

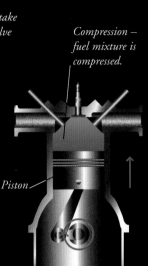

Piston

Power – fuel burns, driving down piston.

Exhaust valve

LET'S EXPERIMENT
MAKING A STEAMBOAT

THIS BOAT HARNESSES the energy of a burning candle. Heat from the flame turns the water in the coil into steam. The steam forces water out of the tubing and drives the boat forward. Immediately, the steam cools, condenses, and shoots back up the tubing as water. This process sails the boat along in a series of pulses. **You will need:** an adult's help; soft plastic bottle; knife; 1/8 in (3 mm)-wide soft metal tubing; tubing cutter or hacksaw; sandpaper; pencil; nail, small candle; adhesive tape; match; container of water.

1 Ask an adult to cut the bottle in half lengthways and to cut the metal tubing to about twice the length of the bottle. Sandpaper the ends of the tube. Gently bend the tubing around a pencil to make a coil. Using a nail, pierce two holes into the back end of the boat and push the tubing through to form a tight fit. Tape the candle to the bottom of the boat and gently bend the tubing so that the coil rests directly above the flame.

2 Fill the tubing with water by placing one end in the water and carefully sucking at the other. Then place the boat on the surface of a large container of water, making sure the tube ends are both under the surface. Light the candle. After a few moments, the boat will begin to move along in a series of pulses. As long as the boat has a heat source and an engine full of water, it should continue to move.

Your steamboat moves along in pulses.

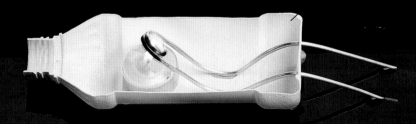

EXPANSION AND CONTRACTION

SOMETIMES THE LIDS ON JARS FIT SO tightly that they're difficult to open. But if you put them under hot water, you'll find that they open more easily. This is because the heat from the water makes the lids expand (get bigger). Most things expand when they are heated. Adding more heat to a substance makes its molecules vibrate, or move around vigorously, and take up more room. On the other hand, when a substance cools, it contracts (gets smaller). Its molecules don't move as much and therefore take up less room. Almost all materials – solids, liquids, and gases – expand or contract when the temperature changes.

EFFECTS ON SOLIDS

When engineers build a long bridge, they don't build it all in one piece. If they did, stresses (forces) occurring when the bridge expanded in hot weather would make it buckle or crack. Instead, the bridge is built in sections with gaps in between. These gaps allow the bridge to expand without causing any damage. For the same reason, concrete roads are laid in sections with expansion gaps in between. Solids don't expand as much as liquids and gases. Iron, for example, expands only by about 100,000th of its length for each 1°C (approximately 2°F) rise in temperature. Brass expands by one and a half times that.

A clinical thermometer

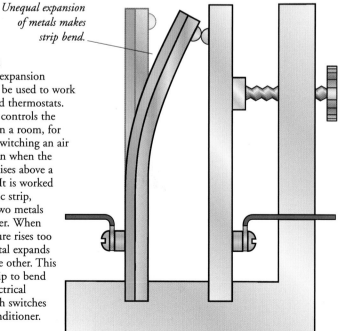

Unequal expansion of metals makes strip bend.

Thermostat

The unequal expansion of metals can be used to work switches called thermostats. A thermostat controls the temperature in a room, for example, by switching an air conditioner on when the temperature rises above a certain level. It is worked by a bimetallic strip, made up of two metals joined together. When the temperature rises too high, one metal expands more than the other. This causes the strip to bend and make electrical contact, which switches on the air conditioner.

MERCURY RISING

In liquids, the molecules are farther apart than they are in solids. This means that they are not so strongly attracted to one another. So when you give them more energy (by heating), they can travel much faster and move even farther apart. We make use of the expansion of liquids in thermometers.

Mercury is a good liquid for thermometers because it is easy to see and expands (and contracts) evenly as the temperature changes. A clinical thermometer has a constriction in the bore to stop the mercury from falling back after the temperature has been taken.

EXPANSION

When explosives are detonated, they produce large amounts of gases and heat. The heated gases expand rapidly and cause a shock wave in the air that we hear as a bang. If a gas can't expand into a bigger volume when the temperature rises, then its pressure goes up. The volume, temperature, and pressure of a gas are related by three fundamental laws known as the gas laws (pp. 28–29). The expansion and contraction of gases explains how heat travels by convection.

The Montgolfiers
Expanding air helped to pioneer early flight. In June 1783, the French brothers Jacques and Étienne Montgolfier built a big linen and paper bag with an opening at the base, and lit a fire beneath it. As the air inside heated up, it lifted the balloon into the air.

An artist's imaginative impression of the first human flight on November 21, 1783.

LET'S EXPERIMENT
GASES AND HEAT

GASES EXPAND A LOT when they're heated, and contract a lot when cooled. You can easily demonstrate this in a simple experiment.

You will need: a plastic bottle; a glass pitcher or other large container; balloon; hot water from the hot faucet (do not use boiling water); ice.

1 At room temperature, stretch the neck of a balloon over the mouth of a bottle. The balloon will hang down limply. Now place the bottle in a large container of hot water. The limp balloon starts inflating and eventually stands upright as the air inside the bottle expands.

2 Now place the bottle in a container of ice and water. The balloon immediately starts deflating, and may eventually be drawn into the neck of the bottle. This happens because the air in the bottle has cooled and contracted.

TRAVELING HEAT

AFTER A FROSTY NIGHT, THE METAL LATCH ON A

wooden gate feels much colder than the wood. Yet they both have the same temperature. This happens because metal conducts (passes) the heat away from your hand faster than wood does. Conduction is one of the three main ways in which heat travels. It happens in all materials – in solids, liquids, and gases. Also all materials give off heat by radiation. In liquids and gases, heat can also travel by convection.

This metal frying pan conducts the heat from the stove to the food.

CONDUCTION

Solids are the best conductors. They are made up of particles (atoms or molecules) held in a rigid framework. They don't change places, but they do vibrate. When a solid is heated in one place, the particles there gain more energy and start vibrating more vigorously. They make neighboring particles vibrate more vigorously too. These do the same to their neighbors, and so on throughout the material. Metals conduct heat particularly well because their loosely-held electrons quickly pass on vibrations from atom to atom.

INSULATION

Polar bears are warm-blooded mammals, yet they live in freezing Arctic temperatures. They retain their body heat because of a thick layer of fat under their skin, as well as a thick coat of fur. Fat and fur are poor conductors of heat, or good insulators. Fur traps small pockets of air, which is an excellent insulator. Wool, wood, and plastic foam trap air too, making them all suitable as insulators.

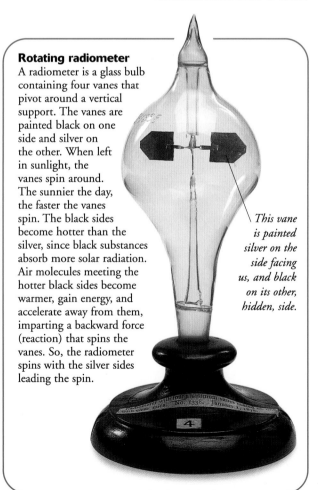

Rotating radiometer
A radiometer is a glass bulb containing four vanes that pivot around a vertical support. The vanes are painted black on one side and silver on the other. When left in sunlight, the vanes spin around. The sunnier the day, the faster the vanes spin. The black sides become hotter than the silver, since black substances absorb more solar radiation. Air molecules meeting the hotter black sides become warmer, gain energy, and accelerate away from them, imparting a backward force (reaction) that spins the vanes. So, the radiometer spins with the silver sides leading the spin.

This vane is painted silver on the side facing us, and black on its other, hidden, side.

Beating the heat
Insulating tiles made of silica cover most of the space shuttle. They shield the craft and crew from high temperatures. These temperatures are caused by air friction when the shuttle plunges into Earth's atmosphere after its journey into space.

Thermal tiles cover the space shuttle orbiters.

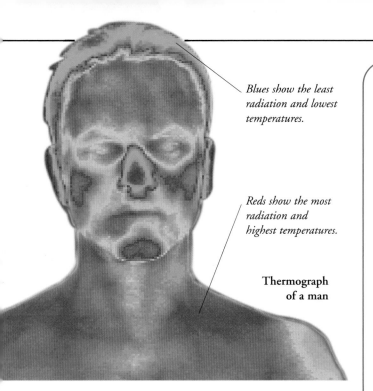

Blues show the least radiation and lowest temperatures.

Reds show the most radiation and highest temperatures.

Thermograph of a man

RADIATION

Did you know that you are a radiator and give off heat like a radiator in a room? Using a technique called thermography, we can see the heat radiation that the body gives off. Every object radiates heat – the hotter it is, the more heat it radiates. Heat rays, or waves, belong to the same family of waves as light – electromagnetic waves (pp. 102–103). Heat waves are called infrared rays. Like all electromagnetic radiation, they can travel through space. That is how the Sun's heat reaches us.

LET'S EXPERIMENT
THE BEST RADIATORS

THE AMOUNT OF HEAT A BODY radiates depends not only on its temperature, but also on the nature of its surface. In this experiment, you'll find out whether a black or a shiny surface is the better radiator. **You will need:** an adult's help; two jars with lids; matte black paint; paint brush; shiny aluminum foil; drill and bit; thermometer; water; modeling clay.

1 Wrap shiny foil around one jar and paint the other matte black. Get an adult to drill a hole in each lid for the thermometer. Fill the jars with hot water from the faucet, screw on their lids and take their temperatures. Place a piece of modeling clay over the lid holes to seal the jars.

2 Every few minutes, take the temperature of each jar. Are they the same? You'll find that they aren't. The black jar cools down faster than the shiny one, because black bodies are the best radiators.

LET'S EXPERIMENT
CONVECTION IN WATER

HEAT IS SPREAD BY CONVECTION in all fluids – liquids as well as gases. In this experiment, you can see convection currents in action when water is heated.
You will need: an adult present; colored paper; hole punch; spoon; water; a heat source (such as a gas burner or a stove); heatproof glass container (if using a stove, use a heatproof glass bowl resting on a saucepan of water).

1 Cut paper dots with a hole punch. Stir them into a heatproof container of water. Place the container over a heat source and gently heat it on one side.

2 View the container from the side. Notice the dots begin to move as the water heats up. The ones directly over the heat source move upward with the rising warmer, lighter (less dense) water. On the other side, the dots move down with the colder, denser water.

CONVECTION CURRENTS

Hang-glider pilots launch themselves off cliffs, riding the warm air currents, which are called thermals, sweeping up from below. The upward currents are created when hot land heats the air above it. The air expands and becomes lighter (less dense) than the air around it, and therefore rises. At the same time colder, denser air descends to take its place. These circulating streams of rising and descending air are convection currents. On a large scale, convection currents cause the winds. On a small scale, they spread heat from radiators around a room.

SOUND VIBRATIONS

IF YOU TOUCH YOUR BICYCLE BELL WHEN IT IS RINGING,
you feel it vibrating. It is these vibrations that produce the
ringing sound you hear. As the bell vibrates outward, it
pushes against the air molecules next to it and starts them
vibrating, too. In turn, these molecules start the next ones
vibrating, and the vibrations, or waves, spread through the
air away from the bell. We hear these vibrations as sound
when they reach our ears. In fact, every sound you hear is
created by something vibrating. Sometimes you can
see the vibration; sometimes you cannot.

VIBRATIONS IN THE AIR

A hummingbird beats its wings as fast as
70 times a second as it hovers in front of a
flower. The rapid beating of its wings creates
vibrations in the air, which produce the
humming noise that gives the birds their name.
It is also the rapid beating of wings that creates
the buzzing sound made by bees and other
flying insects. Male grasshoppers produce their
distinctive sound by rubbing together parts at
the base of their wings called the file and scraper.

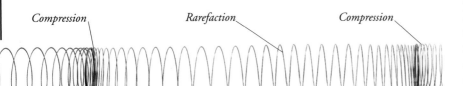

Compression　　　*Rarefaction*　　　*Compression*

Sound waves

Sound waves travel through materials in much the same way as
waves travel through a spring (above). When a sound is made,
the air molecules near the sound are squashed together and
create a high-pressure area called a compression. They, in turn,
jostle up to the molecules next to them and then are pulled back
into place. This action creates a low-pressure area called a
rarefaction. Sound waves are longitudinal. This means that
they vibrate in the direction in which they are traveling.

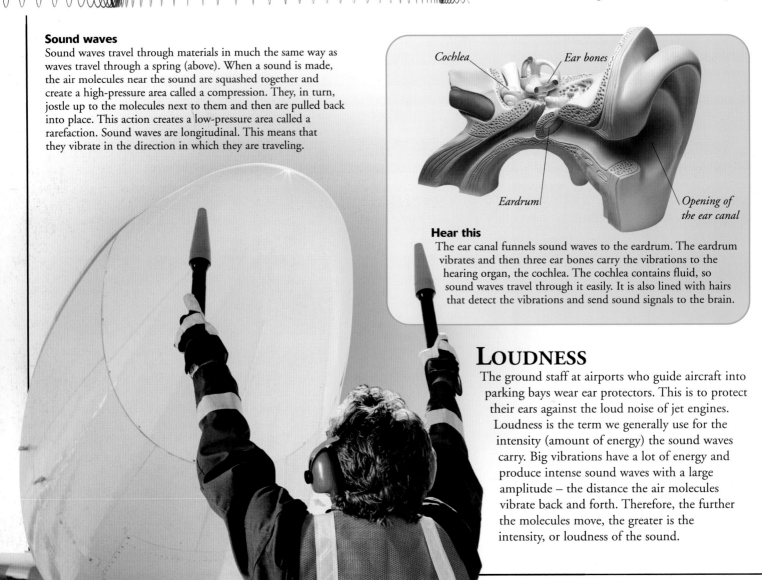

Cochlea　　　*Ear bones*

Eardrum　　　*Opening of
the ear canal*

Hear this

The ear canal funnels sound waves to the eardrum. The eardrum
vibrates and then three ear bones carry the vibrations to the
hearing organ, the cochlea. The cochlea contains fluid, so
sound waves travel through it easily. It is also lined with hairs
that detect the vibrations and send sound signals to the brain.

LOUDNESS

The ground staff at airports who guide aircraft into
parking bays wear ear protectors. This is to protect
their ears against the loud noise of jet engines.
Loudness is the term we generally use for the
intensity (amount of energy) the sound waves
carry. Big vibrations have a lot of energy and
produce intense sound waves with a large
amplitude – the distance the air molecules
vibrate back and forth. Therefore, the further
the molecules move, the greater is the
intensity, or loudness of the sound.

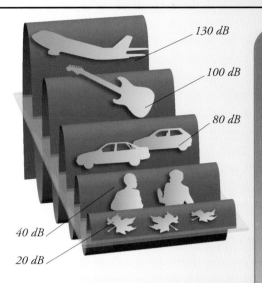

130 dB

100 dB

80 dB

40 dB

20 dB

The decibel scale

We measure sound intensity (loudness) on the decibel (dB) scale. One decibel is one-tenth of a bel, a unit named after Alexander Graham Bell, who invented the telephone. The quietest sound we can hear is 0 dB, while the sound of a jet plane taking off is an ear-splitting 130 dB. But this figure does not mean that the aircraft is 130 times louder than the quietest sound. The decibel scale is logarithmic, which means that an increase of 10 dB increases loudness 10 times. In other words, a sound of 130 dB sounds 10 times as loud as one of 120 dB.

WE CANNOT SEE sound waves in the air, but we can sometimes see the effects of the vibrations. This experiment shows that sound is simply vibration. **You will need:** tuning fork; glass; water.

1 Fill the glass to the brim with water. Strike the tuning fork sharply (preferably on a wooden surface) so that it produces a note.

2 Now touch the surface of the water with the prongs of the tuning fork. The water will immediately splash around, driven by the vibrations of the fork.

ECHOES AND ACOUSTICS

If you shout when you are in a large, empty building, you can often hear the sound of your voice coming back to you as an echo. Echoes are sounds that have been reflected (bounced) off surfaces around you. Hard surfaces reflect sound more effectively than soft surfaces. Soft surfaces tend to absorb sound. The way the design of a building affects sound is called its acoustics. Concert halls and theaters must be carefully designed so that echoes do not interfere with the sounds of speech or music reaching the audience. The Greeks and Romans built amphitheaters (below) with superb acoustics.

Large ears give bats more sensitive hearing.

Locating by echoes

Echoes play a vital role in the lives of most bats. Bats fly at night when ordinary eyes are no good for finding the way, so they use their ears instead. They send out high-pitched sound signals that echo from any object in their path. The bat picks up the signals again and builds a picture of sounds that enables it to navigate its way through the darkness. This technique is known as echolocation.

SPEED AND FREQUENCY

COMPARED WITH LIGHT, SOUND TRAVELS
relatively slowly. When you see someone
hammering in the distance, you hear the
sound after you see the hammer strike. Under
the same conditions, all sound waves travel
at the same speed. But they can vibrate in
different ways. Some vibrate quickly – they
have a high frequency or pitch (like the voice
of a soprano). Others vibrate slowly – they have
a low frequency (like the voice of a bass). We
measure frequency in hertz (Hz), the number
of waves passing a point each second.
Humans can hear sounds between
about 20 and 20,000 Hz.

WHALE SONG

Sound travels more than four times faster in water than in air
and is carried for long distances. The molecules in water are
more densely packed and pass on the vibrations more easily.
Whales can, therefore, communicate with each other by sound
over distances of 20 miles (30 km) or more. Male humpback
whales are noted for their "singing" during the mating season.
Their songs are complex symphonies of repeated melodies
and phrases and may last for a day or more. The whales
sing either to attract a mate or to warn off other males.

*A cloud forms behind the
plane as it breaks the
sound barrier.*

THE SOUND BARRIER

At sea level, sound travels through the air at a
speed of around 760 mph (1,225 kmh). This is
called sonic speed. When a plane travels at below
sonic speed, sound waves travel in front of it. But
when it reaches sonic speed, the sound waves pile
up on the plane to create a shock wave. When
the plane goes supersonic (flying faster than
sound), it leaves a shock wave behind, which is
heard on the ground as a loud bang called a sonic
boom. It was once thought that the shock wave
set off at sonic speed would shatter a plane and
was a barrier, or obstacle, to supersonic flight.
This came to be known as the sound barrier.

ULTRASONICS

Humans cannot hear sound waves with frequencies over about 20,000 Hz. These are called ultrasonic waves. We may not be able to hear them, but we can make use of them. Pregnant women have ultrasound scans to check on the health of their unborn babies. A scanner transmits ultrasonic waves into the womb, where they are reflected by the baby's body. The reflections are picked up and displayed on a screen (left). Ultrasonic waves are also used in sonar, a kind of sound radar that ships and submarines use in navigation. It works in the same way as echolocation in bats (p. 95).

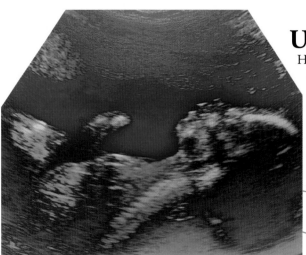

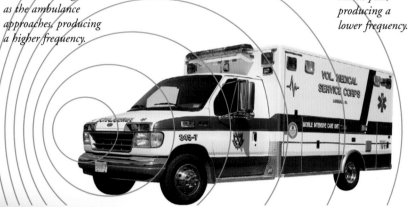

Waves crowd together as the ambulance approaches, producing a higher frequency.

Waves stretch out as the ambulance travels past, producing a lower frequency.

The Doppler effect

When an ambulance races first toward and then away from you, you hear the sound of its siren change pitch, or frequency. This is called the Doppler effect. When the ambulance comes toward you, you hear more waves than usual per second (higher frequency). When the ambulance goes away, the sound waves are stretched out and you hear fewer waves than usual per second (lower frequency).

ANIMAL HEARING

Some animals hear a different range of sound frequencies to humans. Snakes, for example, can hear only a narrow range of frequencies, from about 200 to 800 Hz. Bats, on the other hand, can hear frequencies from about 1,000 Hz to over 120,000 Hz. They use ultrasound for echolocation. Mice and moths hear ultrasounds, too. Other animals can hear sounds with lower frequencies than we can hear. We call sounds at these frequencies infrasounds. Pigeons can hear sounds with frequencies as low as 0.1 to 10 Hz. This means they may have the ability to detect earthquake waves.

LET'S EXPERIMENT
BOUNCING SOUND

SOUND WAVES ARE REFLECTED from surfaces in much the same way as light waves. This is what causes echoes. In this experiment, find out which surfaces reflect sound best – soft or hard. **You will need:** two poster tubes; cardboard; ticking watch (or clock); pieces of foam and fabric.

1 Set up the cardboard and tubes as shown in the picture. Leave a gap of about 2.5 inches (6 cm) between the ends of the tubes and the cardboard. Place the watch at the mouth of one tube, and put your ear to the mouth of the other.

2 You will be able to hear the watch ticking clearly. The sound has traveled along one tube and been reflected by the cardboard into the other. Cover the cardboard first with cloth, then with foam. Do they reflect the sound better or worse than before?

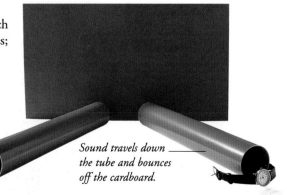

Sound travels down the tube and bounces off the cardboard.

MAKING MUSIC

MUSICAL INSTRUMENTS CREATE SOUNDS by making something vibrate. For example, guitars use vibrating strings. Most musical instruments are "tuned" to produce a set of frequencies, or notes. But the same note sounds different on different instruments. This is because each instrument produces its own distinctive range of vibrations, called harmonics, in addition to a basic vibration. The pattern of sound waves from a musical instrument can be represented as wavy lines, with peaks and troughs showing the change in air pressure as the sound reaches your ear.

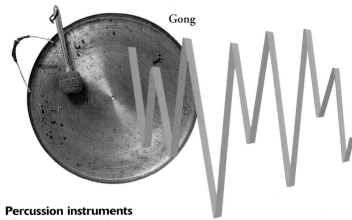
Gong

Percussion instruments
The gong is a percussion instrument, which you hit with a hammer. The sound waves have an irregular pattern, which we hear as a crashing noise. Other percussion instruments include the drum, triangle, and xylophone.

Flute

Wind instruments
The flute is a wind instrument. Players blow over a hole to vibrate the air inside. It produces a very pure sound, with a clean wave form. With other wind instruments, such as the oboe and clarinet, players blow through a reed to make the air vibrate.

The sound waves shown for the flute (above) and the violin (below) are created when each instrument hits the same note. However, they each have their own distinctive wave pattern.

Violin

String instruments
The violin is a string instrument. The strings are made to vibrate with a bow. They produce a complex, "bright" sound with many harmonics. Other bowed string instruments include the viola and double bass. The guitar and harp are string instruments that are plucked to create sounds.

ALL TOGETHER NOW
A gamelan orchestra (above) in Southeast Asia plays traditional music with a distinctive sound. The performers play mainly percussion instruments such as gongs, chimes, and gamelangs, which resemble xylophones. In Western countries, orchestras use a range of instruments, divided into four main types: strings, wind, brass, and percussion. Usually, a conductor keeps the musicians playing in time with each other. The conductor also determines the tempo (speed) of the music.

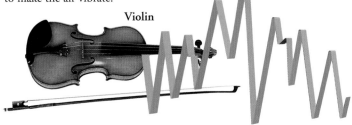

LET'S EXPERIMENT
MUSICAL BOTTLES

WIND INSTRUMENTS WORK by vibrating a column of air. You can make you own wind instrument from a row of bottles. **You will need:** eight identical bottles; water; food coloring (optional).

1 Arrange bottles in a row and fill them with decreasing amounts of colored water. Blow over the mouth of the bottles to make sounds.

2 "Tune" each bottle by adjusting the water level so that it gives you a different note. Now you can play music!

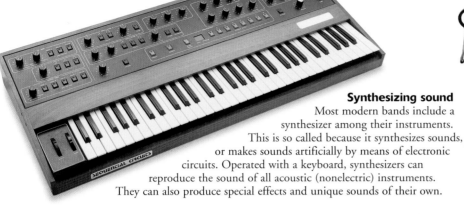

Synthesizing sound

Most modern bands include a synthesizer among their instruments. This is so called because it synthesizes sounds, or makes sounds artificially by means of electronic circuits. Operated with a keyboard, synthesizers can reproduce the sound of all acoustic (nonelectric) instruments. They can also produce special effects and unique sounds of their own.

RECORDING SOUND

At a recording studio, singers sing into a microphone in time with a pre-recorded backing track, which they hear through their headphones. Thomas Edison made the first ever sound recording in 1877, of the words "Mary had a little lamb." He used a needle attached to a vibrating disc moved by sound waves to scratch a groove in aluminum. This groove method is the basis of recording on vinyl discs. Technological developments allowed sound to be recorded onto magnetic tape, while the more recent digitization process led to sound being stored on CDs (compact discs) and as digital audio files on computers and MP3 devices.

Mixing sounds

In a recording studio, the sounds of different instruments and voices are often recorded at different times. Sound engineers then take over to produce the finished recording. They use a device called a mixer to bring all the sounds together. Using the sliders on the mixing console (above), the sound engineer adjusts the loudness and tone of each individual performance to make a perfect blend.

Digital recording

In modern digital recording, the wave forms of sounds are converted into precise numbers, which are then recorded in binary code (using just the numbers 0 and 1). On a CD, these numbers are recorded as pits and "lands" (flat areas), which are read by a laser to play the CD. In most digital audio files, the binary-coded files are shrunk down to about one-twelfth of their original size. These compressed files can then be stored and played on an MP3 player or other digital audio device.

A CD carries sounds as numbers in a spiral track of pits.

A digital audio device can be used to store and play music.

LIGHT AND COLOR

Picture: Rainbows form when sunlight passes through raindrops.
Double bows are sometimes seen when the Sun is bright.

VISIBLE WAVES

LIFE ON EARTH COULD NOT EXIST WITHOUT LIGHT.

It enables plants to grow and animals to survive. Light is a form of energy that we can think of as traveling in waves. It forms the small visible part of the electromagnetic spectrum, which also includes radio and television waves, microwaves, infrared (heat), ultraviolet (UV), X-rays, and gamma rays. Things that do not produce their own light are visible because light from another source is reflected off them. The Sun produces most of the natural light on Earth, while electric lighting is a common source of artificial light.

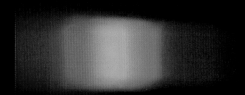

The visible part of the electromagnetic spectrum

NATURAL LIGHT

On Earth, the main source of natural light is the Sun. Nuclear reactions at the core of the Sun create energy in the form of light (and heat). A few organisms, such as fireflies and glowworms, produce natural light in their bodies through a chemical reaction called bioluminescence. For centuries, scientists debated whether light traveled as waves or as particles. In the early 20th century, research by German physicists Max Planck (1858–1947) and Albert Einstein (1879–1955) led to the current theory. Scientists now believe that light can travel both as waves and as tiny particles of energy called photons, but never both at the same time.

INTERFERENCE

When two beams of light meet, they interfere with each other (p. 118). If the peaks of one light wave line up with the peaks of the other, constructive interference occurs and the waves add together to produce a brighter beam. However, if the peaks of one wave line up with the troughs of the other, destructive interference takes place and the beams cancel each other out. This combination results in a pattern of dark and light known as an interference pattern. These patterns can be obtained by shining light through a small glass slide engraved with thousands of narrow lines called a diffraction grating. As the light passes between the lines, it is split up into tiny beams that spread out and interfere with each other.

LASERS

A laser produces a highly concentrated beam of light that can be strong enough to cut through metal. Most lasers have either gas, or a crystal such as a ruby, trapped inside a small space with mirrors at each end. A burst of very bright light or electricity causes the gas or crystal to produce light. The color of this light depends on the substance trapped – rubies give red light, for example. This light reflects to and fro off the mirrors in the cavity. Each time the light passes through the crystal or gas, it

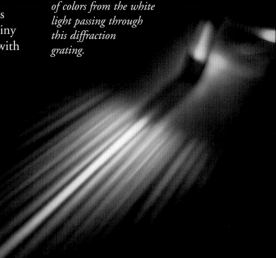

Interference creates streaks of colors from the white light passing through this diffraction grating.

c. 300 BC Greek mathematician Euclid investigates the reflection of light.

c. 1010 Arabian scientist Alhazen describes human vision and explains how lenses work.

1621 Dutch mathematician and physicist Willebrord van Roijen Snell discovers the law of refraction.

1665 English physicist and mathematician Isaac Newton uses prisms to split sunlight into a spectrum of colors.

1801 English physicist Thomas Young discovers interference of light.

1808 French engineer and physicist Etienne Louis Malus discovers polarized light.

Neon lights in Las Vegas

Picture of the Sun taken by the SOHO probe.

When electricity passes through the mercury gas, it gives out ultraviolet light. Because we cannot see ultraviolet light, the insides of the tube are coated with fluorescent crystals which convert the ultraviolet light into visible light. Fluorescence also occurs in nature. For example, a fluorescent rock will glow under an ultraviolet lamp.

LIGHT YEARS

Most stars are an extremely long way from the Earth. Miles or kilometers are not practical ways of measuring such enormous distances. For instance, one of the stars in the constellation Cygnus is approximately 60 million million miles (100 million million kilometers) away from Earth. Astronomers need a larger unit of measurement to describe distances in space, so they use light-years. A light-year is the distance that light travels in one year. Light from our next nearest star, Proxima Centauri, (the Sun is our nearest star) takes 4.3 years to reach us here on Earth, so it is 4.3 light-years away.

Polarized light interference produces colored stress patterns on this plastic hook.

The red beam from this helium-neon laser is used to perform laser eye surgery.

causes them to give off even more light. Finally, an extremely powerful laser beam emerges from a small hole in one of the mirrors. Lasers have many uses, from medical surgery, to creating holograms, to reading the data on compact discs.

POLARIZED LIGHT

Electromagnetic waves such as light waves have two parts, an electric field and a magnetic field. The two fields travel at right angles to the direction of the wave.

The electric field is the part of the light wave that interacts with matter. Normally, the electric field vibrates in many different directions, but if it is restricted to only one direction, the light is said to be polarized. Sunlight reflecting from a road tends to be horizontally polarized. Therefore, wearing sunglasses with polarizing filters that only let through vertically polarized light will block the glare.

FLUORESCENCE

When neon gas is sealed in a glass tube and electricity is passed through it, the neon glows red. Often used in signs, neon lights based on this principle were the forerunners of fluorescent lights. Instead of using neon gas, fluorescent lights use mercury gas inside a glass tube.

1840s English astronomer Sir John Herschel and French physicist Edmond Becquerel take colored photographs of light spectra.

1864 Scottish physicist James Clerk Maxwell concludes that light is an electromagnetic wave forming part of an electromagnetic spectrum.

1880s American scientists Albert Michelson and Edward Morley use interference to determine that the speed of light is constant.

1895 French chemists Auguste and Louis Lumière publicly screen motion pictures.

1905 German physicist Albert Einstein publishes his quantum theory of light.

1948 Hungarian physicist Dennis Gabor invents holograms.

LIGHT AND SHADE

TRANSPARENT SUBSTANCES, SUCH AS GLASS,
let light through, but opaque materials, such as
wood, block light. Light travels in straight lines.
If it falls on an opaque object, a dark shadow is
cast in the shape of the object where the light
could not pass through. Every night we are
plunged into shadow by the Earth. As it rotates,
each place on the surface becomes shielded from
the Sun's light for a few hours by the rest of the
Earth. Shadows also fall over parts of the Earth's
surface during solar eclipses.

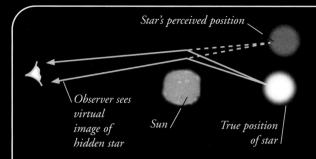

Star's perceived position

*Observer sees
virtual
image of
hidden star*

Sun

*True position
of star*

◄ GENERAL RELATIVITY ►

The German-born theoretical physicist Albert Einstein
(1879–1955) wrote two theories of relativity. His
"general" theory of relativity published in 1916 describes
gravity. It suggests that the force of gravity can bend
light, so the gravity of planets and stars makes them
act like giant lenses. British astrophysicist Arthur
Eddington tested this theory during the solar eclipse of
1919. Eddington photographed stars whose light passed
near to the Sun during the eclipse and
compared them with photographs
of the same stars taken when the
Sun was in another part of the sky.
The stars appeared to have moved
slightly, proving that the Sun's
gravity was indeed bending the light
from them just as Einstein had
predicted. This result made
Einstein famous. **137** ►

Albert Einstein

Gnomon

The shadows of time
Shadows can be used to tell the time.
A sundial marks the time of day by the
shadow cast on its surface as the Sun moves
gradually across the sky. The object on a
sundial that is used to create the shadow
is called a gnomon. On this sundial (left),
the shadow falls on a large metal ring
raised at an angle to the ground. The
ring has the hours of the day marked on
it and the position on which the shadow
of the gnomon falls tells the time.

*The diamond ring
effect during a
solar eclipse*

ULTIMATE SHADOW

A solar eclipse occurs when the Moon blocks out
the Sun's light and casts a shadow on the Earth.
Since the Moon does not completely obscure the
Sun, a blurred shadow is produced. The dark
middle of the blurred shadow is called the umbra,
and the lighter shadow around the edges is the
penumbra. During a solar eclipse, people in
the umbra see a total eclipse, while those in
the penumbra see a partial eclipse. Lunar
eclipses occur when the Moon moves through
the Earth's shadow. During a lunar eclipse,
the Moon usually becomes red rather than
completely dark. This color comes from small
amounts of sunlight refracted (pp. 124–125) by
the Earth's atmosphere that still reach the Moon.
Other planets, moons, and stars also produce eclipses.

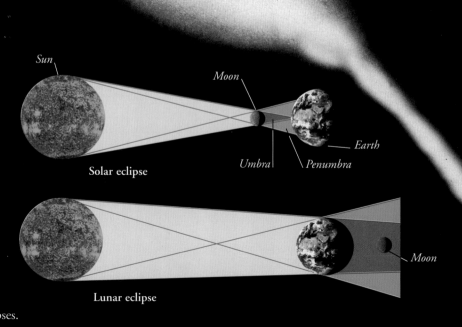

Sun

Moon

Earth

Umbra *Penumbra*

Solar eclipse

Moon

Lunar eclipse

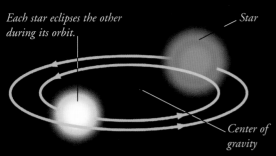

Each star eclipses the other during its orbit.

Star

Center of gravity

BINARY STARS

Many of the stars we see are in fact binary stars. These are pairs of stars attracted by gravity to orbit around each other. Some binaries are a type of variable star called an eclipsing binary. Their position in the sky means that when we look at them from Earth, each star repeatedly passes in front of the other blocking out its light. Astronomers identify eclipsing binaries from these changes in brightness. This nebula (right) photographed by the Hubble Space Telescope has a binary star at its center.

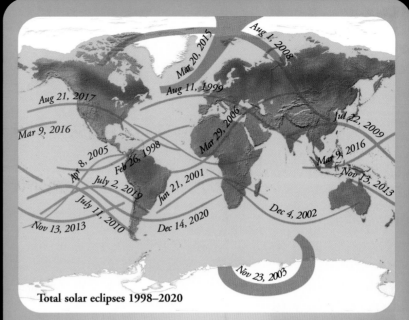

Total solar eclipses 1998–2020

Forecasting an eclipse

A solar eclipse occurs when a "new" Moon passes between the Earth and the Sun, and casts a shadow on the Earth's surface. There is a new Moon every 29.5 days, but solar eclipses only occur about every 18 months. This is because the path of the Moon's orbit around the Earth is tilted at an angle of five degrees compared to the path the Earth takes as it orbits around the Sun. Most of the time therefore, the new Moon's shadow passes above or below the Earth. When viewing a solar eclipse, never look at the Sun without eye protection.

The corona at total eclipse of the Sun

MAKE FUN SHADOWS with shadow puppets. **You will need**: pencil; heavy construction paper or cardboard; scissors; adhesive tape; flashlight.

1 Draw the outline of a character onto the paper. (You may want to copy these ghosts.) Carefully cut out the character and tape it to the end of the pencil.

2 Hold the puppet near a wall, then shine the flashlight on it to make the shadow appear. Or, hold your hands in front of the light and see what patterns you can make on the wall. Try clasping your hands and moving one or more of your fingers. Also note the effect of moving the flashlight to different positions.

History of shadow

Shadow theaters are traditional in parts of Asia. In the 17th century, they spread to Europe, becoming the forerunners of modern movies. The rods attached to these Javanese puppets allow their jointed limbs to be moved.

LET'S EXPERIMENT
SHADOW PUPPETS

REFLECTION

MOST OBJECTS DO NOT
produce their own light. We
only see them because light is
reflected off them. That is why
we cannot see in the dark. Rough
and dark objects reflect less light than
lighter, shinier things. Mirrors reflect
back almost all of the light falling on
them. They can form images of objects
because, unlike rough surfaces, which
scatter reflected light in many directions,
they reflect light rays in one direction and
in the same pattern in which they arrive.

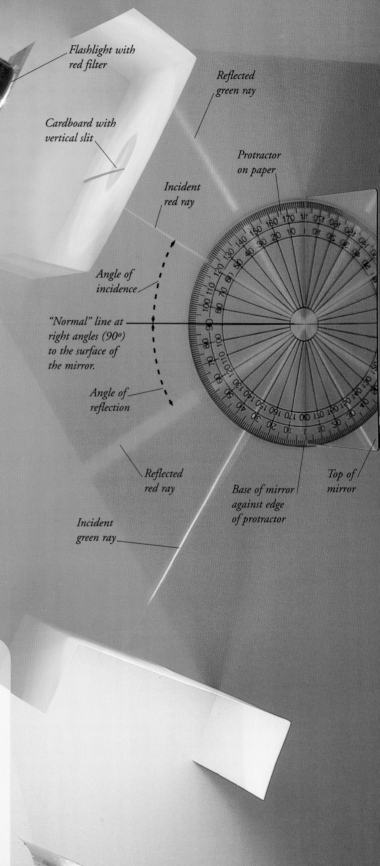

Flashlight with
red filter

Reflected
green ray

Cardboard with
vertical slit

Protractor
on paper

Incident
red ray

Angle of
incidence

"Normal" line at
right angles (90°)
to the surface of
the mirror.

Angle of
reflection

Reflected
red ray

Base of mirror
against edge
of protractor

Top of
mirror

Incident
green ray

LAWS OF REFLECTION

There are always two rays involved in reflection – an
incident (incoming) ray and a reflected (outgoing) ray.
The angle between the incident ray striking any mirror
and an imaginary line called the "normal" that hits the

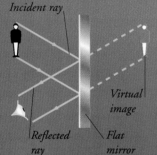

Incident ray

Virtual
image

Reflected
ray

Flat
mirror

mirror at right angles is always
the same as the angle between
the "normal" and the reflected
ray. Both the rays and the
"normal" lie on the same
imaginary flat surface.
Images formed by flat mirrors
are virtual (appearing to be
behind the mirror) and
the wrong way around.

LET'S EXPERIMENT
THE LAWS OF REFLECTION

PROVE THAT THE ANGLE of incidence of light on a mirror equals
the angle of reflection. **You will need:** two flashlights; colored
filters (such as candy wrappers); two pieces of cardboard; scissors;
large sheet of paper; protractor; small mirror; modeling clay; pen.

1 Attach a different
color filter over
each flashlight. Cut a
vertical slit in each
piece of cardboard. Put
the flashlights on the
floor. Place the pieces
of cardboard in front of
each, so a narrow strip
of light shines onto the
mirror (see Step 2).

2 Put the protractor
on the paper on
the floor. Supporting
the mirror with clay,
stand it against the
straight edge of the
protractor. On the
paper, mark the 90°
line, and the incident
ray and reflected ray
for each color.

3 For each color, the
angle between the
90° mark and the
incident ray should
equal the angle
between 90° and the
reflected ray. Move the
flashlights to other
positions. The two
angles will always
be equal.

Flashlight with
green filter

OPTICAL FIBERS

Most of our telephone calls and emails are converted by electronics into pulses of light and carried by optical fiber cables to their destination. On arrival, more electronics turns the light back into sound or data. Optical fibers like the one on the right (pictured with a needle to show its size) are made from a very thin core of glass that can refract (bend) light strongly. This core is surrounded by a coating of glass, known as the cladding, that cannot bend light as much. If light enters the fiber at certain angles, the boundary between the core and the cladding acts like a mirror and reflects it to and fro down the fiber. Light pulses can travel long distances in this way.

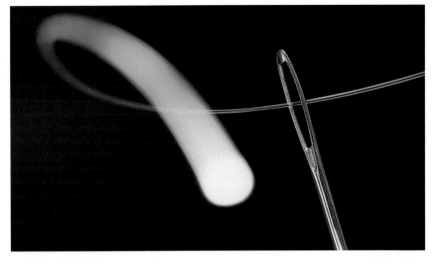

Endoscope
Bundles of optical fibers inside endoscopes (long, thin, medical instruments for seeing inside the body) transmit detailed images to television screens or an eyepiece for doctors to see. The area being studied is illuminated by light delivered by another bundle of fibers. Here surgeons are using an endoscope during keyhole surgery to remove a gallbladder.

Reflecting telescope
A large concave mirror, called the primary mirror, collects the light from stars and planets inside reflecting telescopes. The light reflected off this mirror falls onto a smaller flat mirror and an image is created. The image can either be recorded on photographic film or viewed through the lenses in an eyepiece that magnify it. There are different shapes and arrangements of mirrors in reflecting telescopes. This version (right) was designed by Sir Isaac Newton (1642–1727). The world's largest telescope mirror (left), belonging to the Hobby-Eberly telescope at the McDonald Observatory in Texas is 36 ft (11 m) wide.

The Hobby-Eberly telescope mirror has 91 segments.

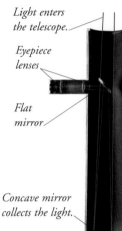

Light enters the telescope.

Eyepiece lenses

Flat mirror

Concave mirror collects the light.

CONCAVE AND CONVEX

Curved surfaces can either be concave, which means that they curve inward, or convex, which means that they curve outward. The mirrors we use to see our reflections are flat because although the images they produce are reversed from right to left, they are the same size and shape as the object. Curved mirrors produce distorted images that can be larger or smaller than the object reflected.

Convex mirror
Rays of light reflected from convex mirrors spread out (diverge), which makes them appear to have come from a focal point behind the mirror. The virtual image formed behind the mirror is smaller than the object, so convex mirrors are used as rearview mirrors in cars to help drivers see as much of the road behind as possible.

Concave mirror
Light reflected from concave mirrors is focused in front of them. Depending on how close the object is, either a magnified, same size, or smaller real image (which lies in front of the mirror) or a magnified virtual image (which lies behind the mirror) is formed. Magnifying makeup and shaving mirrors are concave.

Astronauts' visors behave like convex mirrors.

Rays of light

Virtual focus

Mirror

Real focus

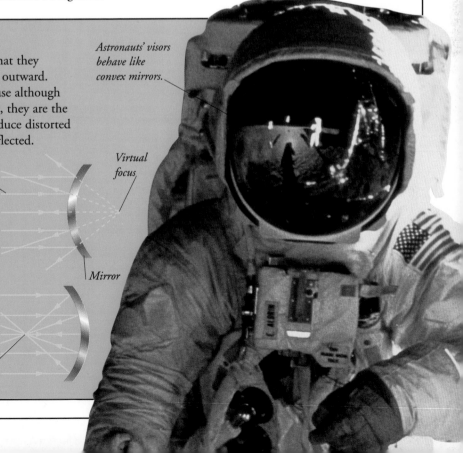

REFRACTION

WHEN LIGHT TRAVELS FROM ONE TRANSPARENT
substance into another, it changes direction slightly.
This bending of light is known as refraction. If you
look down at your legs while standing in water,
they will appear bent. This is because light refracts
as it passes from water to air. Curved pieces of
transparent material that can refract light in a
particular way are known as lenses. Most optical
instruments, including binoculars, telescopes, and
cameras, have lenses that focus light and produce
an image of whatever is being viewed.

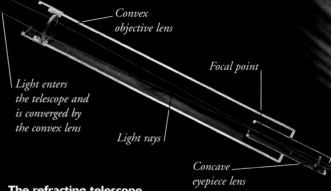

*Convex
objective lens*

Focal point

*Light enters
the telescope and
is converged by
the convex lens*

Light rays

*Concave
eyepiece lens*

The refracting telescope
Lenses inside refracting telescopes are used to produce magnified
images of distant objects such as planets and stars. The large lens
at the far end of the telescope collects light from the object and
creates an image of it. The smaller lens at the near end is the
eyepiece lens, which magnifies the image.

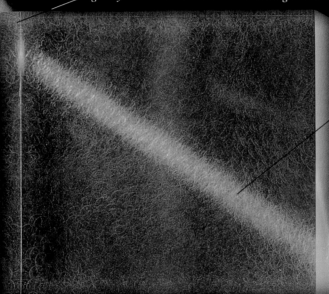

Light ray bends as it leaves the air and enters glass block.

*Light inside
the block
travels in a
straight line.*

*Light ray
bends again as
it leaves glass
block and
enters the air.*

LAWS OF REFRACTION
The picture on the left shows a ray of light bending
as it moves from air into the top of a glass block, and
bending again as it leaves the block at the bottom. In
1621, the Dutch mathematician Willebrord Snell
(1580–1626) discovered that there is a precise
mathematical relationship between the
angle at which a light ray enters a
substance that refracts it, and the
angle it is refracted to. This
relationship produces a
number known as the
refractive index and
tells us how strongly a
substance refracts light.

Willebrord Snell

LENSES
Transparent materials such as glass and
plastic are used to make lenses. Lenses
refract light. Convex lenses cause light
rays to converge (come together). The light
focuses where the converging rays meet.
Convex lenses make objects look larger
or smaller, depending
on their distance from
the lens. Concave
lenses cause light
rays to diverge (spread
out) and appear to
come from a virtual
focal point the same
side of the lens as the
light enters. Concave
lenses make objects
look smaller.

Convex lens

*Direction of
light rays*

Concave lens

Near-sighted
For the human eye to see clearly, light
rays coming into the eye should focus
on the retina. A near-sighted person
can see close objects clearly, but distant
objects are blurred. This is because
their eyes are too long, so light rays
focus before reaching the retina,
rather than on it. Glasses with
concave lenses correct the problem.

Far-sighted
Distant objects look clear to a
far-sighted person, but closer objects
look blurred. Their eyes are too short,
so light rays from close by focus
behind the retina, rather than on it.
A young person's natural lens can
correct for this, otherwise glasses
with convex lenses are used.

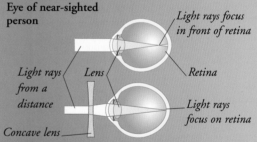

**Eye of near-sighted
person**

*Light rays
from a
distance*

Lens

*Light rays focus
in front of retina*

Retina

Concave lens

*Light rays
focus on retina*

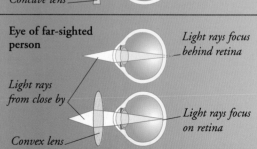

**Eye of far-sighted
person**

*Light rays
from close by*

*Light rays focus
behind retina*

Convex lens

*Light rays focus
on retina*

SEE HOW LIGHT is refracted when it passes through transparent objects. **You will need:** cardboard box; scissors; small lamp; white cardboard; transparent jars, bottles, and lenses.

1 Remove the top and bottom of the box and cut narrow slits in each of its sides. Experiment by cutting a different number of slits in each side, for example, cut seven close together on one side and three spaced out on another.

A water-filled jelly jar makes a great convex lens

2 Put the lamp on the sheet of white cardboard and place the box on top of it. Make a roof with cardboard so that light does not escape through the top of the box.

3 Darken the room, then place the transparent objects in the path of the light rays coming from the box. See how these objects act as convex lenses, bringing the rays to a focal point. Try a concave lens as well (below).

Cardboard roof prevents light from escaping out the top of the box.

Focal point

Fill a small bottle with water and stand it in the path of the light rays. The bottle acts as a convex lens, refracting and converging the rays. The rays of light meet at a place called the focal point.

Position a convex lens in front of the light rays. The more curved a lens is, the closer it will focus the light. So the bottle (above) focuses the light nearer than the lens.

Concave lens

Concave lens bends light outward.

Concave lens
Place a concave lens in one of the light ray paths. See how the light diverges as it does in this picture (left).

Focal point

Fresnel lighthouse lens

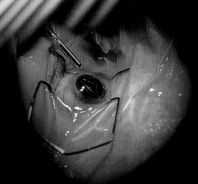

Cataract surgery
Old age and certain diseases can cause an opaque area – through which light cannot pass – called a cataract to form on the normally transparent lens of the eye. Cataracts cause blurred vision or blindness. To correct this, the affected lens is removed in an operation and replaced by a plastic lens.

LIGHTHOUSE
Ships can be warned of potential danger, and find where they are, by the light from a lighthouse like this one in South Africa. French physicist Augustin Fresnel (1788–1827) designed a lighthouse lens like this one in the 1820s. The lens gives a strong beam of light, and versions of it are used today to project beams visible for 28 miles. The first lighthouse was built around 280 BC, and guided ships into the harbor at Alexandria in Egypt.

OPTICAL ILLUSIONS

MOST OF THE TIME OUR BRAINS INTERPRET THE signals coming from our eyes correctly. But occasionally we're tricked into thinking we see something that isn't really there. We call this an optical illusion. Some optical illusions, such as mirages, occur naturally. Others, such as the illusion of depth on a flat surface, or pictures with impossible shapes, are artificially created for fun. The way we interpret information from our senses is called perception. Past experience of sensing things is a factor that can shape perception.

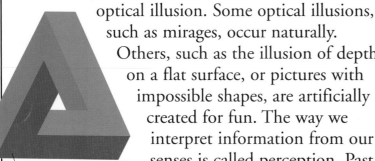

Our brains interpret this tribar as an impossible 3D shape.

MIRAGES

If a layer of warm air forms near the ground beneath a cooler layer of air, an effect known as an oasis mirage may occur. Light rays from distant objects are refracted (bent) as they pass from cool air into warmer air. The light rays bend upward to our eyes and appear to be coming from the ground. We therefore see an upside-down image of the object – as in this mirage (above) photographed in the Western Desert

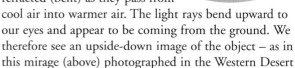

in Egypt. It appears to be in a pool of water, which is in fact an image of the blue sky. No wonder mirages have driven many thirsty travelers to despair!

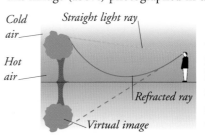

Cold air
Straight light ray
Hot air
Refracted ray
Virtual image

PERSPECTIVE

In real life, objects appear more blurred, and paler and bluer in color, the further into the distance they are. Artists mimic this effect when painting landscapes to give a three-dimensional (3-D) illusion on a two-dimensional (2-D) canvas. This technique is called atmospheric perspective. When looking into the distance, we also see any parallel lines – such as the sides of a long, straight road – converge. They appear to meet at an imaginary "vanishing point." Artists use this optical illusion, known as linear perspective, as another way of giving a picture depth. Objects are drawn smaller and closer together the nearer they are to the vanishing point.

LET'S EXPERIMENT
HOLE IN YOUR HAND

WE USUALLY SEE through both eyes at the same time. We are not aware of seeing with two separate eyes, because our brains add the images from each eye together, as you will see in this experiment. **You will need:** a sheet of paper.

1 Roll the paper into a tube and hold it with your right hand to your right eye. Look down the tube while keeping your left eye open.

2 Position your left hand with the palm toward you against the tube, about two-thirds of the way down its length (as shown, right). You should now see a hole in your hand as your brain adds together the two separate images from each eye.

Tube of paper

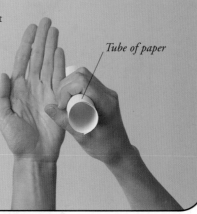

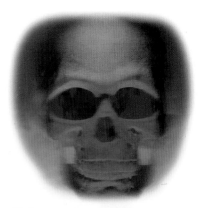

Holograms
Three-dimensional photos called holograms are created with lasers. One half of a laser beam is shone onto a special holographic film while the other half is scattered off the subject. The pattern of light recorded on the film where the beams meet represents both how bright and how far away from the film each part of the subject is. Shining a light at the developed film from a certain angle reveals a 3-D image.

2-D ILLUSIONS

Some optical illusions work because our brains do not have enough information to interpret correctly what we are seeing. We fill in the missing pieces by guesswork based on our knowledge of the world around us. Other illusions occur when the surroundings of what we are looking at change. Colors can look different depending on what colors they are surrounded by, and shapes can seem altered with different backgrounds.

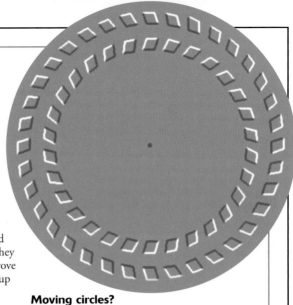

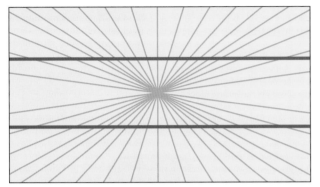

Straight lines?
The thick lines going across this drawing appear to bend outward at the middle. In fact they are straight. You can prove this by putting a ruler up against them. It is the pattern of lines behind them that has tricked you into thinking they are curved.

Moving circles?
Pictures cannot really move around a page, but they can appear to move. Stare at the spot in the middle of these circles while moving the page toward then away from your eyes. The circles seem to rotate.

STEREOGRAMS

We can see three dimensions because each of our eyes views an object from a different angle and produces a slightly different image of it. Our brains interpret these two images as a single image that not only has shape, but depth and distance as well. Pictures with hidden 3-D images are called stereograms (the one below creates a depth illusion). They are made by laying a two-dimensional, repeating pattern over a 3-D picture to disguise it. It can be difficult to see the hidden image. One way is to focus your eyes on a more distant object, then look at the stereogram without altering the focus of your eyes.

Can you tell what this is?

Image recognition
We identify different things because our brains compare what we see with images of objects stored in our memories. When a match occurs, we recognize whatever it is. If objects are blurred or disguised in some way, as in this picture, recognition becomes harder. If this picture were more heavily disguised, our brains might mistake it for something similar, such as a tiger.

MORE THAN THE EYE CAN SEE

THE HUMAN EYE CAN SEE A SURPRISINGLY LONG WAY into the distance. Even neighboring planets are visible on a clear night, although it is impossible to make out much detail without telescopes or binoculars. We cannot see details on very small things either, so use microscopes to reveal more about them or to see objects that are so small they are invisible to our unaided eyes. By using night-vision devices we can even see in the dark. Such devices amplify the small amounts of light present at night to produce a visible image.

Naked-eye astronomy
Before the invention of telescopes in the 17th century, astronomers observed the night sky unaided. This photograph shows Jupiter (top), Venus (center) and the Moon (near the horizon) as they appear to the naked eye.

The head of a fruit fly magnified 45 times

BINOCULARS

Like telescope lenses, the lenses in binoculars collect and magnify the light from objects. Light passes through the objective lenses, which produce an upside-down reversed image of the object (pp. 114–115). Inside the binoculars are specially shaped prisms that reflect light from two of their faces. There are two prisms in each half of a pair of binoculars. One prism turns the image the right way up, and the other turns it the right way around. The four successive reflections provide a long path for the light within a small space, allowing binoculars to be made much shorter and more portable than telescopes.

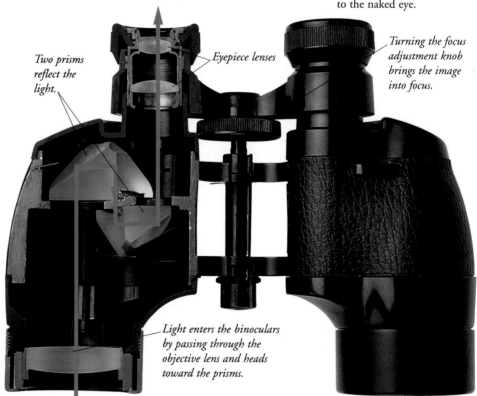

Two prisms reflect the light.

Eyepiece lenses

Turning the focus adjustment knob brings the image into focus.

Light enters the binoculars by passing through the objective lens and heads toward the prisms.

Night vision
This picture of security police on a training exercise shows what an onlooker with a night-vision device could see. Night-vision equipment amplifies the moonlight and starlight reflected from objects so they appear many times brighter. It does this by converting each photon (pp. 102–103) of light into an electron (pp. 42–43), then multiplying each electron into many more electrons. A screen at the end of the device then glows brightly whenever one of these electrons hits it, producing a visible image. Military personnel as well as nature and bird watchers use this type of powerful equipment.

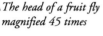

Hubble Space Telescope
The Earth's atmosphere distorts the images obtained by ground-based telescopes. By orbiting Earth above the atmosphere, the Hubble Space Telescope, launched in 1990, can obtain very clear images of stars and planets. This picture taken by Hubble shows a spiral galaxy 60 million light-years away. The outer stars are younger than those in the center.

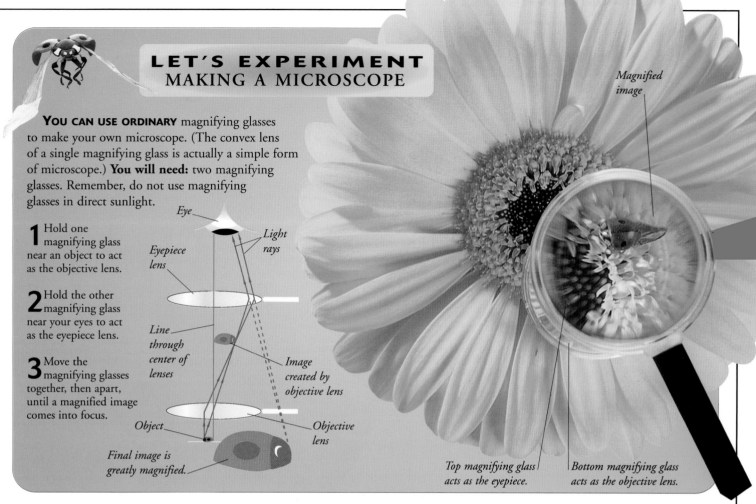

LET'S EXPERIMENT
MAKING A MICROSCOPE

YOU CAN USE ORDINARY magnifying glasses to make your own microscope. (The convex lens of a single magnifying glass is actually a simple form of microscope.) **You will need:** two magnifying glasses. Remember, do not use magnifying glasses in direct sunlight.

1 Hold one magnifying glass near an object to act as the objective lens.

2 Hold the other magnifying glass near your eyes to act as the eyepiece lens.

3 Move the magnifying glasses together, then apart, until a magnified image comes into focus.

Eye

Light rays

Eyepiece lens

Line through center of lenses

Image created by objective lens

Object

Objective lens

Final image is greatly magnified.

Magnified image

Top magnifying glass acts as the eyepiece.

Bottom magnifying glass acts as the objective lens.

OPTICAL MICROSCOPE

Most optical microscopes are compound microscopes containing at least two lenses. These lenses are convex (curved outward). The objective lens (or lenses) near to the specimen collects light reflected from it and forms a magnified image. The eyepiece lens (or lenses) that scientists look through then magnifies the image even more. Magnifications up to about 1,000 times are possible. The picture on the right shows onion cells magnified 330 times by an optical microscope.

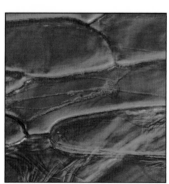

Electron microscope
To magnify things hundreds of thousands of times, electron microscopes, which use beams of electrons rather than light, are needed. Very small objects cannot be seen through optical microscopes. Light won't reflect off the specimen because the length of the light waves is much larger than the object. However, tiny objects can interact with electron beams, which behave like incredibly small waves, to form images such as the one shown here of an ant's head.

The first microscopes
English physicist Robert Hooke (1635–1703) carried out experiments with compound microscopes like this replica (below) of his design. In 1665, he published a book called *Micrographia* containing drawings of what he saw through his microscope, including this illustration of the stinging spines on a nettle leaf. Around this time, Dutch microscopist Anton van Leeuwenhoek (1632–1723) made hundreds of simple microscopes and used them to discover many new things, including bacteria.

Hooke's microscope screwed up and down for focusing.

Water-filled sphere helped focus light onto specimen.

Specimen mounted on metal spike

PICTURE THIS

WE CAN RECORD IMAGES OF objects using a camera. Cameras work in a similar way to our eyes. All cameras have a lens to focus the light reflected from objects, a film (or rows of electronic devices) on which to record the image, and a system for controlling the amount of light that falls on the film. In order to see the photographs taken with a camera, the film must be developed and printed. French inventor Joseph Niepce (1765–1833) took the first permanent photograph in 1826 on a pewter plate coated with light-sensitive bitumen. Modern film has a coating of silver salts to record the image.

High-speed action photo

Shutter release button

Viewfinder

Aperture controls amount of light in camera

Solid lines show path of light rays.

Film

Dotted line shows light falling onto film when mirror moves and shutter opens.

Retractable mirror

Lens

SLR CAMERA

All cameras have the same basic parts, but there are many different designs. In the single-lens reflex (SLR) camera, small mirrors and a prism reflect the image produced by the lens onto the viewfinder, so that it is exactly the same as the image that will be recorded. When the shutter-release button is pressed, the mirror moves out of the path of the light coming from the lenses and the shutter in front of the film opens. Light now falls onto the film at the back of the camera, recording the image. In many cameras, the image that is produced by the lens and recorded is not quite the exact image seen through the viewfinder.

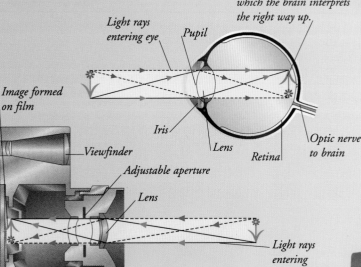

Image formed on retina, which the brain interprets the right way up.

Light rays entering eye

Pupil

Iris

Lens

Retina

Optic nerve to brain

Image formed on film

Viewfinder

Adjustable aperture

Lens

Light rays entering camera

EYE VERSUS CAMERA

A camera has much in common with the human eye. In the human eye, the muscles in the iris cause the small hole in the middle (the pupil) to contract in bright light or enlarge in dim light. A camera has a hole called an aperture that can be made larger or smaller to control the amount of light entering through the lens. The lens in the eye focuses light rays onto a light sensitive layer at the back of the eye called the retina. Cells in the retina send signals along the optic nerve to the brain, which interprets them as an image. In a camera, the lens focuses light onto a film, and the image is revealed when the picture is printed.

Digital photography

Light entering a digital camera is focused onto rows of small electronic devices at the back of a digital camera where the film would normally be. These devices convert the light into electronic signals which are saved onto a memory card in the camera. A small liquid-crystal display at the back of the camera acts as a viewfinder, and allows pictures in the memory to be viewed. Pictures taken on digital cameras can be stored on computer discs, viewed on a computer screen, and printed out.

MAKE A SIMPLE MODEL CAMERA to show how a real camera works. Your model camera will form an image in a similar way to a real camera, but it will not be able to make a photograph. **You will need**: cardboard box (such as a tissue box); scissors; cardboard tube (from toilet paper or paper towel roll); pen; adhesive tape; tracing paper; magnifying glass.

1 Carefully cut the bottom off the cardboard box. Hold the cardboard tube against the opposite side of the box and draw around it to make a circle.

2 Carefully, cut out the circle in the box. Put the tube into the circular hole so that about 2 in (5 cm) sticks out of the top of your box. Tape in position.

3 Tape tracing paper over the large opening in the bottom of the box. This is where you will see the image.

4 The magnifying glass provides the lens for the camera. Hold it near the end of the tube and focus by moving the magnifying glass nearer or farther from the tube.

5 Find a well-lit object to look at. Hold the model camera so that you are looking at the end with the tracing paper.

6 An upside-down and reversed image of the object will form on the tracing paper. If the image is out of focus, try moving the magnifying glass until you see a sharp image. In a real camera, this image would be formed on photographic film.

Cardboard tube fits into hole in box.

The magnifying glass acts as the lens.

An upside-down image is formed on the tracing paper.

PROCESSING PICTURES

Photographic film is coated with a light-sensitive emulsion containing silver salts. Light falling on the emulsion causes a chemical change in the salts. The first stage of film processing creates a record of these changes. The film is soaked in developing chemicals that convert the exposed silver salts into metallic silver. A fixing solution washes away the unexposed silver salts, leaving a negative image that is darkest where the brightest light fell onto the film. Light is then shone through the negative onto photographic paper. The paper makes a print that is brightest where the negative is darkest, reproducing the photographed scene.

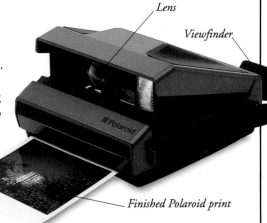

Lens

Viewfinder

Finished Polaroid print

Color negatives
Color film has three layers of emulsion, one for each primary color of light – blue, green, and red. During developing, each layer produces a dye of the opposite (complementary) color to the light that fell on the film – yellow dye for the blue layer, magenta for the green layer and cyan for the red layer. Each dye in the negative absorbs light of its complementary color. After printing, the complementary colors formed by the dyes in the paper absorb and reflect the colors in white light. This results in the original colors of the subject.

Polaroid pictures
Instant photographs are available with a Polaroid camera. The American inventor Edwin Land (1909–1991) demonstrated the Polaroid camera in 1947. It uses a special type of film that is combined with printing paper. Developing chemicals are stored in packets between the negative and print layers of the Polaroid film. Once the film has been exposed, it passes through rollers which break the storage packets and release the developing chemicals. Modern Polaroid cameras produce pictures in less than a minute.

MOTION PICTURES

A MOVIE IS MADE UP OF A SEQUENCE OF STILL
pictures. The continuous movement seen on the movie
screen is an illusion. The human brain remembers an
image for about a tenth of a second after the image
disappears. This effect is called persistence of vision.
When two pictures appear in quick succession,
persistence of vision blends the first picture into the
second, so that a single moving image is seen. The
still pictures that make up a movie are called frames.
At the movies, 24 frames per second are projected
onto the screen. The frames blend together, creating
the illusion of a continuous moving image – a movie.

EARLY FILMS

The American inventor George Eastman (1854–1932)
brought flexible film onto the market in 1889. A year
later, William Dickson (1860–1935), an assistant to
the American inventor Thomas Edison, developed
a way of moving this film through cameras and
projectors. He punched tiny holes down the sides,
so that metal claws could pull the film along. The
first motion picture to be screened for the public was
shown in Paris in 1895. It was a silent movie made
by French brothers Auguste (1862–1954) and Louis
Lumière (1864–1948). Early films had only 16 frames
per second. This meant that the pictures seemed to
flicker on the screen, instead of blending into a
continuously moving image. In 1927, *The Jazz
Singer*, starring Al Jolson, became the first "talking"
feature film, adding sound to moving images.

*An early movie
recorded on
Eastman's film*

Blue screen effects
Amazing special effects
can be created on film
with the help of a giant blue
screen. First, the scene is filmed
in front of the blue screen. A computer is
then used to remove the blue and replace it with
another background that has been filmed separately.
These pictures show a scene from the film *The Perfect
Storm* (2000). The actors were filmed on the boat
against a giant blue screen. Then the blue was
replaced by a raging storm in the background
to create the final scene (inset).

LET'S EXPERIMENT
MAKE A FLICK BOOK

MAKE YOUR OWN simple motion picture.
You will need: small notebook; pen.

1 Draw a picture on the top page.
Change the picture slightly on
the following pages to create a sense
of movement. For example, to make
this figure wave his arm, copy your
original drawing several times
over, moving the arm slightly
higher in each picture.

2 Flick the pages of the
notebook. The figure
appears to be waving in a
continuous moving image
because your brain blends
the pictures together.

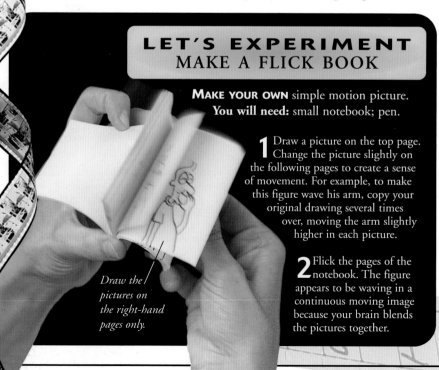

*Draw the
pictures on
the right-hand
pages only.*

IMAX CINEMAS

Most films are shot on 35mm film, but IMAX
films are recorded on 70mm film, which has
frames 10 times bigger than normal. IMAX
screens are curved so that the picture fills the
viewer's entire field of vision. Some IMAX
films are three dimensional (3-D). Human brains
combine the separate images from our eyes into
a single image that has depth and shape. A 3-D
camera mimics this by recording images from two
lenses. The movie is projected by switching from
the "left eye" film to the "right eye" film 96 times
per second. Viewers wear special headsets that
stop light from reaching the right eye while the
left eye image is on the screen, and vice versa.
The result is a lifelike, 3-D film experience.

ANIMATION

Thousands of drawings are needed to make our favorite cartoon characters come to life. A cartoon feature film contains about 65,000 pictures. Animators draw the characters in different stages of motion onto pieces of transparent film called cels. A succession of these transparent cels are laid over the top of a background drawing which remains the same. For each sequence, animators draw the extremes of movement first, like the takeoff and landing of this squirrel, before completing the in-between stages. The outline of the character is drawn on the front of each cel, then the color is painted onto the back.

Colors must be consistent throughout.

Extremes of movement are drawn first.

Shifting the background behind the cel is another way of giving the character a sense of motion.

Finished cel

3-D animation

Like 3-D film, 3-D animation adds visual depth to the images. Modeling clay is used to create characters like the one shown on the left. Each frame is filmed separately so that the position of the limbs and facial expressions can be changed slightly in between, giving the impression of continuous movement in the film. Some models have a range of cable or radio controlled motors, allowing the puppeteer to move them via remote control during normal filming. Models are also used in ordinary films to create special effects.

Wire frame image of CGi character

COMPUTER ANIMATION

Many films now use computer generated images (CGi) to create different effects. To produce a CGi character like this dragon from the film *Dragonheart* (1997), a 3-D representation called a wire frame is created on a computer (see right). This acts like a skeleton for the character. Muscles are added to the digital skeleton, then color and fine detail put on top. Computer software enables the CGi character to move in a realistic way. Separately filmed background footage can be combined with the CGi later (see below) to create the finished scene.

WAVES AND COLORS

LIGHT TRAVELS IN THE FORM OF TINY WAVES.

These light waves have peaks and troughs like waves on the sea. The distance between two peaks is known as the wavelength. Different colors are different wavelengths of visible light. However, white light, such as sunlight, is not just a single wavelength. The famous English scientist Isaac Newton (1642–1727) discovered that sunlight is made up of the spectrum of colors that we see in a rainbow – red, orange, yellow, green, blue, indigo, and violet. Red has the longest wavelength, while violet has the shortest.

Wavelength of red light

Wavelength of violet light

Comparative wavelengths of red and violet light

SPLITTING SUNLIGHT

When sunlight shines on a triangular block of glass called a prism, we can see that it is made up of a combination of different colored light waves. The prism bends (refracts) the beam of sunlight. Each color is refracted by a slightly different amount, separating the sunlight into the familiar spectrum of red, orange, yellow, green, blue, indigo, and violet.

A beam of sunlight shines onto a prism.

Some light is reflected by the bottom of the prism.

The prism bends the light.

The light separates into the colors of the spectrum.

NEWTON'S PRISMS

Isaac Newton discovered the light spectrum in 1665 by conducting an experiment similar to the one shown below. (Read the diagram from right to left.) Sunlight shines through a slit in the window shutters and onto a prism. The prism splits the sunlight into the seven colors of the spectrum. The separated light waves then pass through a lens that focuses them onto a second (upside-down) prism. There, the colors recombine to produce another beam of white light. As the beam passes through a third (right way up) prism, the light disperses yet again, displaying the color spectrum onto the screen. When Newton blocked out individual colors before they reached the lens, he noticed that these colors did not appear in the final spectrum on the screen.

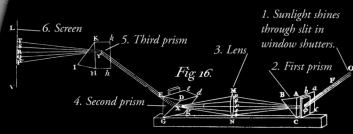

6. Screen
5. Third prism
3. Lens
1. Sunlight shines through slit in window shutters.
2. First prism
Fig 16.
4. Second prism

This diagram from Newton's book, *Opticks*, published in 1704, shows the dispersion and recombination of the light spectrum.

INTERFERENCE

The changing colors of certain objects are produced by interference. These colors are called iridescent. For example, a compact disc has tiny grooves that separate a ray of light into hundreds of smaller beams. Where these beams meet, they interfere with each other. If constructive interference occurs for a particular color, the light waves combine and become brighter. If destructive interference occurs, this color is cancelled out. When viewed from different angles, the colors change. Soap bubbles have iridescent colors that are created when the light reflected by the outer surface interferes with the light reflected by the inner surface.

Stellar spectra

The color of light often indicates temperature. For instance, we can tell how hot a star is by its color. The hottest stars are blue, while the coolest are red. Yellow stars like our Sun are in between, with a surface temperature of approximately 9,900°F (5,500°C). Most light emitted by a star is of a particular wavelength, but other colors do appear in the spectrum. Astronomers can analyze the spectrum to find out which chemical elements are present (below).

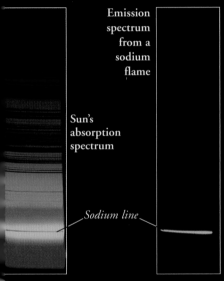

Emission spectrum from a sodium flame

Sun's absorption spectrum

Sodium line

Spectroscopy

Different types of atoms absorb and emit different colors of light, so a spectrum can be used to identify elements in a substance. An absorption spectrum is obtained by shining a white light through a substance, then splitting the light into a spectrum. Dark lines on the spectrum represent atoms that absorb that specific color. The Sun's spectrum (above left) shows several dark lines. One line shows an absorption of yellow light by sodium in the Sun's outer layers. An emission spectrum shows the color of light emitted from a substance. A sodium flame gives off yellow light, as shown in this emission spectrum (above right).

RAINBOWS

When there is sunshine and rain at the same time, a rainbow may appear. Sunlight is bent (refracted) as it enters a raindrop. It is then reflected off the back of the raindrop before being refracted again as it leaves the drop. Each color in the white sunlight bends by a slightly different amount as it enters and leaves the drop. This splits the sunlight into the familiar colors of the spectrum – red, orange, yellow, green, blue, indigo, and violet. Occasionally, you can see a double rainbow with a fainter, secondary rainbow outside the primary one. The secondary rainbow forms when sunlight enters the bottom of the raindrops instead of the top. The sunlight is then reflected twice off the inner surface of the drop, which means that the order of the colors in a secondary rainbow are reversed.

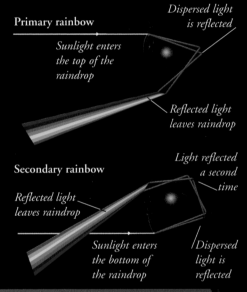

Primary rainbow

Dispersed light is reflected

Sunlight enters the top of the raindrop

Reflected light leaves raindrop

Secondary rainbow

Light reflected a second time

Reflected light leaves raindrop

Sunlight enters the bottom of the raindrop

Dispersed light is reflected

MIXING COLORS

WHITE LIGHT IS MADE UP OF ALL the colors in the spectrum (pp. 118–119). It is also possible to make white simply by adding together the three primary colors of light – red, blue, and green. Amazingly, by combining these primary colors in different proportions, you can produce any color you wish. This process is known as "color addition," and it is how a range of colors is produced on television screens. However, unless an object is a source of light, for example a flashlight, it does not give out its own distinct color. The things that surround us appear to be colored because they reflect a single color or a mixture of colors back to our eyes from the white light that falls on them, while absorbing all other colors. Paints and pigments work in the same way. Forming colors like this is called "color subtraction" because colors are taken away from white light to make the color that we can see.

Light beam

Blue and green make cyan.

Red, blue, and green make white light.

Red and green make yellow.

Red and blue make magenta.

PRIMARY COLORS OF LIGHT

Red, blue, and green are the primary colors of light. Combinations of these three primary colors can make any other color (see above). A mixture of red light and green light gives yellow, while mixing blue light and red light makes magenta. Blue light and green light together produce a bright turquoise blue called cyan. Varying the amounts of each light in any mixture allows many more colors to be produced. Mixing all three primary colors together in equal amounts produces white light. Color addition like this is used to produce the different colors on the screens of color televisions.

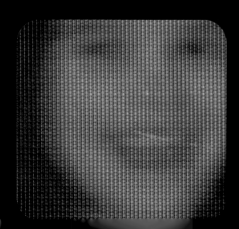

Television
Tiny dots or strips of phosphor are arranged all over color television screens in groups of three (left). In each group, one dot will emit red light, another blue, and the remaining one green. Varying the amounts of each of these primary colors of light creates a full range of different colors when the screen is viewed from a distance.

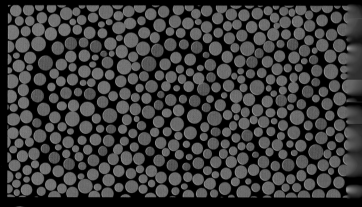

COLOR VISION

Light is focused on the retina inside the eyes, and millions of light-sensitive cells send signals along the optic nerve to the brain. Rods and cones are the two main types of such cells. Rods work in dim light and cannot detect color. Cones come in three types – one responds to blue light, another to red, and the third to green. As these are the primary colors of light, all other colors can be seen as they stimulate different combinations of cones. Not everyone can see all colors. People who are color blind have defective cones, so they confuse colors. Color blindness can be diagnosed using tests like this picture (above). People who cannot see the difference between red and green do not see the number 683.

SPINNING DISC

Colored cardboard disc before spinning

YOU CAN SHOW THAT white light is made up of a mixture of colors. Each color painted on a disc will reflect a different color of light. When you spin the disc, these colors will mix together to produce white. **You will need:** piece of cardboard; saucer; pencil; scissors; protractor; colored paints; pencil sharpener.

1 Place the saucer on the piece of cardboard and draw around it. Carefully cut out the disc, and use a protractor to divide it into seven equal segments.

2 Color in the segments with the colors of the spectrum in the order that they appear in a rainbow – red, orange, yellow, green, blue, indigo, and violet.

3 Sharpen the pencil and carefully push it through the center of the disc. Position the disc halfway along the pencil's length.

4 Stand the pencil on its point and use the other end to spin the disc as quickly as possible. The colors merge together and the disc looks almost white.

The colors disappear as the disc spins.

PRIMARY COLORS OF PIGMENTS

Magenta

Yellow

Black

Cyan

Pigments absorb certain colors from the light that falls on them and reflect others. Magenta, cyan, and yellow are the primary colors of pigments, and each absorbs one of the primary colors of light. For example, yellow pigment absorbs blue but reflects green and red light, which our brains add together so we see yellow. Different combinations of primary pigments produce every color except white. If equal amounts of all three primary pigments are mixed together, they absorb all three primary colors of light and we see black (left). When painting, red, blue, and yellow are used as primary colors instead.

Cadmium red

Viridian

Cadmium yellow

Natural dyes and pigments

Many of the dyes and pigments that we use today are artificially created, but in the past they were made from natural substances. The earliest cave paintings used colors made from ground-up rocks and clays, charcoal, and chalk. Cave painters only used a limited range of colors – mainly reds and browns – but by the Middle Ages a much larger variety of dyes and pigments had been discovered. Many were made from crushed minerals, which produced vivid colors. Viridian, for example, is a bluish-green mineral called chromium oxide found in a type of clay called "terre verte." Cadmium yellow is a bright yellow pigment that contains the metallic compound cadmium sulfide.

ELECTRICITY AND MAGNETISM

Picture: Lightning bolts strike Tucson, Arizona. Lightning occurs when electrical charge builds up in clouds.

THE RIGHT CONNECTION

PEOPLE HAVE BEEN AWARE OF THE

forces of electricity and magnetism for a very long time. The ancient Greeks carried out electrical experiments. They were also aware of naturally magnetic rocks. As early as the 11th century, it is thought that magnetism was used in China to help with navigation. However, it was only in the 19th century that a link was discovered between electricity and magnetism, and the power of electricity could be put to use. Electricity is the major source of power for much of the world today and enables electronic devices and computers to work.

3-D MRI scan (with false colors) of a human brain as viewed from above

The word "electricity" comes from the Greek word for amber – elektron. If rubbed with wool or fur, amber becomes electrically charged and can attract light objects.

MRI SCANS

Magnetism has many useful applications. For example, doctors can produce pictures of the insides of our bodies through a technique called magnetic resonance imaging (MRI). The patient is placed in a large magnetic field. About 65 percent of the human body is made from water. The magnetic field allows the hydrogen atoms in this water to absorb high frequency radio waves in a certain way. When the radio waves are switched off, the hydrogen atoms emit the energy they have absorbed as much weaker radio waves. Each type of tissue emits waves of different lengths and strengths. A computer turns the radio waves into images that help to diagnose diseases.

PACEMAKERS

The human heartbeat is triggered by tiny electrical impulses from an area of the heart called the pacemaker. If the impulses are impaired, an artificial pacemaker can be implanted in the chest. This has a battery that enables it to produce the required electrical impulses. A machine called an electrocardiograph monitors the electrical activity of our hearts via sensors placed on the body. Problems with the heart show up as changes in the electrocardiogram (ECG), which is the wavy line made by the machine.

c. 600 BC Greek philosopher and astronomer Thales of Miletus discovers that rubbing amber produces an electrical charge.

c. 1000 It is believed that the magnetic compass is invented in China.

1600 English scientist and physician William Gilbert tries to explain the magnetic properties of Earth.

1729 English scientists Stephen Gray and Jean Desaguliers discover that some substances are electrical insulators, while others are electrical conductors.

1752 American scientist and statesman Benjamin Franklin discovers the electrical nature of lightning.

1820 Danish physicist Hans Christian Oersted discovers the link between electricity and magnetism.

Timeline

MAGNETIC STORMS

The Sun constantly gives out a stream of charged particles into space called the solar wind. Sometimes the Sun has violent reactions on its surface called solar flares

Certain types of eruption on the Sun can cause magnetic storms on Earth.

and coronal mass ejections. The huge numbers of high-energy particles emitted in these explosions produce a disturbance in the Earth's magnetic field. This is known as a magnetic storm. Magnetic storms can damage satellites and cause huge surges of electricity in power transmission lines that can blow out power stations. They also interfere with radio reception and cause compass needles to change direction.

ELECTRONIC DEVICES

Many familiar electrical devices, from televisions to microwave ovens, contain components that work by using varying

A simple type of electronic toy

electrical signals to represent information. These components are electronic devices. In 1947, the invention of an electronic device called a transistor enabled electronic goods to be made small enough to be practical. In some electronic equipment,

such as the game shown below left, all of the electronic components needed to work the device are contained on a tiny piece of silicon known as a chip. More complicated equipment usually contains several chips, along with separate electronic components mounted on a printed circuit board.

TRANSDUCERS

Electronic systems contain devices called transducers. Transducers change one form of energy into another form. They can change electrical energy to mechanical energy or mechanical energy into electrical energy, for example. Microphones and loudspeakers are examples of transducers. A microphone contains a diaphragm that is mechanically vibrated by sound waves. The vibrating movement causes a fluctuating electric current to be produced that represents the original sound waves. In a loudspeaker, the reverse occurs, with alterations in an electric current from the amplifier causing a diaphragm to vibrate and produce sound waves.

Microphone components

COMPUTERS

It is hard to imagine a world without computers and the internet, but computers have only been available for personal use since the mid-1970s. Since then, there have been huge advances in processing speed and much larger amounts of data can be stored in a computer's memory. These advances continue today. Computers have many uses, from helping engineers design bridges and buildings to predicting the weather. Computers store and process information in the form of binary digits (bits). These bits have only

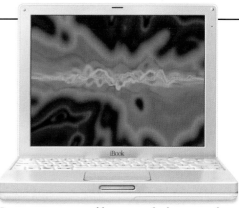

Laptop computers enable us to work almost anywhere.

two possible values – "0" and "1." Many computers currently process information one step at a time. Scientists are hoping to build much faster quantum computers in the future that can compute several possibilities simultaneously.

PARTICLE ACCELERATORS

For some experiments, physicists need to accelerate charged subatomic particles to incredibly high speeds. They use huge pieces of scientific equipment called particle accelerators to do this. Electricity makes the particles accelerate, while magnetic fields keep the particles on the correct path as they speed along inside the accelerator. By studying what happens when these high-speed particles hit atoms or other particles, scientists can learn more about the structure and nature of the atoms and particles.

Tunnel housing two particle accelerators at Fermilab in the US

1823 English mathematician Charles Babbage begins designing mechanical computing machine.

1831 English physicist and chemist Michael Faraday discovers that magnetism can be used to produce electricity.

1876 Scottish inventor Alexander Graham Bell patents the telephone.

1911 Dutch physicist Heike Kamerlingh-Onnes discovers superconductivity.

1947 American physicists John Bardeen, Walter Brattain, and William Shockley invent the transistor.

1958 American electronics engineer Jack Kilby produces the first integrated circuit.

1958 American company Bell introduces modems.

ELECTRICITY AT REST

WHEN WE THINK OF ELECTRICITY, WE IMAGINE IT flowing through electrical devices. However, electricity does not always move. Static electricity causes lightning strikes and makes some clothes crackle as we take them off. Objects can develop a positive or a negative charge when they rub against each other. The rubbing knocks electrons, which have a negative charge, off the atoms in one object so it becomes positively charged, while the other object is negatively charged as freed electrons move to its atoms. Although static electricity is often undesirable, it is put to good use inside photocopiers.

LIGHTNING

Water and ice particles inside thunderclouds collide and become charged with static electricity. Smaller positively charged particles move to the top of the cloud, while heavier ones with a negative charge collect at the bottom. The negative charge from the base of the cloud induces a positive charge on the ground beneath. If it is strong enough, the charge in the cloud forces its way through the air to the ground and discharges as lightning.

Franklin's lightning experiment
The American statesman Benjamin Franklin (1706–1790) proved that lightning was static electricity by performing a dangerous experiment (above). He attached a key to the string of a kite, then flew the kite in a thunderstorm. The wet string acted as a conductor, so when he brought his hand near the key he felt a shock and saw sparks like those in laboratory experiments on static electricity.

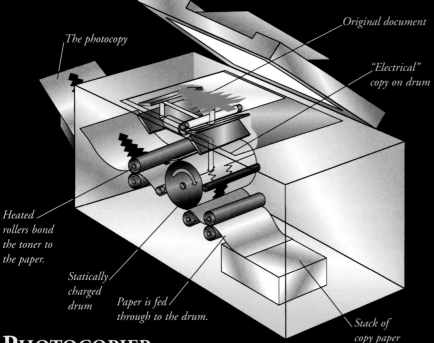

The photocopy

Original document

"Electrical" copy on drum

Heated rollers bond the toner to the paper.

Statically charged drum

Paper is fed through to the drum.

Stack of copy paper

PHOTOCOPIER

When someone presses the "copy" button on a photocopier, light is shone at the document. The light reflects off the white areas of the page but not off the parts covered with ink. A metal drum inside the machine is charged with static electricity. Wherever light reflected from the document falls on this drum, it neutralizes the charge. This leaves the drum charged up only in the areas where the ink was on the original document. The drum is coated with toner (powdered ink), which only sticks to the charged parts. When the drum spins, the toner is transferred onto paper, which is also charged, to make the copy.

Van de Graaff generator

Static electricity can be built up using a Van de Graaff generator, which was invented by American physicist Robert Van de Graaff (1901–1967). A small version of this machine (above) produces amazing effects. When someone touches the metal dome, negative electrical charges pass through them. As the strands of their hair become charged, they stand on end because like charges repel each other.

Antistatic clothing

Static electricity can be uncomfortable when it makes clothing stick to us (above) and crackle as we take it off. When we move, opposite charges can build up on our bodies and the garments we are wearing, making them cling to us. Anti-static yarns help to drain away the charge or prevent charge build-up, reducing these effects.

LET'S EXPERIMENT
MAKE AN ELECTROSCOPE

YOU CAN BUILD an electroscope to measure static electric charges. **You will need:** an adult's help; foil candy wrapper; drinking glass; piece of cardboard; pencil; scissors; wire (cut from a coathanger); glue; adhesive tape; plastic pen; some silk.

1 Flatten the foil, and cut out a long rectangular piece to act as the leaves of the electroscope. Roll the remaining foil into a ball.

2 Place the glass upside down on the cardboard. Draw around it, then carefully cut out the disc.

3 Push the wire carefully through the middle of the disc and glue it in place. Ask an adult to bend the end of the wire. Suspend the foil leaves from it using a drop of glue. Lower the wire into the glass, and tape the cardboard disc to the rim. Push the foil ball onto the end of the wire.

4 Rub the pen with the silk to give it a positive charge. Hold it near the foil ball. Negative charges in the wire are attracted toward the ball, which gives the leaves of the electroscope a positive charge. Since they have the same charge, the leaves repel each other.

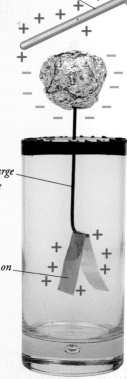

Positively charged pen

Negative charge moves up the wire toward the ball.

Like charges on the leaves make them move apart.

ELECTRICITY THAT FLOWS

MANY MACHINES REQUIRE A CONTINUOUS FLOW OF
electricity, known as an electric current. Static electricity
(pp. 126–127) cannot be used to power electrical devices.
The simplest way of generating an electric current is
provided by a battery, which is a useful and portable
source of power. Some batteries, such as those in cars,
are rechargeable so they can be used again and again.
Materials that electric currents can flow through are
known as electrical conductors. Metals are particularly
good conductors, so electrical wires are made of metal.

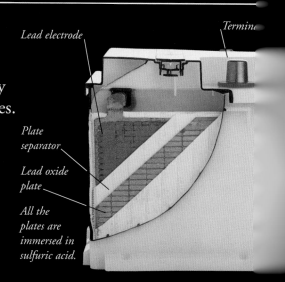

Lead electrode

Termina

Plate separator

Lead oxide plate

All the plates are immersed in sulfuric acid.

ELECTRIC CURRENT

A current is a flow of electric charge that
occurs when electrons that are free to move
inside a conductor – usually a metal – travel in
a particular way. Normally the electrons move
randomly in different directions (right). However,
if the conductor is connected to a battery, the
electrons, which have a negative charge, flow
toward the battery's positive terminal,
and a current is produced (inset).
The rate of flow of electric charge
is measured using a device
called an ammeter.

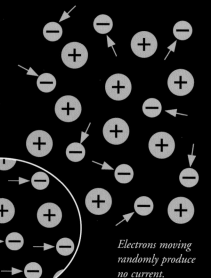

Electrons flowing in one direction produce an electric current.

Electrons moving randomly produce no current.

BATTERIES

All batteries contain two metal elec
separated by a conducting mixture
electrolyte. The mixture causes a ch
reaction at each electrode, which p
current. The batteries in flashlights
radios are known as dry batteries. T
contain a carbon rod and a zinc cy
separated by a conducting paste. T
chemical reaction in a dry battery c
ceases, and the battery stops workin
However, some batteries can be rec
by applying an electric current tha
the chemical reaction. Cars contain
rechargeable lead-acid batteries (ab
supply current to start the engine.

LET'S EXPERIMENT
MAKING A BATTERY

YOU CAN MAKE a working battery.
You will need: an adult present;
vinegar; a glass container; electrical
cables with metal clips on the ends;
a strip of zinc; a strip of copper; a
small 3-volt light bulb.

1 Pour some vinegar
into the container.
Connect a cable to the
end of each strip. Clip
the other ends of these cables to
either side of the bulb as shown.
Immerse the strips in the vinegar.

2 A chemical reaction starts
to dissolve the zinc strip.
Electrons from the zinc atoms
collect on the strip, making
it negative. These flow
through the completed
circuit to the copper strip,
which has become positively
charged by losing electrons
to the acid. The bulb lights
as the current flows.

The first battery
The Italian physicist Alessandro
Volta (1745–1827) built the first
practical battery in 1800. His
"voltaic pile" (right) was based
on three types of disc. A zinc disc
and a copper disc were separated
by a pasteboard disc that had been
soaked in salt solution or weak
acid. The zinc and copper discs
acted as electrodes and the moist
pasteboard as the electrolyte.
Volta stacked up several sets of
these discs to produce a greater
amount of electricity.

Copper disc

Zinc disc

Pasteboard disc

*Heating elements
from an electric heater
are made from
conducting wire.*

CONDUCTORS

Materials containing atoms with one or
more electrons that are free to move can
conduct electricity and are known as conductors.
Materials whose electrons cannot move around are
unable to conduct electricity and are known as insulators.
Semiconducting materials also exist (pp. 144–145). Metals
are especially good conductors as they have large numbers of free
electrons. The cables that connect electrical devices to electricity supplies
are made from conducting metal wire – usually copper – surrounded by an
insulator such as rubber or plastic. The insulator ensures that the current only
flows through the conductor and cannot harm anyone who touches the cable.

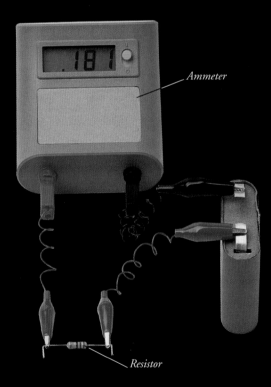

Ammeter

Resistor

Measuring current

There are several different types of ammeter
used for measuring electric currents. One is
based on the fact that an electric current
produces a magnetic field. This field deflects
a needle, which points to a different position
on a scale, depending on the strength of the
current. Another type measures how much
the current heats up a thin wire inside the
ammeter. Most modern ammeters have a
digital display instead of a mechanical pointer.

LET'S EXPERIMENT
TESTING FOR CONDUCTORS

YOU CAN USE A BATTERY and a light bulb to discover whether
or not a material conducts electricity. Handle batteries with
care and always follow instructions. **You will need:** an adult
present; electrical cables with metal clips on the ends; a 9-volt
battery; a small light bulb; items to test (for example, a piece
of string, a wooden ruler, a screwdriver, a fork).

1 Connect the cables to the terminals
of the battery. Clip one cable to the
light bulb, then connect the other side
of the light bulb to one end of the
test object as shown.

2 Next clip the other cable from the
battery to the opposite end of the
test object to form a complete circuit.
If the object is a conductor, the bulb
will light up. If the object is an
electrical insulator, the bulb
will remain unlit.

*A selection of
objects to test*

*Conductors light
the bulb.*

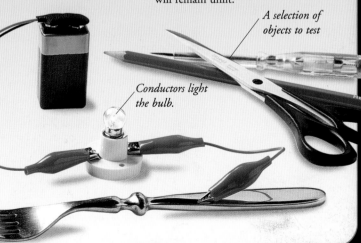

ELECTRICAL CIRCUITS

ELECTRICITY WILL ONLY FLOW IF IT HAS A COMPLETE
circuit to go around. The three basic components of a
circuit are a conductor for the electricity to flow through
(such as copper wire), something for the circuit to power
(for example a light bulb), and an energy source to drive
the current (such as a battery). Once a
circuit is complete, electricity will only stop
flowing if the circuit is broken or the energy
runs out. Switches allow the current to be
turned off when it is not needed. Scientists
use standard symbols to represent the
components of electrical circuits in
circuit diagrams (drawings).

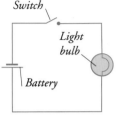

Switch
Light bulb
Battery

Symbols of a simple circuit

Tungsten filament

RESISTANCE

All conductors have a certain amount of resistance to the flow
of current. For example, around 10 percent of the power from
electricity generating stations is lost before it reaches homes
and industries because of resistance by the transmission cables.
When a conductor resists an electric current, the electrical
energy is turned into heat. This effect is made use of in many
domestic electrical appliances. Electronic devices called resistors
(right), which are made from materials that have high resistance,
are used in many circuits to control the current in various ways.

Heating and lighting
Appliances such as stoves and
irons have heating elements
made from conducting wire
that has a high resistance to
electric current. As the element
resists the current flowing
through it, it gets hot. The same
principle enables an electric light
bulb to produce light. Light
bulbs contain a filament made
of tungsten, which has very high
resistance. When electricity passes through the
filament, it becomes so hot that it glows white.

Metal contact

LET'S EXPERIMENT
SIMPLE CIRCUITS

YOU CAN SEE HOW simple circuits work using some
basic equipment. Handle batteries with care and always
follow instructions. **You will need:** an adult present;
a 9-volt battery; some cables with metal clips on
the ends; two small light bulbs; paper clips.

1 To set up a series circuit, connect the bulbs
to the battery so the circuit is a continuous
loop (right). Use a paper clip to switch the
current on and off. Both lamps only
light dimly, as the resistance of the
bulbs reduces the amount of
current passing through the circuit.
If your circuit does not work at first,
check that there is good contact between
each of the wires and the components.

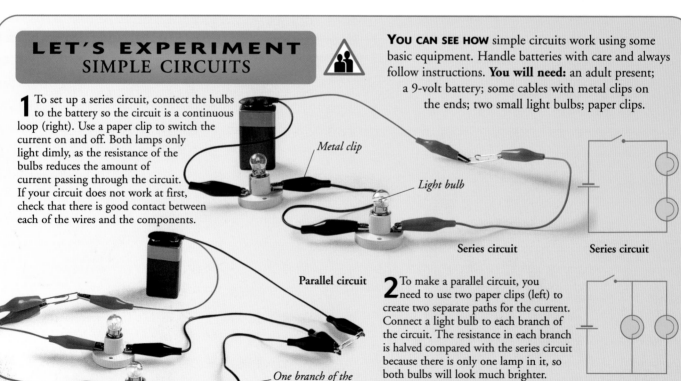

Metal clip
Light bulb
Parallel circuit
One branch of the parallel circuit

Series circuit
Series circuit

2 To make a parallel circuit, you
need to use two paper clips (left) to
create two separate paths for the current.
Connect a light bulb to each branch of
the circuit. The resistance in each branch
is halved compared with the series circuit
because there is only one lamp in it, so
both bulbs will look much brighter.

Parallel circuit

ELECTRICITY IN THE HOME

Houses that are connected to the power grid have an electrical circuit that runs in a loop. The cables run through all the rooms, supplying current to light fixtures and to the wall sockets for electrical appliances. Some countries require a heavy-duty loop to supply current to heavy appliances such as the washing machine. There is a box where the current enters the house containing a meter that records how much electricity is used and a circuit breaker or fuse for each loop. It is dangerous to play with electrical sockets.

Superconductivity
When some materials are cooled to extremely low temperatures, they lose their resistance to electric current and become "superconductors." Many materials including tin, aluminum, and lead have shown superconductivity. The effect was first seen in mercury in 1911 by Dutch physicist Heike Kamerlingh Onnes. Mercury must be cooled below -452°F (-269°C) to become a superconductor. Electric currents on a superconductor's surface produce a magnetic field that can repel and levitate a small magnet (above).

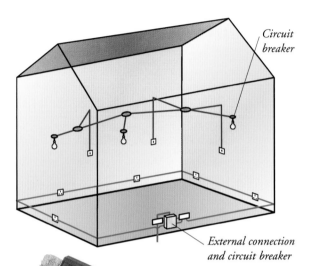

Circuit breaker

External connection and circuit breaker

Circuit breakers
If too high a current flows through a wire, it could overheat and start a fire. To prevent this, fuses or circuit breakers are used. Fuses (left) contain metal wires or strips that melt if more than a certain current passes through them. So if a fault develops in a particular circuit and too large a current flows around it, the fuse will "blow" and break the circuit.

ELECTRONIC CIRCUITS

Many modern products including televisions and computers contain complex electronic circuits that enable them to work. Instead of being connected by wires, the electronic components in these circuits are usually attached to a printed circuit board (PCB) like the one shown below. PCBs are made from a layer of electrically insulating material coated with a conducting substance such as copper. The copper is removed in the places where it is not needed, leaving a pattern of connections between the various components. Electric currents can then flow along these copper tracks.

Capacitor

Copper connection

Diode

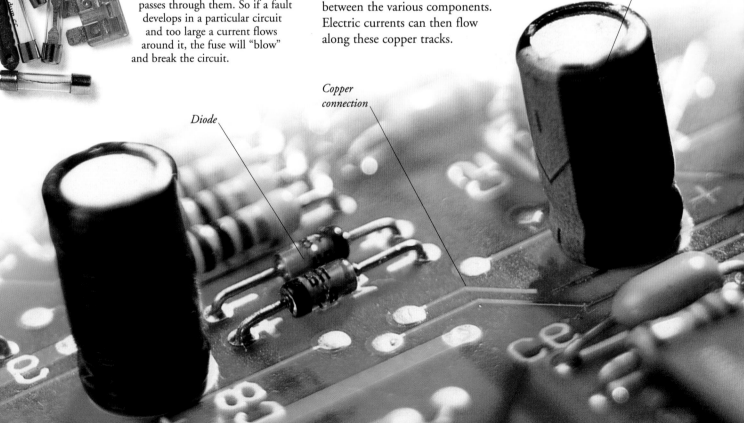

ELECTRICAL CHEMISTRY

WE TEND TO THINK OF ELECTRICAL CONDUCTORS AS being solids, such as metal wires, but some liquids can also conduct electricity. When electricity is passed through a conducting liquid, called an electrolyte, a chemical reaction takes place. If the electrolyte is brine (salt and water), the electricity splits the solution into chlorine gas and sodium hydroxide (caustic soda). If the electrolyte is a solution containing a metal, the current will separate the metal out of the solution. This process is known as electrolysis. Today electrolysis has many uses, including extracting some metals from rough ores and coating objects with a thin layer of a precious metal.

LAWS OF ELECTROLYSIS

Michael Faraday (1791–1867)

The British physicist and chemist Michael Faraday carried out many detailed experiments on electrolysis and discovered two laws of electrolysis. Faraday's first law states that the mass of substances formed during electrolysis is proportional to the amount of electricity used. However, the amount of electricity needed to form each separate substance depends on the charge and the mass of the substance. Faraday's second law explains this scientific principle mathematically.

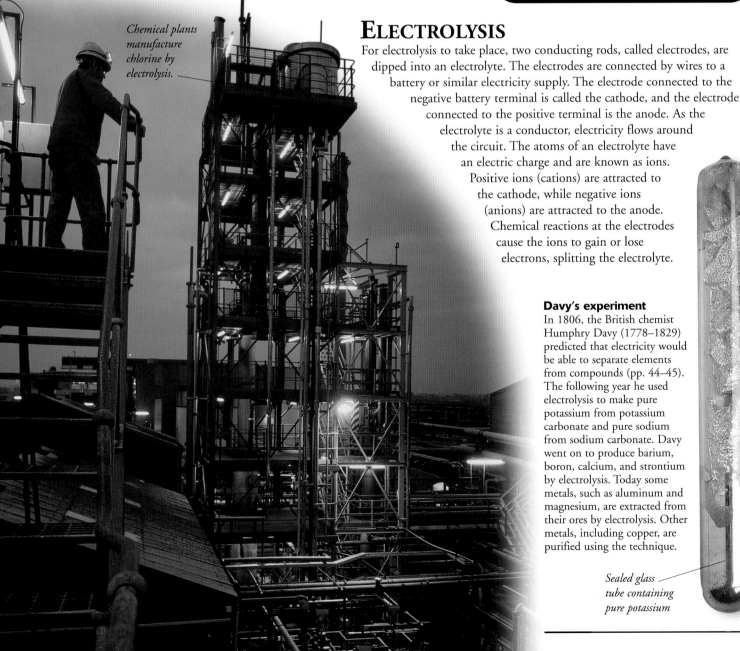

Chemical plants manufacture chlorine by electrolysis.

ELECTROLYSIS

For electrolysis to take place, two conducting rods, called electrodes, are dipped into an electrolyte. The electrodes are connected by wires to a battery or similar electricity supply. The electrode connected to the negative battery terminal is called the cathode, and the electrode connected to the positive terminal is the anode. As the electrolyte is a conductor, electricity flows around the circuit. The atoms of an electrolyte have an electric charge and are known as ions. Positive ions (cations) are attracted to the cathode, while negative ions (anions) are attracted to the anode. Chemical reactions at the electrodes cause the ions to gain or lose electrons, splitting the electrolyte.

Davy's experiment

In 1806, the British chemist Humphry Davy (1778–1829) predicted that electricity would be able to separate elements from compounds (pp. 44–45). The following year he used electrolysis to make pure potassium from potassium carbonate and pure sodium from sodium carbonate. Davy went on to produce barium, boron, calcium, and strontium by electrolysis. Today some metals, such as aluminum and magnesium, are extracted from their ores by electrolysis. Other metals, including copper, are purified using the technique.

Sealed glass tube containing pure potassium

YOU CAN PROVE that adding salt to water makes it a better electrical conductor. Handle batteries with care and always follow instructions. **You will need:** an adult present; electrical cables with metal clips on the ends; 9-volt battery; glass container; water; tape; small bulb; table salt; plastic spoon.

1 Connect a cable to each battery terminal. Place the free end of one of the cables in the container of water, and tape the wire to the container. Connect the end of the other cable to the light bulb, then clip another cable to the other side of the bulb and place the free end of this cable in the water an inch or two away from the first cable and tape it down.

2 Slowly add salt to the water, stirring it in carefully without moving the cables. The bulb will light up more and more brightly as more salt is added. If you repeat the experiment with fresh water and add sugar instead of salt, the bulb will not light up because sugary water is not an electrolyte.

Battery

Electrodes

The bulb glows brighter as more salt is added.

Saltwater electrolyte

ELECTROPLATING

Electrolysis can be used to give objects a coating of metal about 0.002 in (0.05 mm) thick. This process, known as electroplating, is used to coat cutlery made from cheap metal with an expensive metal. For example, to silverplate a spoon it is first cleaned, then made into a cathode by being connected to the negative terminal of a battery. A silver bar is used as the anode, and both electrodes are dipped in a solution containing a silver compound. Positively charged silver ions from the solution are attracted to the negatively charged spoon, which ends up with an even coating of silver if it is rotated slowly.

Nickel spoon

Silver-plated spoon

Rust proofing
Electroplating can be used to protect objects from corrosion. For example, car bodies can be electroplated with zinc to help prevent them from rusting. During the manufacturing process, the metal vehicle body is dipped into a huge bath containing a solution of zinc. The body is electrified so that it behaves like a cathode and attracts the positive zinc ions from the solution. The ions quickly cover every part of the car, leaving it with a coating of zinc.

MAGNETISM

ALL MAGNETS ARE SURROUNDED BY A FORCE FIELD THAT IS STRONGEST
at the "poles" (the ends) of the magnet. Poles can be "north" or "south."
Opposite magnetic poles attract each other, while like magnetic poles
(for example, two south poles) repel each other. The Earth produces
a magnetic field and behaves as if it has a huge magnet
inside it. The south pole of this imaginary magnet
is near the geographical North Pole at a
point known as the magnetic north
pole. Compasses always point
north because the north
poles of their needles are
attracted to the Earth's
internal south pole.

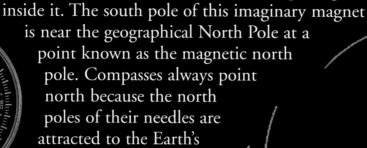

EARTH'S MAGNETIC FIELD

The Earth's core consists of solid iron surrounded by liquid
iron. Electric currents flowing in the outer core are thought
to produce the Earth's magnetic field. Scientists are uncertain
how these currents are generated, but they are probably linked
to the Earth's rotation. Earth's magnetic field extends out
into space, and any particles entering a region known as the
magnetosphere will be affected by it. Over long periods of
time, the Earth's magnetic poles slowly move. This means
that at some points in history the magnetic south pole has
been in the magnetic north pole's present position. This
computer simulation (right) shows the Earth's magnetic
poles changing position over thousands of years.

COMPASSES

One of the easiest ways to find
out which direction you are facing
is to use a magnetic compass.
The compass needle always points
toward the magnetic north pole,
but this is not in the same place as the
geographic North Pole. It is also slowly
changing position over time, so in order
to use a magnetic compass accurately,
corrections must be made with
the help of special charts.

Compasses at sea
Sailors need a reliable means of navigation
to avoid being lost. Today some motor boats
and kayaks have adventure compasses (right)
to show the way. Ships are built of metal,
which can affect the readings of a magnetic
compass, so a nonmagnetic compass called
a gyrocompass is used instead. Gyrocompasses
are based on a device called a gyroscope
(p. 73). The indicator in a gyrocompass
always points to geographic North.

Earth

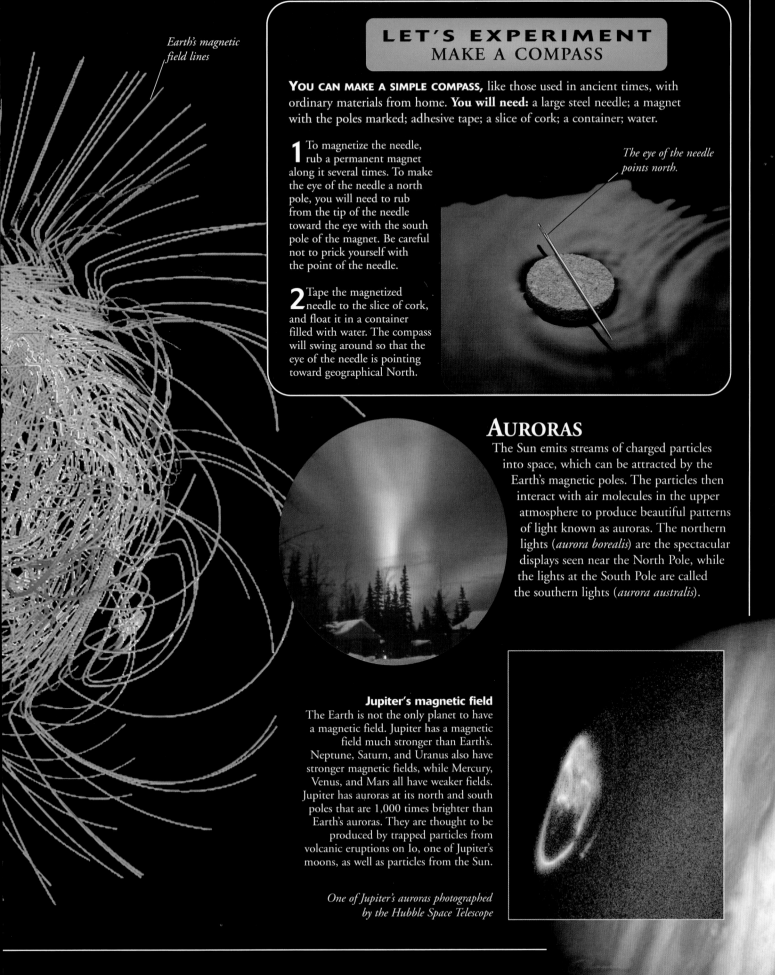

Earth's magnetic
field lines

AURORAS

The Sun emits streams of charged particles into space, which can be attracted by the Earth's magnetic poles. The particles then interact with air molecules in the upper atmosphere to produce beautiful patterns of light known as auroras. The northern lights (*aurora borealis*) are the spectacular displays seen near the North Pole, while the lights at the South Pole are called the southern lights (*aurora australis*).

Jupiter's magnetic field

The Earth is not the only planet to have a magnetic field. Jupiter has a magnetic field much stronger than Earth's. Neptune, Saturn, and Uranus also have stronger magnetic fields, while Mercury, Venus, and Mars all have weaker fields. Jupiter has auroras at its north and south poles that are 1,000 times brighter than Earth's auroras. They are thought to be produced by trapped particles from volcanic eruptions on Io, one of Jupiter's moons, as well as particles from the Sun.

One of Jupiter's auroras photographed by the Hubble Space Telescope

MAGNETS

ANY SUBSTANCE THAT CAN ATTRACT OR REPEL IRON is classed as a magnet. Other materials are also attracted to magnets, and all these and iron are known as magnetic materials. There are two types of magnetic material, and both become magnetized in a magnetic field. "Soft" magnetic materials, such as nickel and iron, lose their magnetism when they are removed from the field. "Hard" magnetic materials, such as alloys of iron, nickel, cobalt, and aluminum, become permanent magnets once magnetized. Iron or steel compass needles may be magnetized by being rubbed with a magnet.

LODESTONES

Today most magnets are artificially made, but the first compasses were made from the naturally occurring magnetic mineral lodestone – now called magnetite. This lump of magnetite (left) is attracting some iron filings. The word magnet comes from Magnesia, a place in Turkey where magnetite is found. It is believed that the ancient Chinese made the first compass from magnetite in the 11th century, but the reason why magnets point north was not understood until much later. In 1600, the English scientist William Gilbert (1544–1603) explained that the Earth acts like a giant magnet and attracts compass needles.

MAGNETIC TYPES

We think of materials such as wood that are not attracted to magnets as nonmagnetic. In fact all substances are "diamagnetic," which means that when they are exposed to a magnetic field, they make their own field in a way that makes them repel the external field. Some substances are also "paramagnetic," which is a much stronger effect that covers up their diamagnetism. Paramagnetic materials are moderately attracted to magnetic fields. Some paramagnetic materials are also "ferromagnetic." Ferromagnetic materials, such as iron and nickel, are magnetized by weak magnetic fields and are those we normally think of as magnetic. All magnetized materials produce magnetic force fields around themselves. These photographs (right) show how iron filings can be used to reveal magnetic force fields.

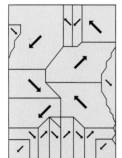
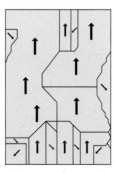

Unmagnetized material   Magnetized material

Magnetic domains

The atoms in magnetic materials are arranged in groups, or domains, which behave like tiny magnets. Normally these domains point in all directions, canceling out their magnetism. However, in a magnetic field, the domains line up in the same direction as the field, making the material strongly magnetic. Hammering or heating destroys the magnetization, by causing the domains to point in all directions again.

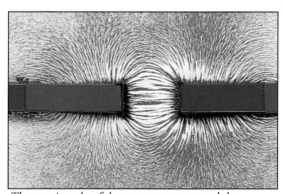

The opposite poles of these magnets attract, and the magnetic field between them is strengthened.

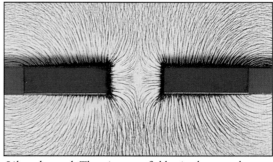

Like poles repel. There is a zero field point between them.

NORMALLY THE FORCE FIELD around a magnet is invisible, but iron filings can reveal where it is. When they are brought near a magnet, the iron filings become magnets themselves with a north and south pole, and move to line up with the magnet's field. Wash your hands after touching iron filings. **You will need:** an adult's help; a permanent magnet; a large piece of paper; iron filings; a compass.

1 Place the magnet on the piece of paper. Ask an adult to sprinkle the iron filings carefully all over the paper around the magnet. Gently nudge the paper. The filings will line up along the magnetic field lines as shown.

2 A small compass can also be used to reveal the magnetic field as the compass needle lines up with the field lines. The stronger the magnetic field at any place, the closer together the field lines will be.

The iron filings cluster near the poles, where the magnetic field is strongest.

Diamagnetic levitation

When living creatures, plants, plastic, and any other objects that are diamagnetic are placed in a magnetic field, all their atoms become slightly magnetic. Their electrons produce a weak magnetic field that opposes the field of the magnet they are near. This means that the atoms are repelled by the magnet. If this repelling force is as strong as the force of gravity that the object normally feels pulling it toward the ground, the object can be levitated above the magnet.

The atoms in this frog are repelled by the magnet below it.

MiniDisc

Audio signals are stored in digital form on a magnetic layer inside a MiniDisc. When something is recorded, the playback laser heats the magnetic layer to about 356°F (180°C), while a magnetic recording head induces areas of north or south polarity. Areas left with a north pole represent digital "1"s, while those with a magnetic south pole represent "0"s. To play the recording, the laser beam operates at a lower power. Spots with south poles interact with the laser beam in a different way to those with north poles, which allows the data to be decoded and turned back into sound.

Disc drive motor

Recording head

ELECTRIC CONNECTION

MOST OF THE ELECTRIC MACHINES
in use today rely on electromagnets –
magnets whose power can be
switched on and off by an electric
current. The discovery in the
19th century of the connection
between electricity and magnetism,
known as electromagnetism, led to
the development of new machines for
a wide variety of tasks. Electromagnets
have many uses, ranging from lifting heavy
metal objects to providing propulsion in
levitating trains and allowing telephones
to work. Electromagnetism also forms the
basis for electric motors and generators.

*Horseshoe shaped
core of soft iron*

*Coiled
copper wire*

*Compass needle is
deflected by current.*

*Clamps hold the
current-carrying wire.*

ELECTROMAGNETISM

The link between electricity and magnetism was discovered
by the Danish physicist Hans Christian Oersted (1777–1851).
When he brought a compass near a current-carrying wire, the
needle moved. This showed that an electric current produces a
magnetic field. The French scientist André-Marie Ampère (1775–1836)
carried out further experiments and found that the strength of the
magnetic field around a wire increased as the current increased.

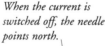

*When the current is
switched off, the needle
points north.*

ELECTROMAGNETS

In many electric devices a magnetic field
is only required some of the time. For
example, a doorbell uses an electromagnet
instead of a permanent magnet.
Electromagnets usually consist
of a coil of conducting wire around a
core of soft magnetic material such as
iron. When the electric current is
switched off, the magnet has no strength
(above). When a current flows through
the coil, the electromagnet is magnetized
(above right). If the direction of the
current changes, the north pole of the
electromagnet will become the south
pole and vice versa. The greater the
current flowing through the coil, and
the more wire it contains, the stronger
the electromagnet becomes.

Iron filings

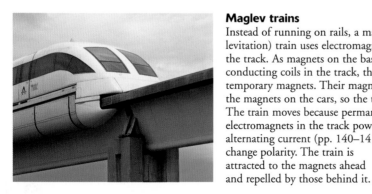

Maglev trains

Instead of running on rails, a maglev (magnetic
levitation) train uses electromagnetism to float above
the track. As magnets on the base of the cars pass
conducting coils in the track, the coils become
temporary magnets. Their magnetic force repels
the magnets on the cars, so the train floats.
The train moves because permanent
electromagnets in the track powered by
alternating current (pp. 140–141)
change polarity. The train is
attracted to the magnets ahead
and repelled by those behind it.

Connections to
electric current

Coiled
copper wire

Iron filings
cling to
the magnet.

TELEPHONES

Electromagnets inside a telephone handset allow
the caller to hear another person speaking. The
mouthpiece contains a diaphragm that is vibrated
by sound waves from a voice. These vibrations are
converted into a varying electric current and sent
down the telephone line. The signals can be heard
because the receiver in the handset contains
another diaphragm and an electromagnet. The
variations in the current traveling down the
telephone line vary the magnetic field that the
electromagnet produces, making the diaphragm
vibrate and reproduce the sound waves.

Modems

It is not just conversations
that can be transmitted by
telephone lines. Computers
can send emails and files to each other via a
modem (above right). The modem converts
binary information from a computer into
tones, which are sent down telephone lines.
The tones are then converted by another
modem back into data. Most computers and
some mobile phones have built-in modems.

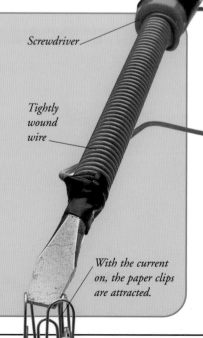

Screwdriver

Tightly
wound
wire

With the current
on, the paper clips
are attracted.

LET'S EXPERIMENT
MAKE AN ELECTROMAGNET

YOU CAN MAKE your own electromagnet
that will lift small magnetic objects.
Handle batteries with care and always
follow instructions. **You will need:** an
adult present; a screwdriver with a plastic
handle; some copper wire; adhesive tape;
a 9-volt battery; some paper clips.

1 To turn the screwdriver into an electromagnet, first
wind the copper wire tightly around the middle of it
as shown (right). Use tape to secure the wire at each end.

2 Connect one end of the wire to the positive terminal
of the battery and the other end to the negative
terminal. With both wires connected to the battery, the
screwdriver becomes magnetized. Be careful when
handling the screwdriver as the copper wire may be hot.

3 The screwdriver electromagnet can now be used to
pick up paper clips and other objects made from
magnetic materials. When the electromagnet is
disconnected from the battery, it starts to lose its
magnetism and drops whatever it is holding.

GENERATING ELECTRICITY

A CURRENT IS CREATED IN A CONDUCTING WIRE,
either when the wire moves past a magnetic field, or when
a magnet moves past a stationary wire. This effect, called
electromagnetic induction, was discovered independently by
the American physicist Joseph Henry (1797–1878) in 1830
and the British scientist Michael Faraday (1791–1867) in
1831. Nearly all of the electricity we use today is created by
electromagnetic induction, through enormous generators
that turn mechanical energy into electrical energy.

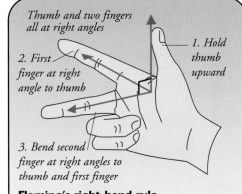

Thumb and two fingers all at right angles

1. Hold thumb upward

2. First finger at right angle to thumb

3. Bend second finger at right angles to thumb and first finger

Fleming's right-hand rule
Use your right hand to indicate the flow of an
electric current when a wire moves through a
magnetic field: thumb – direction of moving
wire; first finger – direction of magnetic field;
second finger – direction of induced current.

GENERATORS

There are two types of generators. A dynamo produces direct current (DC), which
flows in one direction all the time. An alternator produces alternating current (AC),
which constantly changes direction. In both types of generator, the electric current
is induced in a rotating coil of wire (armature) when it passes through a
magnetic field. The electricity we use every day is AC from alternators,
while DC from dynamos is used for industrial electrolysis, such
as electroplating and chemical manufacturing.

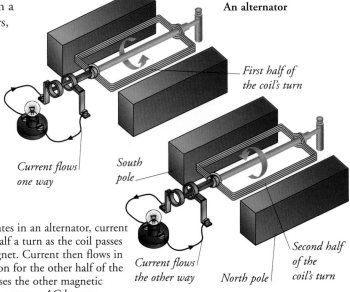

An alternator

*First half of
the coil's turn*

*South
pole*

*Current flows
the other way*

North pole

*Second half
of the
coil's turn*

Dynamo
As the wire coil rotates in a dynamo, one side passes
the south pole of a permanent magnet, inducing
a current in one direction. When the wire
passes the north pole, a current flows in the
opposite direction. A device called
a commutator ensures that the
current in the external circuit
flows in only one direction.

A dynamo

South pole

North pole

Armature

Commutator

External circuit

Alternator
As the wire coil rotates in an alternator, current
flows one way for half a turn as the coil passes
one pole of the magnet. Current then flows in
the opposite direction for the other half of the
turn, as the coil passes the other magnetic
pole. Power stations generate AC because
it is easier to transmit over long distances.

*Current flows
one way*

POWER STATIONS

Inside power stations are huge generators
that are driven by the rotating shaft in
an engine called a turbine. In coal and
oil-fired power stations, heat from the
burning fuel converts water into steam.
The pressure of the steam rotates the
turbine shaft. In nuclear power stations,
the heat that converts water into steam
comes from nuclear reactions, generally
using uranium as fuel. Hydroelectric
power stations use turbines driven by
water rather than steam. Smaller amounts
of electricity are being generated by solar
power and wind power.

**A turbine and generator inside a
nuclear power station**

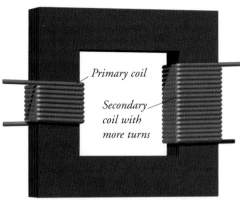

Primary coil

Secondary coil with more turns

Step-up transformer

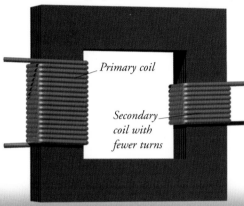

Primary coil

Secondary coil with fewer turns

Step-down transformer

ELECTRICITY SUPPLY

A network of substations, overhead wires, and underground cables called a grid delivers electricity from power stations to homes and businesses. To be transmitted effectively, a higher voltage of electricity is needed. A lower voltage is needed for use at its destination. To increase and decrease the voltage, a transformer is used. Transformers have two separate coils of wire wound around an iron core. When alternating current (the type that constantly switches directions) flows through the primary coil, it creates an alternating magnetic field. This field induces an alternating electric current in the secondary coil. A step-up transformer has a secondary coil with more turns than the primary coil, increasing the voltage enough for transmission. A step-down transformer has a secondary coil with fewer turns, decreasing the voltage to a suitable level for use in homes and businesses.

Electric fish
Some fish, such as electric eels and electric rays (above), have special muscle cells that generate and store electric currents. They produce strong electric shocks to stun or kill prey and as defense from predators. They also generate weaker electric pulses to help recognize prey and to navigate in murky water.

Solar cell panels

Experimental solar-powered car

Solar energy
Sunlight can be converted into electricity in a device called a solar cell. Solar cells are made from two layers of silicon. Each layer has a different element added to it that alters its electrical properties. When sunlight falls on the surface of a solar cell, an electric current is generated across the junction between the layers. A small individual solar cell cannot produce much electricity, so many solar cells are usually connected together to form a solar panel. Solar panels are used to power electronic equipment in satellites and spacecraft. They are also used for home electricity generation and in experimental vehicles.

Solar cells

Solar-powered wing
The *Helios* solar-powered flying wing was built as part of a NASA research project. It has a total wingspan of 247 ft (75 m), which is larger than the wingspan of a Boeing 747 aircraft. The pilot flies the *Helios* via remote control.

MAKING MOTORS

THE LINK BETWEEN ELECTRICITY AND MAGNETISM WAS
discovered when a compass needle swung around as it was
brought near a wire carrying an electric current (p. 138).
A year later, in 1821, British scientist Michael Faraday
built the first electric motor, in which a wire carrying
an electric current rotated around a fixed magnet. An
electric motor is the opposite of an electric generator.
In a generator, motion is used to create
electricity, but in a motor, electricity
is used to create motion.

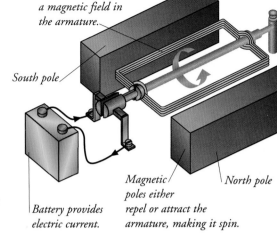

*An electric current creates
a magnetic field in
the armature.*

South pole

*Magnetic
poles either
repel or attract the
armature, making it spin.*

North pole

*Battery provides
electric current.*

ELECTRIC MOTORS

When an electric motor is switched on, a current flows through a coil of
wire called an armature, which is located between the poles of a permanent
magnet (above). The current creates a magnetic field in the armature with
like poles in the armature facing like poles of the magnet. The like magnetic
poles repel each other, pushing the armature around. As the armature turns,
the poles approach the opposite poles of the magnet, and become attracted.
The direction of the current is then reversed, and the poles on the armature
switch over. As a result, the armature is repelled by the magnet again, and
the rotation is complete. As long as there is an electric current, the armature
spins between the poles of the magnet, creating motion. Electric motors
range in size from relatively small, as in electrical appliances such as
hairdryers, to very large, such as the motors used in electric trains.

**Disk
drive**
This electric
motor is from
the floppy disk
drive of a computer.
An electric current causes
small electromagnets on the
turntable to generate a magnetic
field that enables it to spin.

ELECTRIC RAILROADS

Most locomotives used to pull trains are
powered by electric motors. An electric
train receives the current needed to drive
its motor either from an overhead cable or
from a third rail on the track. To pick up
the current from an overhead cable, a
locomotive must have a flexible steel connector
attached to its roof. Many intercity trains use this
system. To obtain the power from a third rail, a locomotive has metal
plates called shoes located underneath it, which make contact with
the electrified rail. Local rail services often use this system. Trains on the
London Underground in the UK (above) receive power from a third rail.

TGV
The large motors used in
electric trains provide a lot
of power, enabling trains to
move very quickly. One of the
fastest types of train is the
TGV (Train à Grande Vitesse)
in France (left), which can
reach speeds of more than
180 mph (300 kmh). The
TGV receives its power from
overhead cables. Its
streamlined shape allows
it to speed along with a
minimum of air resistance.

Fleming's left-hand rule

Hold your left hand as shown to indicate which way a wire carrying an electric current moves through a magnetic field. The thumb shows the direction that the wire moves; the first finger, the direction of the magnetic field; the second finger, the direction of the electric current.

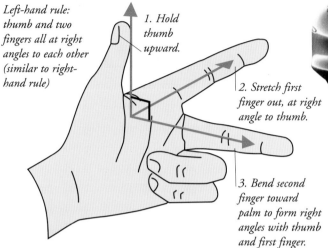

Left-hand rule: thumb and two fingers all at right angles to each other (similar to right-hand rule)

1. Hold thumb upward.

2. Stretch first finger out, at right angle to thumb.

3. Bend second finger toward palm to form right angles with thumb and first finger.

Electric cars

It is possible for cars to be powered by electric motors, although electric cars are not common. In most types of electric car, a rechargeable battery provides an electric current to run the motor. Many electric cars cannot travel very fast, and their batteries frequently need recharging. Although electric cars themselves do not pollute, their batteries must be recharged using electricity from power stations, which may produce pollution. A more successful type of electric car, known as a hybrid (above), uses both electricity and another power source. The battery is partially recharged when braking.

LET'S EXPERIMENT
MAKE A MOTOR

MAKE YOUR OWN electric motor. Although it will not be very powerful, your motor will work in the same way as larger motors, and the armature (the moving part of the motor) should spin fairly quickly. Handle batteries with care and always follow instructions.
You will need: an adult present; about 3 ft (1 m) of copper wire; cardboard tube (from toilet paper roll); small amount enamel or acrylic paint; two large paper clips; rubber bands; D cell battery (1.5 volt); bar magnet; glue.

About seven loops in coil

Wrap ends of wire around sides of coil, leaving ends sticking straight out.

1 Use the copper wire to make the armature. Leaving about 2 in (6 cm) free at each end, wrap the wire around the cardboard tube. It should go around about seven times, with the two ends of the wire ending up on opposite sides of the coil (above). Slide the coil off the tube, then wrap the two free ends around the sides of the coil to hold it together.

Paint top of wire end.

2 Paint the top half of one end of the wire using enamel or acrylic paint. Wait for it to dry. The paint is an electrical insulator, so once the motor is operating, it will break the electric circuit for half of each revolution.

Bend paper clip at this point.

3 Bend two large paper clips in the middle (above). These will act as supports for the armature. Loop large rubber bands around the battery. Hook one paper clip to each end of the battery, using the rubber bands to keep the clips securely in place (below).

4 Glue the bar magnet to the side of the battery. Hook the ends of the coil onto the paper-clip hooks and spin. If it does not work at first move the copper coil closer to the magnet or place it near a more powerful magnet.

Magnet

One clip overlaps painted wire.

Make sure paper clips are held securely to battery.

Paper clips support ends of coil.

Spin the armature gently to help start it revolving.

ELECTRONICS AND CHIPS

CRYSTAL WAFERS NOT MUCH BIGGER THAN YOUR thumbnail are the "brains" behind computers and video games, mobile phones, and robots. They contain miniature components and circuits that control and manipulate flows of electrons. The study of electricity flowing through crystals, and also through gases or a vacuum, is known as electronics. The crystal wafers (chips), which have caused such a revolution in recent years, are made out of materials called semiconductors, or semimetals (pp. 46–47), which conduct just a little electricity.

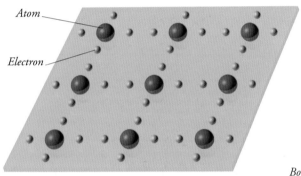

In pure silicon, the atoms have four electrons, which are negatively charged, in their outer shells. Overall, the atoms are electrically neutral.

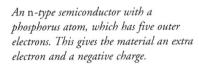

An n-type semiconductor with a phosphorus atom, which has five outer electrons. This gives the material an extra electron and a negative charge.

CLEVER CRYSTALS

Diodes and transistors are two of the most versatile components used in electronic circuits. They are both crystal devices, made up of semiconductor material. Diodes have two terminals and pass electric current only in one direction. Some give off light, and are called LEDs (light-emitting diodes). Transistors have three terminals – base, emitter, and collector. They can be used as switches (as in the experiment at right) or as amplifiers, to amplify (strengthen) weak currents.

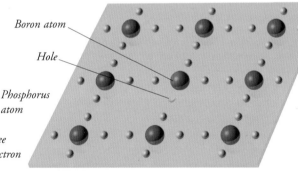

A p-type semiconductor with a boron atom, which has only three outer electrons. When boron replaces a silicon atom, there is one electron less, creating a positive hole.

HOW SEMICONDUCTORS WORK

Elements like silicon and germanium become semiconductors when traces of certain impurities are introduced into them. Adding traces of boron to silicon creates a material with positively charged "holes." Under suitable conditions, these holes move around, allowing current to flow. This kind of semiconductor is called a *p* (positive)-type. Adding phosphorus or arsenic to silicon creates a material with spare electrons, which can flow to form a current. This is called an *n* (negative)-type semiconductor.

INTEGRATED CIRCUITS

Electronic circuits were once made up of separate components, such as transistors and capacitors, linked together by wires. Now, most electronic devices have complete circuits in miniature, integrated in a single slice, or chip, of semiconductor material. They are called integrated circuits. The silicon chips used in the latest personal computers are made up of integrated circuits containing billions of components. Single chips can contain all the circuits that carry out processing in the computer (right), and are often called microprocessors or microchips.

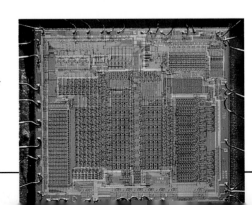

The crucial invention

In 1947, a team of US scientists at Bell Laboratories in New Jersey made one of the crucial inventions of the 20th century. William Shockley, John Bardeen, and Walter Brattain developed the transistor. Their new device was much smaller, tougher, and consumed less power than the vacuum valves that it replaced in electronic circuits. In 1956, the men were jointly awarded the Nobel Prize for Physics.

MAKING CHIPS

Silicon chips are produced hundreds at a time on a circular slice of pure silicon crystal. The circuits and different components (such as transistors and capacitors) are built up in a series of layers. Each layer is made by impregnating certain parts of the silicon with different elements, such as boron and phosphorus. When all the layers are complete, a layer of gold or aluminum is laid down to form the connections between the various components. Then the chips are inspected by probes and faulty ones are marked.

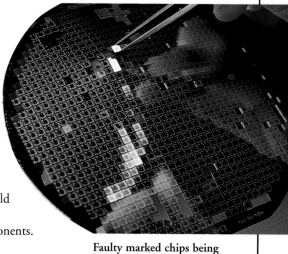

Faulty marked chips being removed from a slice of silicon

LET'S EXPERIMENT
MAKING A TRANSISTOR SWITCH

YOU CAN USE A TRANSISTOR as a switch to turn an LED (light-emitting diode) on and off. You do so by altering the connections to the transistor's base terminal. Handle batteries with care and always follow instructions. **You will need:** an adult's help; *n-p-n* transistor (BC108); an LED; 220 and 10,000 ohm resistors; battery pack (2 x 1.5-volts); electric cables with clips; insulated wire; short nails; eyelets; short lengths of wire; 2 wooden baseboards; soldering equipment; hammer.

1 Attach the battery pack to a baseboard and connect lengths of wire to the battery terminals. Attach the other ends of the wires to the eyelets. Ask an adult to hammer nails into the other baseboard as shown (below). Connect the circuit as shown in the photograph (right), wrapping the connecting wires of the components around the nails. Make sure that the transistor terminals – base, emitter, and collector – are the right way around.

2 Ask an adult to solder the connecting wires to the nails and check that they are firm. Touch the end of the piece of insulated wire (the loose wire) to the middle nail on the negative side of the circuit, and the LED remains switched off. Touch it to the middle nail on the positive side, and the LED switches on.

Wire from negative battery terminal

The wires from the terminals connect with the electric leads at the eyelets.

Insulated wire

Wire from positive battery terminal

Middle nail of negative side

Base

Emitter

Transistor

Collector

LED

Middle nail of positive side

10,000 ohm resistor

220 ohm resistor

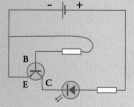

Base (B) connected to negative terminal, collector (C) connected to positive terminal. LED stays off.

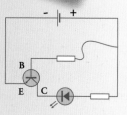

Base (B) and collector (C) both connected to positive terminal. Transistor switches on, lets current flow through LED.

ON THE RADIO

RACING ALL AROUND US AT THE SPEED OF light are invisible waves carrying voices and music, messages and pictures, and even signals from outer space. They are radio waves, which are at the heart of most modern systems of communications. We pick up radio waves by tuning electronic circuits in our radios, televisions, and mobile phones. But what exactly are radio waves? They are tiny electrical and magnetic disturbances in space. These electromagnetic waves belong to the same family as light but have a much longer wavelength (up to several miles).

PHONES ON THE MOVE

Using mobile phones, people can stay in touch with each other wherever they are by voice, text messaging, and, on WAP (wireless application protocol) phones, by emailing. Mobile phones work by radio waves. They send signals to an antenna up to a few miles away, which serves a small area called a cell. Signals picked up by the antenna are routed by computer via ordinary telephone links to a landline number, or to another mobile phone via the antenna of the cell in which it is located.

CARRIER WAVES

How can sounds be sent through the air on radio waves? First, they are changed into electrical signals by a microphone. Then these signals are made to alter a radio wave, called the carrier wave, in a characteristic way. This process is called modulation. In amplitude modulation (AM), the voice signals are made to vary the amplitude of the carrier wave – the amount it vibrates up and down. In frequency modulation (FM), the voice signals vary the frequency of the carrier wave – the number of vibrations passing a certain point per second. FM transmissions suffer less from interference than AM.

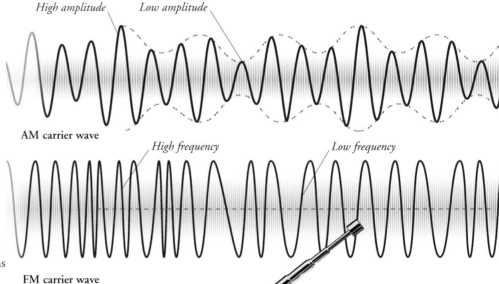

High amplitude   *Low amplitude*

AM carrier wave

High frequency   *Low frequency*

FM carrier wave

LET'S EXPERIMENT
MAKING RADIO WAVES

MOST ELECTRICAL DEVICES emit radio waves of some kind when they are switched on or off. The sudden surging or draining of current through their circuits disturbs the electrical and magnetic properties of the space around them.
You will need: a radio that has AM bands; flashlight.

1 Switch on the radio and select an AM band. Bring the flashlight up close to the antenna and switch it on, then off. You should hear clicks on the radio.

2 Tune the radio to different frequencies and repeat. Do the clicks get quieter or louder? What noise do you hear when you bring the radio near a television set?

SONY   TUNE ●

FM/u 88 92 96 100 104 108 MHz
SCALE 0 1 2 3 4 5 6 7 8 9 10
AM/M 5.3 6 7 8 10 12 14 16 ×100 kHz

FM AM

RADAR WAVES

Aircraft and ships use radio waves not only for communications, but also for navigation. They use radar to see the traffic around them. The word radar stands for radio detection and ranging. Radar sets transmit pulses of radio waves and pick up any echoes when the beams are reflected from nearby objects. The reflections are displayed on a screen. The time it takes for the echoes to return gives the range (distance away) of the objects.

Radar screen showing objects surrounding a ship (center).

Scanning coil sweeps beams back and forth across the screen.

Shadow mask allows each beam to strike the appropriate colored phosphor.

Phosphor stripes will glow red, blue, or green when electron beams hit them.

Anode and cathode (inside tube)

Three electron guns (not visible) produce beams representing red, green, and blue colors in the picture.

Inside a television set

AS SEEN ON TV

Radio waves carry television picture signals to a receiver, which converts them into images. The key device in the receiver is the cathode-ray tube (CRT). Electronic circuits sort out the incoming signals into four main sets: three representing the colors red, green, and blue in the picture being transmitted, and one set of scanning signals. The color signals are fed to electron guns, which fire beams of electrons at the screen, where they strike phosphors (p. 120) that glow with the appropriate color. The scanning signals make the beams scan across the screen. This happens so quickly that our eyes see a full-screen picture.

‹ TUNING IN ›

In 1932, a US electrical engineer named Karl Jansky detected radio waves coming from space, and launched radio astronomy. Astronomers pick up radio waves from space with huge, dish-shaped radio telescopes. Their study of the radio universe led to the discovery of new astronomical bodies, such as quasars, pulsars, and radio galaxies. **113** ▸

Parkes radio telescope in New South Wales, Australia, has a dish 210 ft (64 m) across.

147

COMPUTING

WHEN THE SPACE SHUTTLE BLASTS OFF THE
launch pad, 300,000 operations must be
performed every second to ensure that all its
systems function properly. Human astronauts
could not possibly cope with such demands, which
is why liftoff is controlled by computers. Within
their electronic circuits, computers are capable of
carrying out millions of operations every second.
Exactly what a computer does depends on the
way it is programmed (instructed). It may be
used to play games, design the molecules of
new medicines, pilot airliners, write novels,
or create imaginary, virtual worlds.

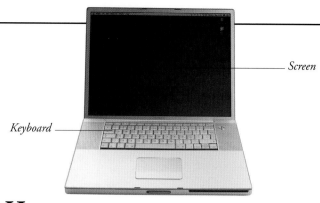

Screen

Keyboard

HARDWARE

The pieces of equipment that make up a computer are
called the hardware. The key component is the CPU (central
processing unit), the computer's main control unit. Other
chips hold the computer's memories, the permanent ROM
(read-only memory), and temporary RAM (random-
access memory). Information is fed into the computer
by keyboard, mouse, and from storage discs,
usually CDs (compact discs) or DVDs (digital
versatile discs). Information and graphics
(pictures) are displayed on a screen, and
may be printed out as "hard copy."

*Car designed
with a program
called CAD
(computer-assisted
design), which uses
advanced 3-D graphics*

SOFTWARE

The programs and data
(information) fed into a
computer are called the software.
Before it can be handled by the computer,
software has to be translated into binary
code, in which information is represented
by the two digits 1 and 0. These digits
can then be represented in the computer's
electronic circuits by the flow (1) or non-
flow (0) of electricity. (This is achieved by
switching electric current on and off with
transistors.) Each 1 or 0 is called a bit; a
set of eight bits is called a byte. Computer
programmers write their programs in
"computer language," such as BASIC
or COBOL, which the computer can
recognize and translate into binary
code (machine code).

Like the real thing
A pilot "flies" a fighter in a
computer-generated landscape
(left). The plane responds to the
pilot's actions just like a real plane
would. The ultimate in this kind of
computer simulation is virtual reality,
in which you can enter a virtual (created)
world that the computer produces. You
wear a helmet that shows the virtual
world on screens before your eyes.
You can "touch" virtual objects
using a glove wired-up with sensors.

SURFING THE NET

Through your computer, you can join a worldwide computer network known as the internet, which you can access via the telephone. The "net" allows access to an almost unlimited amount of information on every subject you can think of. It also lets you communicate with other computer users by electronic mail (email). On the net, companies, universities, stores, special interest groups, and individuals provide information through different websites. From them, you can download (put onto your computer) text, graphics, photographs, and even video footage and music. Search engines provide a quick way of looking for the information you want.

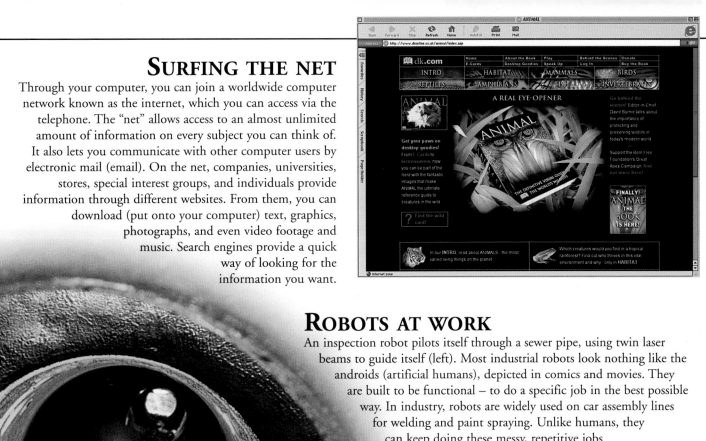

ROBOTS AT WORK

An inspection robot pilots itself through a sewer pipe, using twin laser beams to guide itself (left). Most industrial robots look nothing like the androids (artificial humans), depicted in comics and movies. They are built to be functional – to do a specific job in the best possible way. In industry, robots are widely used on car assembly lines for welding and paint spraying. Unlike humans, they can keep doing these messy, repetitive jobs indefinitely without getting tired.

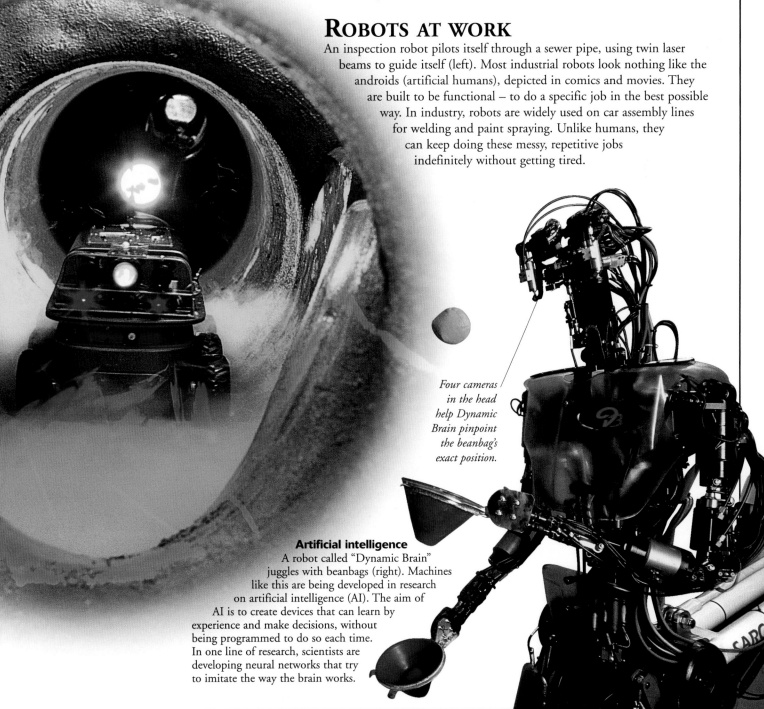

Four cameras in the head help Dynamic Brain pinpoint the beanbag's exact position.

Artificial intelligence

A robot called "Dynamic Brain" juggles with beanbags (right). Machines like this are being developed in research on artificial intelligence (AI). The aim of AI is to create devices that can learn by experience and make decisions, without being programmed to do so each time. In one line of research, scientists are developing neural networks that try to imitate the way the brain works.

GLOSSARY

Absolute zero: lowest temperature possible, when all molecular motion ceases, 0K or -273.15°C (-460°F)

Absorption: (1) In physics, taking in of energy (e.g. heat, light, sound) by a substance. (2) In chemistry, the take-up of a gas by a liquid or solid, or of a liquid by a solid.

Acceleration: rate of change of velocity, expressed in units such as metres per second per second.

Acid: compound containing hydrogen that splits up in water to produce positive hydrogen ions.

Acid rain: rain containing acids produced in the air from polluting gases, such as sulphur dioxide.

Acoustics: study of sound. The sound properties of a building are called its acoustics.

Adhesion: attraction between the atoms or molecules of different substances.

Aerodynamics: study of gases (particularly air) in motion and of objects moving through them.

Aerofoil: wing-shape that cuts through the air, creating lift.

Air resistance: *See Drag.*

Alchemy: early chemical science in which people (alchemists) investigated chemicals and reactions in an effort to make, for example, gold from base metals.

Alkali: base that dissolves in water.

Allotropes: different forms of the same element, e.g. oxygen and ozone.

Alloy: mixture of two or more metals, or of a metal and a non-metal.

Alpha rays: stream of particles given off by radioactive substances, consisting of the nuclei of helium atoms.

Alternating current (AC): electric current that flows first in one direction, then in another, at a constant frequency. Mains electricity is AC.

Alternator: electric generator that produces alternating current.

Ammeter: instrument that measures electric current.

Ampere (amp): unit of electric current.

Amplifier: device that magnifies or strengthens electrical signals.

Amplitude: maximum height plus depth of a wave.

Angular momentum: momentum possessed by a rotating object.

Anion: negatively charged ion that moves to the anode during electrolysis.

Anode: positive electrode.

Antimatter: matter made up of particles that are exact opposites of the ones in ordinary matter. Positrons (positively charged) are the antiparticles of electrons (negatively charged).

*Red cabbage can be used as an indicator to test the level of **acid** in a substance.*

Artificial element: element produced artificially by nuclear bombardment.

Atmospheric pressure: pressure of the air in the atmosphere, about 100 kilopascals or 1 kg per square centimetre (14.7 pounds per square inch) at sea level.

Atom: smallest particle of an element that can exist and still have the properties of that element.

Atomic energy: *See Nuclear energy.*

Atomic number: number of protons in the nucleus of an atom.

Atomic weight: *See Relative atomic mass.*

Barometer: instrument that measures air pressure.

Base: in chemistry, a compound that reacts with an acid to produce a salt and water only.

Battery: series of electric cells joined together to produce and store electricity.

Beta rays: streams of electrons given off by radioactive substances.

Binary number: number system based on two digits, 0 and 1.

Biochemistry: study of the chemical reactions that take place in living organisms.

Biology: study of living things, comprising two main branches – botany, the study of plants and zoology, the study of animals.

Bioluminescence: light without heat produced by living organisms (such as glow-worms).

Black hole: a region of space with such intense gravity that nothing can escape it, not even light.

Boiling point: temperature at which a liquid bubbles and changes into gas.

Bonds: attractions between atoms or ions that hold molecules and other compounds together. *See also Covalent, Ionic, and Metallic bond.*

Bubble chamber: device for detecting charged atomic particles. The particles leave a trail of bubbles behind when they pass through it.

Buoyancy: upward force exerted on a body immersed in a fluid.

Burning: *See Combustion.*

Capacitor: device in electronic circuits that stores electric charge.

*The circulating streams of rising and descending air that enable this glider to fly are known as **convection** currents.*

Capillary action: movement of a liquid up or down a narrow tube because of attraction between its molecules and those of the tube.

Carbohydrate: energy-giving compound made up of carbon, hydrogen, and oxygen.

Carbon chemistry: *See Organic chemistry.*

Carrier waves: radio waves that carry signals, as in radio and TV.

Catalyst: substance that speeds up a chemical reaction without itself undergoing chemical change.

Cathode: negative electrode.

Cathode-ray tube (CRT): vacuum tube in which a stream of electrons (cathode rays) makes phosphors on a screen fluoresce, or give out light.

Cation: positively charged ion that moves to the cathode during electrolysis.

Cell: (1) in biology, the basic unit from which all organisms are made up. (2) In electricity, a device that produces electricity through chemical changes. *See also Battery.*

Celsius: temperature scale devised by Anders Celsius (1701–44), on which water freezes at 0 degrees.

Central processing unit (CPU): principal part of a computer, which carries out the processing of data.

Centre of gravity (or mass): point in a body in which all its weight (or mass) seems to be concentrated.

Centripetal force: force in rotating bodies which acts inwards to keep them turning in a circle.

Chain reaction: reaction that continues on its own. In a nuclear chain reaction, particles produced when one atom splits (undergoes fission) trigger more atoms to split.

Charge (or electric charge): a property of many subatomic particles that makes them attract or repel one another. It takes two forms – negative and positive. The electron has a single negative charge, a proton a single positive charge.

Chemical reaction: process in which substances (reactants) undergo chemical change and form new substances (products).

Chemistry: study of the properties and makeup of substances and the changes they undergo.

Chromatography: method of separating substances in a mixture by passing it through a medium (such as filter paper). The

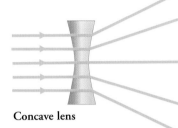

Concave lens

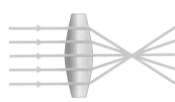

Convex lens

Concave lenses cause light rays to diverge (spread out), whereas convex lenses cause light rays to converge (come together).

substances separate because they flow through at different speeds.

Circuit: path through which an electric current can flow. *See also Integrated circuit.*

Cohesion: force of attraction between particles of the same substance.

Combustion (or burning): chemical reaction in which substances combine with oxygen in the air to produce heat (and usually light as flames).

Composite: material made of different substances, such as plastic reinforced with fibers.

Compound: substance formed by the combination of two or more different elements in fixed proportions.

Concave lens: lens that curves inward, like a dish.

Condensation: change of state from a gas (or vapor) into a liquid.

Conduction: process in which heat, sound, or electricity passes through a substance.

Conductor: substance that passes heat, sound, or electricity well.

Conservation of energy: energy cannot be created or destroyed, merely changed from one form to another.

Contraction: shrinking in size, as when a hot body cools.

Convection: transfer of heat through a liquid or a gas by moving currents.

Convex lens: lens that curves outward, bulging in the middle.

Corrosion: chemical or electrochemical attack on a metal surface. *See also Rusting.*

Covalent bond: bond formed when atoms share pairs of electrons with one another.

Cracking: oil refining process in which catalysts are used to help break down heavy oil fractions into lighter, more useful products.

Cryogenics: study of materials at very low temperatures, such as liquid gases.

Crystal: solid substance with a regular shape due to the internal arrangement of its particles. *See also Lattice.*

Data: information.

Decibel: unit used to measure the intensity (loudness) of sound.

Deliquescence: absorption of moisture from the atmosphere by a substance to the point that it eventually dissolves.

Density: mass of a certain volume of a substance (such as pounds per cubic foot or kilograms per cubic meter). *See also Relative density.*

Deoxyribonucleic acid (DNA): chemical that makes up the chromosomes in the cells of living things. It forms the genes that pass on characteristics from one generation to another.

Detergent: chemical that helps dirt and grease dissolve in water; used for cleaning.

Diffraction: spreading out of waves when they pass through a thin slit.

Diffusion: mixing of different substances as a result of the movement of their particles.

Diode: crystal semiconductor device that passes current only one way. *See also Light-emitting diode.*

Direct current (DC): electric current that flows in only one direction through a circuit.

Distillation: process for purifying or separating liquids. The liquid (or liquid mixture) is boiled into vapor, which is then condensed.

Drag: force of resistance an object experiences when it travels through a fluid (gas or liquid), caused by friction with the surrounding molecules.

Dynamo: electric generator that produces direct current.

Echo: sound heard again after it has been reflected from an object.

Echolocation: method of detection and navigation using echoes, used in nature by bats and dolphins. Radar and sonar employ the same principles.

Eclipse: shadow cast by the Moon on the Earth when the Moon passes in front of the Sun, or by the Earth on the Moon.

Effort: force needed to move a load.

Elasticity: property of a material allowing it to return to its original size after it has been stretched.

Electric current: flow of electrons or ions in a circuit.

Electricity: effects resulting from the movement of electric charges (in current electricity) or from stationary charges (in static electricity).

Electrochemistry: study of the chemistry involved with ions in solution, as in electric cells and electrolysis.

Electrode: conductor that emits or collects electrons in a cell, semiconductor, or circuit.

Electrolysis: production of a chemical reaction by passing an electric current through an electrolyte.

Electrolyte: liquid that conducts electricity, as in electrolysis.

Electromagnetic radiation: waves of energy that are tiny electric and magnetic disturbances in space.

Electromagnetic spectrum: family of electromagnetic waves, which differ in their wavelength. They range from the shortest-wave (or highest-frequency) gamma rays to the longest-wave (lowest-frequency) radio waves.

Electromotive force (emf): driving force of a cell or generator, which "pushes" the electrons around a circuit. *See also Potential difference.*

Electron: one of the three main particles in an atom (with the proton and neutron). It carries a negative charge. Electric current is a flow of electrons.

Electron gun: device that produces electrons in a cathode-ray tube and "shoots" them at the screen.

Electronics: study of the flow of electrons in semiconductor crystals, gases, and a vacuum, and the design of devices that rely on such flow. *See also Integrated circuit, Semiconductor.*

Electron microscope: microscope that uses electron beams in order to produce magnified images.

Electroplating: coating one metal with another by means of electrolysis.

Electroscope: device for detecting electric charge.

Electrostatics: study of electric charges at rest and the force fields around them.

Element: substance that cannot be broken down into simpler substances. There are about 90 naturally occurring elements and 19 artificial ones.

Elementary particles: *See Fundamental particles.*

Emulsion: tiny particles of one liquid dispersed (scattered) in another.

This toy has elasticity, which allows it to return to its original shape after it has been stretched.

Endothermic reaction: chemical reaction in which heat is taken in. *Compare Exothermic reaction.*

Energy: ability to do work. *See also Conservation of energy.*

Enzyme: protein that acts as a catalyst in the chemical reactions that take place in living things.

Equation: in chemistry, a shorthand method of representing a chemical reaction, using symbols to represent the elements involved, as in the burning of hydrogen: $2H_2 + O_2 = 2H_2O$.

Equilibrium: balanced state; for example, a lever is in equilibrium when the effort balances the load.

Evaporation: change of state in which a liquid changes into a gas (or vapor). It can take place at any temperature above the liquid's freezing point.

Exothermic reaction: chemical reaction in which heat is given out. *Compare Endothermic reaction.*

Expansion: increasing in size, as when a body gets hotter.

Fahrenheit scale: temperature scale named after Gabriel Fahrenheit (1686–1736), on which water freezes at 32 degrees. *See also Celsius scale, Kelvin scale.*

Fermentation: common chemical reaction in which yeast converts sugars into alcohol, with carbon dioxide being given off.

Fiber optics: *See Optical fibers.*

Field: region in which a body experiences a force. Fields exist around magnets (magnetic field), charges (electric fields), and massive bodies because of their gravity (gravitational field).

Fission: *See Nuclear fission.*

Floppy disc: flexible plastic disc with a magnetic coating, used to store data and programs in computing.

Fluid: substance that flows – a liquid or gas.

Fluorescence: visible light given off by some substances when they absorb ultraviolet radiation.

Focus: point at which light rays converge after passing through a lens or after reflection by a mirror.

Force: something that changes the speed, direction, or shape of a body.

Force field: *See Field.*

Formula: set of chemical symbols that represents the composition of a substance, as in $CaCO_3$, which is calcium carbonate or chalk.

Fossil: remains of a once living organism.

Fossil fuel: coal, oil, or natural gas, which are the remains of organisms that lived hundreds of millions of years ago.

Freezing point: temperature at which a liquid changes into a solid.

Frequency: of a wave form, the number of complete waves passing a certain point each second; measured in hertz (Hz).

Frequency modulation (FM): method of changing (modulating) the frequency of a radio wave to carry signals.

Friction: force that resists the movement of one surface over another.

Fuel cell: electric cell in which electricity is produced directly from a fuel. The space shuttle uses fuel cells in which hydrogen reacts with oxygen to produce water.

Fulcrum: point at which a lever pivots.

Fundamental forces: four main forces of the Universe, which are gravity, electromagnetic force, strong force, and weak force. The last two act only at very short distances within the nucleus of atoms.

Fuse: safety device in an electric circuit that breaks the circuit if the current rises too high.

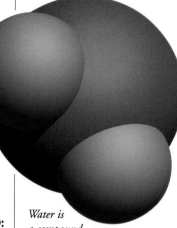

*Water is a compound of two atoms of **hydrogen** and one of atom of oxygen.*

Galvanized: coated with a thin layer of zinc, to protect metals such as iron or steel from rust.

Galvanometer: instrument for detecting and measuring small electric currents.

Gamma rays: electromagnetic rays of very short wavelength that are emitted by certain radioactive substances.

Gas: state of matter in which the particles are far apart and move around randomly and quickly.

Generator: machine that converts mechanical energy into electricity. *See also Alternator, Dynamo.*

Geothermal energy: heat tapped from rocks deep in the Earth's crust.

Global warming: increase in the world's atmospheric temperature, probably caused by an increased greenhouse effect.

Gluons: particles within protons and neutrons that hold quarks in place.

Gravity: force of attraction between any two bodies. It is the Earth's gravity that keeps our feet on the ground and makes objects fall when we drop them. Gravity is one of the fundamental forces of the Universe. *See also Fundamental forces.*

Greenhouse effect: buildup of certain gases in the atmosphere (such as carbon dioxide) that is causing the atmosphere to behave like a greenhouse, trapping heat

*Gyroscope resists having its direction of movement changed because of **inertia**.*

from the Sun.

Grid: network of transmission lines by which electricity is distributed around the country.

Group: vertical column in the Periodic Table containing elements with similar chemical properties. *See also Periodic Table.*

Gyroscope: fast-rotating wheel, which resists disturbance because of its angular momentum. Once set spinning, its axis always keeps pointing in the same direction, a property used in the gyrocompass.

Halogen: group VII in the Periodic Table containing reactive elements like fluorine and chlorine.

Hardware: pieces of equipment that make up a computer system.

Heat: a form of energy transferable from one body or system to another because of a difference in temperature.

Heat engine: machine for converting heat energy into work, such as a steam or gasoline engine.

Heat transfer: movement of heat from a hotter to a colder body, by conduction, convection, or radiation.

Holography: method of producing a three-dimensional image using laser light.

Humidity: amount of water vapor in the atmosphere.

Hydraulics: study of fluids at rest and in motion, particularly with regard to the design of machines that work by fluid pressure.

Hydrocarbon: compound containing hydrogen and carbon only; oil and natural gas are made up mainly of hydrocarbons.

Hydrodynamics: study of fluids in motion.

Hydroelectric power: electricity produced by harnessing the energy in flowing water.

Hydrogen: simplest and most abundant element in the Universe. It has two allotropes, deuterium and tritium.

Hydrometer: device for measuring the density of a liquid.

Hydrostatics: study of liquids at rest.

Immiscible: term that describes two liquids that do not mix, such as oil and water.

Imperial units: units used in some English-speaking countries, including the pound, inch, foot and mile. *See also SI units.*

Indicator: substance used to show (indicate) the pH (acidity or alkalinity) of a solution by its color.

Inert gases: *See Noble gases.*

Inertia: property of a body that makes it resist any change in motion. Mass is a measure of inertia.

Infrared rays (IR): invisible electromagnetic radiation with a wavelength longer than red light; produced by hot bodies.

Infrasound: sound waves with too low a frequency to be detected by the human ear.

Inorganic chemistry: the study of compounds that are not carbon-based.

Insulator: material that is a poor conductor of heat, electricity, or sound.

Integrated circuit: miniature electronic circuit in which all the components (e.g. capacitors, resistors, transistors) are integrated (contained) in one piece of semiconductor.

Interference: disturbance produced when two or more waves (e.g. light, sound) interact.

Internal combustion engine: engine in which fuel is burned inside the engine.

Ion: atom or group of atoms that has lost or gained one or more electrons to become electrically charged. *See also Anion, Cation.*

Ionic bond: bond formed between positive and negative ions, formed when one or more electrons is transferred from one atom to another.

Isotopes: atoms of the same element with the same number of protons in the nucleus, but with different numbers of neutrons.

Jet propulsion: propulsion of a body by a jet of gas or liquid. The action (force) of the jet moving backward produces a reaction (force in the opposite direction) that propels the body forward.

Joule: unit of energy and work in the SI system.

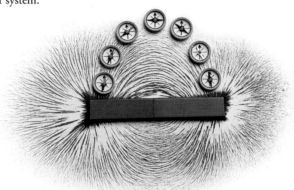

*Iron filings reveal the **magnetic field** around a magnet.*

Kelvin: unit of temperature in the SI system, widely used in science. Named after physicist Lord Kelvin (1824–1907), it begins at absolute zero, which is 0 kelvin (K). The freezing point of water is about 273 K.

Kilogram: unit of mass in the SI system.

Kinetic energy: energy a body has because of its motion.

Kinetic theory: *See Particle theory.*

Laser: device that produces an intense beam of pure light (of a single wavelength). Laser stands for light amplification by the stimulated emission of radiation.

Latent heat: heat that is taken in or given out when a substance changes state.

*The fat and fur of a polar bear are poor conductors of heat, therefore they are good **insulators** – the heat built up in the bear's body cannot travel well and escape easily.*

Lattice: regular arrangement of the particles (e.g. atoms, ions) in a crystal.

Lens: curved piece of glass or other transparent material that brings light rays to a focus. *See also Concave lens, Convex lens.*

Lepton: class of fundamental particle that includes the electron.

Lever: simple machine consisting of a rigid beam turning around a pivot, or fulcrum. A force (effort) is applied at one point to lift a force (load) at another.

Lift: upward force produced on a wing or airfoil when it moves through the air.

Light: electromagnetic radiation that our eyes can detect. White light is a mixture of all the colors of the rainbow, which form the visible spectrum.

Light-emitting diode (LED): Crystal diode that gives off light when electric current passes through it.

Light year: distance light travels in a year which is about 5.9 trillion miles (9.5 trillion km).

Liquid: state of matter between a solid and a gas, in which the particles move around in bundles but are still close together and attract one another.

Liquid crystal: substance that flows like a liquid but has its particles arranged in an ordered structure, like a crystal.

Liquid crystal display (LCD): Sets of liquid crystals that, in an electric field, can twist light passing through them to produce dark segments that can make digits (numbers), for example.

Litmus: common indicator that turns red in acid solutions, blue in alkaline.

Longitudinal wave: wave in which vibrating particles vibrate in the direction in which the wave is traveling. Sound is a longitudinal wave.

Loudness: intensity of sound, measured in decibels.

Lunar eclipse: eclipse of the Moon, when it passes into the Earth's shadow in space.

Magnetic field: field of force that exists around a magnetic body.

Magnetism: property of some materials, especially iron, to attract or repel like materials.

Mass: amount of matter in a body; a measure of the body's inertia. *Compare Weight.*

Matter: anything that has mass and occupies space.

Mechanical advantage: measure of the effectiveness of a machine to magnify effort to move greater loads.

Melting point: temperature at which a solid turns into a liquid.

Meniscus: curved upper surface of a liquid in a tube.

Metal: element that conducts heat and electricity well and is usually solid, hard, and shiny.

Metallic bond: bond in metals in which the electrons can flow freely between the atoms.

Microchip: silicon chip that carries miniaturized electronic circuits.

Microgravity: condition experienced in an orbiting spacecraft, where gravity is reduced to about one ten-thousandth of its value at the Earth's surface. Also called zero-g or weightlessness.

Microscope: instrument with lenses that produces an enlarged image of an object. *See also Electron microscope.*

Microwaves: electromagnetic waves with wavelengths between infrared rays and radio waves.

Mineral: naturally occurring inorganic substances; the main constituents of rocks.

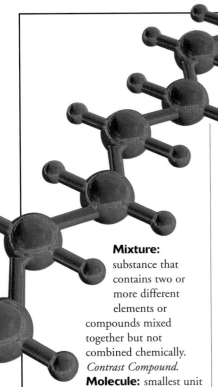

Mixture: substance that contains two or more different elements or compounds mixed together but not combined chemically. *Contrast Compound.*

Molecule: smallest unit of an element or compound which is made of two or more atoms bonded together.

Momentum: tendency of a body to keep on moving, measured by its mass multiplied by its velocity.

Monomer: small molecule that is the basic building block of a polymer.

Neutralization: reaction in which an acid reacts with a base to produce a salt and water.

Neutrino: subatomic particle that has neither mass nor charge, only spin energy; one kind of lepton.

Neutron: particle found in the nuclei of all atoms except hydrogen. It has a similar mass to the proton but no electric charge.

Newton (N): unit of force in the SI system.

Noble gases: gaseous elements that don't react easily with other elements. Once called rare gases and inert gases.

Nonmetals: elements that don't behave like metals and are typically poor conductors of heat and electricity. They include solids like sulfur and gases like chlorine.

Nuclear energy: energy released when the nucleus of an atom is split (fission) or joined to another (fusion).

Nuclear fission: nuclear reaction in which the nuclei of heavy atoms split, releasing energy.

Nuclear fusion: nuclear reaction in which the nuclei of light atoms join together, releasing energy.

Nuclear reactor: device in which a nuclear reaction can be controlled to produce a steady flow of energy.

Nucleus: center part of an atom, made up of protons and neutrons. It contains most of the atom's mass and has a positive charge.

Optical fibers: fine glass or plastic fibers that transmit light by total internal reflection.

Orbit: path of one body around another.

Ore: mineral from which a metal can be extracted; often profitably.

Organic chemistry: chemistry of the carbon compounds, some found in living things.

Organism: living thing, made up of one or more cells.

Oxidation: chemical reaction in which a substance combines with oxygen. Combustion and rusting are common examples of oxidation. *Contrast Reduction.*

Particles: basic units from which all substances are made, such as atoms and molecules. Subatomic particles are particles smaller than an atom, such as protons.

Particle accelerator: machine that accelerates beams of charged particles (protons, electrons) to high energies. Also called an atom-smasher.

Particle theory: theory that all matter is composed of particles in constant motion. The way they interact explains the three states of matter – solids, liquids, and gases – and the way they change from one to the other. Also known as kinetic theory.

Periodic Table: table in which all the elements are listed in order of atomic number and arranged so that elements with similar properties are together.

Petrochemicals: chemicals produced from petroleum at an oil refinery, by processes such as distillation and cracking.

pH: measure of how acidic or how alkaline a solution is. pH 0 or 1 is highly acid, pH 14 is highly alkaline.

Photon: particle that is the smallest unit of electromagnetic radiation, consisting of a single quantum of energy.

Photosynthesis: process by which plants make food in their leaves, using the energy in sunlight. They combine carbon dioxide (which they take in from the air) with water (which they take in with their roots) to make sugars.

Physics: study of energy and forces. Nuclear physics, for example, studies the energy and forces within the nuclei of atoms.

Plasma: state of matter that exists at very high temperatures (like in stars) in which the atoms are separated into electrons and ions.

Plastic: synthetic product consisting of long-chain molecules, or polymers. Thermoplastics (like nylon) soften when heated, but thermosets (like Bakelite) remain rigid.

Polarized light: light whose waves vibrate in only one plane. Ordinary light waves vibrate in all planes.

Pollution: poisoning of the environment (air, water, and land) by substances such as oil, chemicals, and nuclear waste.

Polymers: substances with long chains of atoms, made up of repeated units. Plastics are synthetic polymers made by polymerization, a chemical process that combines small molecules (monomers) to form big ones (polymers).

Potential difference: difference in electrical energy between two points in an electric circuit. It provides the driving force for electric current. Measured in volts.

Potential energy: energy stored for later use. Gravitational potential energy is the energy stored in a body because of its position, such as a roller coaster.

Pressure: force acting against a certain area, usually measured in pascals (newtons per square meter) or pounds per square inch.

Primary colors: colors from which all other colors can be produced. In light, the primary colors are red, green, and blue. In paints and pigments, the primary colors are yellow, magenta (reddish-blue), and cyan (bluish-green).

Prism: triangular wedge of glass or other transparent material that can split up white light into a spectrum of colors.

Program: set of instructions to make a computer perform certain operations.

Proton: one of the two main particles found in the nucleus of atoms. It has the same mass as the neutron, but has a positive charge.

Quantum: a tiny "packet" of energy. Electromagnetic radiation is thought of as a stream of quanta (the plural of quantum) known as photons.

Quantum mechanics: science explaining the properties and behavior of atoms and molecules, based on the idea that energy is emitted in quanta.

Quarks: fundamental particles from which protons and neutrons are made.

Radar (radio detection and ranging): detection of objects by bouncing radio beams off them and listening for the echoes.

Radiation: energy traveling as electromagnetic waves (such as light). Also, the rays given off by radioactive substances, such as alpha, beta, and gamma rays.

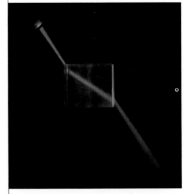

Refraction occurs when a beam of light is passed through a glass block. The light beam bends as it moves from air to glass.

Radioactivity: breakdown of the nucleus of certain elements, causing radiation to be given off.

*The **surface tension** of the milk is broken as detergent is dripped onto it.*

Random-access memory (RAM): temporary memory in a computer, in which data can be stored and retrieved.

Reactants: substances that take part in a chemical reaction.

Read-only memory (ROM): permanent memory in a computer, which cannot be altered.

Reduction: reaction in which a substance loses oxygen or, more broadly, gains electrons. The opposite of oxidation.

Reflection: bouncing back of a wave (such as light) from a surface.

Refraction: bending of a beam of light as it passes from one medium to another (such as air to water).

Relative atomic mass: means of comparing the masses of atoms. It is the ratio of the mass of an atom to one-twelfth of the mass of the carbon-12 atom. Formerly called atomic weight.

Relative density: density of a substance compared with the density of a reference substance, usually water.

Resistance: in electrical circuits, the property that opposes the flow of electricity. Resistors are components that have a known resistance.

Rusting: process by which iron and steel combine with the oxygen in the air to form iron oxide. Rusting is the most common form of corrosion.

Salt: substance formed when an acid reacts with a base or a metal.

Scalar quantity: quantity that just has magnitude, such as temperature.

Semiconductor: crystalline solid that can conduct small amounts of electric current under suitable conditions. Semiconductors (such as silicon) are the basis of modern integrated electronic circuits.

Semimetal: element that has properties between those of a metal and those of a nonmetal. Including boron, silicon, germanium, and arsenic, they are useful as semiconductors.

Shock wave: high-pressure wave set up when air compresses then expands very rapidly and when an object travels supersonically (faster than the speed of sound) through the air.

SI units: system of standard measuring units used in science. SI stands for *Système International d'Unités*. It has replaced the former Imperial and c.g.s. (centimeter-gram-second) units.

Software: programs and data fed into a computer. *Compare Hardware.*

Solar cell: electric cell that converts the energy in sunlight directly into electricity.

Solute: substance that dissolves in a liquid to form a solution.

Solution: special kind of mixture in which a gas, solid, or liquid is dissolved in a liquid.

Solvent: liquid that dissolves substances to form a solution.

Sound: vibration that travels through a medium (gases, liquids, and solids).

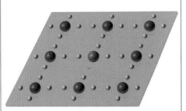

*Silicon becomes a **semiconductor** when certain impurities, such as boron, are added.*

Spectrum: arrangement of electromagnetic radiations, such as light, from shortest to longest wavelengths. The visible spectrum is the spread of colors formed when a beam of white light is split into its separate wavelengths by, for example, a prism.

Streamlining: shaping an object so that it travels with the least resistance, or drag, through the air or through water.

Subatomic particle: particle that is smaller than the atom, such as a proton or an electron.

Sublimation: change of state in which a solid turns into a gas without melting into a liquid first.

Supernova: explosion of a massive star that blasts most of its matter into space, leaving behind either a very dense body called a pulsar or a black hole.

Supersonic: traveling faster than the speed of sound.

Surface tension: force on the surface of a liquid that makes it behave as if it has a skin.

Synthetics: substances produced from chemicals, particularly from petrochemicals. Some synthetic products, such as synthetic rubber, are designed to imitate natural products.

Temperature: measure of how hot or how cold something is. Three main temperature scales are in use: Fahrenheit, Kelvin, and Celsius.

Transducer: device for converting nonelectrical energy or signals (such as light or sound) into electrical signals, or the other way around. The microphone and loudspeaker are transducers.

Transistor: electronic device consisting of a "sandwich" of semiconductor materials. It can be used to amplify signals, or as a switch (as in computer circuits).

Ultrasound: sound with a frequency higher than the human ear can detect.

Ultraviolet (UV) light: invisible electromagnetic radiation with a shorter wavelength than the violet rays in the visible spectrum. UV rays in sunlight can burn skin.

Vector quantity: one that has both magnitude and direction, such as velocity.

Velocity: speed and direction of an object.

Viscosity: measure of how thick a liquid is, or how easily it flows.

Wavelength: distance between the crest of one wave (light, sound, water) and the next. Wavelength is related to frequency – a wave with a short wavelength has a high frequency, and one with a long wavelength has a low frequency.

Weight: force exerted on a body by gravity. The more mass the body has, the greater its weight.

Weightlessness: popular term for the near absence of gravity experienced in an orbiting spacecraft. *See Microgravity.*

Work: work is done when a force moves a body a certain distance. It is a measure of energy transferred from one system to another and, like energy, it is measured in joules.

Velocity is demonstrated with a homemade rocket.

X-rays: penetrating electromagnetic waves with wavelengths between those of gamma rays and ultraviolet rays.

Zero-g: alternative term for weightlessness.

INDEX

Numbers in **bold** refer to
main entries; numbers in *italic*
refer to experiments and
demonstrations.

ACKNOWLEDGMENTS

Picture Credits

The publisher would like to thank the following for their kind permission to reproduce their images:

Position key: c=center, b=bottom, l=left, r=right, t=top, a=above

Bryan And Cherry Alexander Photography: 92cl.
Sportsphoto: Brian Bahr 73tr.
Aquarius Library: 117cr; Claudette Barius (SMPSP) 116tr; ILM 116cr, 117b.
Blackpool Pleasure Beach: 63tc, 75tr.
Stevebloom.com Images: 109br.
Bridgeman Art Library, London / New York: Private Collection – Church Interior by Abel Grimmer (1570-1619) 110cr.
CERN: 43cl.
Corbis: 3bc, 25bl, 35bl, 47cl, 70tr, 70br, 85cl, 93br, 94tr, 98cl, 100-101, 112bl, 127bl, 134bc, 145tl; Aaron Horowitz 70-71; Amos Nachoum 32tr; Bettmann Archive 79bl, 117c–background; Bill Ross 62tr; Gilbert Lundt; TempSport 57tl; James A. Sugar 70cl; Jay Dickman 119; NASA/Roger Ressmeyer 71bl; Neil Beer 56br; Owen Franken 71cr; Ralph White 32bl; Richard A. Cooke 77br; Rick Doyle 119br; Roger Ressmeyer 69tl.

Steve Cross Partnership: 137br.
Denoyer-Geppert: Intl. 94cr.
Ecoscene: 52cl.
EDFA: 74br.
Empics Ltd: 34b.
Mary Evans Picture Library: 88tr, 91cr.
Eye Ubiquitous: David Forman 95bl.
Gables: 62bl.
Robert Harding Picture Library: 34-35t, 37tl.
Heritage Image Partnership: Science Museum 80bl.
Hibbert / Ralph: 116-117t
High Field Magnetic Laboratory, University of Nijmegen, the Netherlands: 137bl.
Hovertravel Limited: 66bl.
Robin Hunter: 115bc
The Image Bank / Getty Images: 2clb, 30cr, 73tl, 81tr, 86tc; Frans Lemmens 74c; Kenneth Redding 14l; Leo Mason. Split Second 66-67c.
ImageState: 12br.
BFI London Imax Cinema: BFI London Imax Cinema 116br.
Memoflex: Memoflex from Aspex 13br.
Museum of Moving Image: 105bl1, 105bl2.
N.A.S.A.: 2tr, 46tr, 65tl, 112br, 119tl, 135br; Kennedy Space Center 84cl.
Stephen Oliver: 36r, 136t.
Oxford Scientific Films: 114tl; Peter O'Toole 48br; Vinay Parelkar / Dinodia 56tr.
Pictor International: 71tl; Steve Vidler 70br.
Brian Pitkin: 25tl, 57bl.

Powerstock Photolibrary / Zefa: 2c, 76b.
Rail Images: 142b.
Santa Pod Raceway: 69cr.
Science Museum: 62br, 92br, 107tr, 108l, 109cr, 112cr, 113br, 114tl, 138cl, 141cl.
Science Photo Library: 2-3, 24tr, 26tr, 26cl, 31cl, 35tr, 36br, 37bl, 38-39, 41cr, 43cr, 43br, 44tr, 44cl, 44cr, 44bc, 44bc, 46cl, 46cr, 47tc, 47r, 53tr, 54cl, 54br, 54-55b, 55tl, 57br, 64bl, 84br, 84-85t, 85cb, 87bl, 87br, 88bl, 88br, 89tr, 90c, 91tl, 93tl, 96-97b, 97tl, 104cr, 105cr, 107cl, 107c, 107br, 108cr, 109bl, 112tl, 112tr, 113tl, 113c, 113bl, 114bc, 122-3, 124tr, 125br, 126br, 126r, 127tr, 129t, 131tr, 131b, 132tr, 132bl, 134-5, 138bl, 140bl, 142cl, 144tr, 144br, 145tr, 147tl, 147tr, 147br, 148cl, 148bc, 148-9c, 149br; A.B Dowsett 58tr; Adam Hart-Davis 14-15c, 75cl; Astrid & Hanns-Frieder Michler 14bl; Biophoto Associates 59cl; BSIP 14cr; Colin Cuthbert 51tl; Damien Lovegrove 110tr; David Nunuk 81br; Dr Gary Settles 82-83; Francoise Sauze 56c; Gary Ladd 32bc; I. Andersson, Oxford Molecular Biophysics Laboratory 16tc; J-L Charmet 67tr; James Bell 8-9; James Holmes 48c;

Jerrican Godfryd 33bl; Jerry Mason 48tr; Kent Wood 49b; L.Medard / Eurelios 41tl; Lawrence Berkeley 11tr; Lawrence Berkeley Laboratory 40bl; Manfred Kage 58-59c; Martin Bond 78tr; Mehau Kulyk 56l; NASA 19cb, 69cl; Pekka Parviainen 58b; Philippe Plailly 40tr; R. Maisonneuve 1011tc; Renee Lynn 18br; Richardson / Custom Medical Stock Photo 59br; Rosenfeld Images Ltd 50cl; Scott Camazine 59tl; Stephen Dalton 68cl; TRL LTD 64tl.
Skyscan: 70cl, 71c.
Still Pictures: 52b.
Stone / Getty Images: 26bl, 64tr, 75br, 79cl, 94bl, 99tr, 99cl; David Leah 60-61c; George Lepp 68-69b.
Telegraph Colour Library / Getty Images: 19br, 133br; Michael Dunning 11b; Phil Boorman 68cr.
Art Directors & TRIP: S. Grant 86cb.

All other images © Dorling Kindersley. For further information see: **www.dkimages.com**
Artworks:
Darren Holt 89cr.
Robin Hunter 20-21c, 25br, 30l, 34cl,

47b, 49tl, 55tr, 55br, 63br, 90bl, 95tl, 98r, 104tr, 106 cl, 107br, 110cra, 119cr, 127tl, 128cl, 130cl,114bl, 130br, 131tr, 136bl, 140tr, 140cl, 140cr, 142tr, 143bl, 144c, 145c.
Martin Wilson 28tr, 28b.
John Kelly 42b, 43t, 45.

Dorling Kindersley would like to thank the following people for their contributions to the making of this book:

Design assistance:
   Polly Appleton,
   Ann Cannings,
   Darren Holt,
   Clair Watson.
Editorial assistance:
   David John,
   Margaret Hynes.
Proof reading:
   Lee Simmons.
Lynn Bresler for the index;
Roger Langston at King's College London, University of London, for kindly loaning scientific equipment;
Craig Outhwaite at Evans Cycles, The Cut, London SE1 for the loan of the bicycle for the "Gears and Pulleys" experiment on p. 78.